Tuesdays With Tony

Volume 2
June 2022-May 2023

Tony Eldridge

"Scripture quotations are from The ESV® Bible (The Holy Bible, English Standard Version®), copyright © 2001 by Crossway, a publishing ministry of Good News Publishers. Used by permission. All rights reserved."

When more than one translation is quoted in printed works or other media, the foregoing notice of copyright should begin as follows:

"Unless otherwise indicated, all Scripture quotations are from . . . [etc.]"; or, "Scripture quotations marked (ESV) are from . . . [etc.]."

"ESV," the "English Standard Version," the "Global Study Bible," and the ESV logo are registered trademarks of Crossway, registered in the United States of America. Use of any of these trademarks requires the prior permission of Crossway.

When quotations from the ESV text are used in non-saleable print and digital media, such as church bulletins, orders of service, posters, transparencies, or similar media, a complete copyright notice is not required, but the initials (ESV) must appear at the end of the quotation. Publication of any commentary or other Bible reference work produced for commercial sale that uses the English Standard Version (ESV) must include written permission for use of the ESV text. Permission requests that exceed the above guidelines must be directed to Crossway, Attn: Bible Rights, 1300 Crescent Street, Wheaton, IL 60187, USA. Permission requests for use of the anglicized ESV Bible text that exceed the above guidelines must be directed to: HarperCollins Religious, The News Building, 1 London Bridge Street, London SE1 9GF, UK.

The Holy Bible, English Standard Version (ESV) is adapted from the Revised Standard Version of the Bible, copyright Division of Christian Education of the National Council of the Churches of Christ in the U.S.A. All rights reserved.

All italics in quotations of Scripture have been added by the authors.

The ESV Global Study Bible is based on the ESV Student Study Bible, copyright © 2011 Crossway, and on the ESV Study Bible, copyright © 2008 Crossway.

Tuesdays With Tony

Copyright © 2023 Tony Eldridge

All rights reserved.

ISBN: 9798391002871

DEDICATION

This book is dedicated to my wife, Emily. Many of the things in this book are here because she has taught me, by her demeanor and devotion to God, what the lessons are that I learned from Scripture. She has taught me patience, forgiveness, and the sacrifice of agape love. I have become a better person with her as my helper, and I am trying to be the helper to her that God would have me to be. If you want to know what grace is, you need only to look at her steadfast faithfulness to me when I didn't deserve it. I will always love her and I look forward to spending an eternity in heaven with her.

TUESDAYS WITH TONY

Introduction 11
What Will Precipitate The Return Of Jesus? 22
Jesus Is God 30
Love Like Jesus Loves 34
Jesus, Our Bridegroom 40
Finding Joy When We're Late To The Party 50
In the Beginning Was The Word 57
Taking A Vacation From God 62
Be Salt In A Wicked Land 69
The Drip Drip Drip of Satan 74
Only A Step Between Me And Death 80
The Feeding of the Multitudes 84
Chapter 1 Excerpt: What Is Sovereignty? 87
Jesus, Son of Man 91
Gentiles Who Sought Jesus 103
A King Who Can Forgive Anything 107
Coffee (Or Tea) With Jesus 115
Do We Think Like The Scoffers? 123
Tough Talk From Jesus 130
My God Knows Me 136
Excruciating Pain 143
Choosing Righteousness 150

Jesus, Matthew 25, and Grace vs Works 156

Excerpt: The Potter and the Clay 160

Ask And It Will Be Given To You 169

Why Sadducees Do Not Believe In A Resurrection 174

Is There A Little Naaman In Each Of Us? 179

The Wonderful Lack Of Detail In The Parable Of The Good Samaritan 181

Banquets and Invitations 186

Patience With God 193

How Can A Loving God Send People To Hell? 198

What Went Through Saul's Mind When He Was Blind? 205

The Silence Of Jesus 211

Another Perspective On Luke 16: The Rich Man And Lazarus 217

Preparing My Heart For Kingdom Living 229

Preparing My Heart For Kingdom Living: Read The Bible Daily 234

Preparing My Heart For Kingdom Living: Pray Without Ceasing .. 242

Preparing My Heart For Kingdom Living: Put Good In 250

Preparing My Heart For Kingdom Living: Seek Out Daily Service Moments 256

Preparing My Heart For Kingdom Living: Build Relationships 262

Preparing My Heart For Kingdom Living: Confess Jesus Daily 269

Wisdom Is Not Always Found With The Aged 276

Be Thankful Every Day For The Lord's Providence 283

Choosing God 291

We Can Do Right Wrong 296

Against You Only Have I Sinned 303

Jacob I Have Loved and Esau I Have Hated 308

Love Believes All Things 312

Introduction

This is the second volume of *Tuesdays With Tony*, a collection of Facebook posts that center on the lessons I learn as I study God's word. Many posts are single lined observations while others are fleshed out studies.

For the most part, this book contains the posts that I wrote in the order that I published them on Facebook. They also contain the same content, written the same way they were published. I do, however, reserve the right to edit the posts for grammar as I see the opportunity.

The idea for these posts came from one of the elders in the congregation I attend. When I was satisfied to keep my writings to myself as study aids to help me when I opened the Word of God, Terry encouraged me to share my notes on Facebook. I reluctantly agreed and *Tuesdays With Tony* was born on June of 2021.

The agreement I made with myself when I decided to publish these posts, observations, and studies was that they would be a way I would glorify my Lord and King, Jesus. To that end, I freely share with anyone who wishes to use anything in this, or any of my books to help bring honor to God.

If you wish, you may resproduce the lessons in any form with two exceptions.

1. I ask that you do not sell the reproduction of this work, though you may cite and quote from this book within a larger work you may produce. Simply, please do not reproduce this book to sell for your own profit.
2. You may quote me in whole, or in part, but please do not alter what I have written. To the best of your ability, please represent my work as an honest reproduction of what I have written.

Short of these two exception, consider the material in this book yours to share as you please. As you do, I ask that you join with me in prayer that God, if He wills, may use these lessons in a way that glorifies Himself while shielding any glory from me. Truly, to God, and God alone, may all praise, glory, and honor be given.

Thank you for picking up this book and for sharing it with whomever you feel may benefit from it. And if I may presume upon you, please pray for me that God will use me as His steward as I continue this work. May this book, and others I may write, be evidence of the confession I make before men of my Lord and Savior, Jesus, who is my King and my Creator.

June 1st, 2022

Hezekiah was one of the greatest kings of Judah. He began to reign when he was 25 and started off his reign by cleansing the temple. As he began this work, he gathered the Levites and priests to direct them toward the work of returning to the one true God of Israel. This is what he said to them:

> "Now it is in my heart to make a covenant with the LORD, the God of Israel, in order that his fierce anger may turn away from us." (2 Chronicles 29:10 ESV).

It is in my heart… What an important phrase. While our hearts are not the foundation of truth, it is the beginning of our service to God. When it is in our heart to make a covenant with the Lord, we will do what Hezekiah did that made him a great king. We will search out the will of God. We will humble ourselves before Him. We will repent and turn away from our sins.

We do not let our heart determine how we follow God. But we must have a heart that is eager and willing to make a covenant with the Lord to do His will. Otherwise, we may go through the motions of worship merely to ease our conscience and make others happy.

But when we take ownership of making a covenant with the Lord in our hearts as King Hezekiah did, then we let His word guide and mold us. Not because it's an expectation, but because it's something we are actively seeking.

Have you made a covenant in your heart with the Lord, a covenant that has you actively seeking to serve Him and learn more about His will for you? If so, then you will find the Lord. But until you first make the covenant in your heart with God, you can never find Him.

> "The LORD is good to those who wait for him, to the soul who seeks him." (Lamentations 3:25 ESV).

***

Today is the last day I have been given to lock myself up in a cabin and work on my book, The Sovereignty of God. I have written a lot, though I will still have a bit left to do when I get back home.

I am finishing up my chapter on God's Sovereignty Seen In Job. I thought you'd be interested in reading an unedited excerpt from the conclusion of that chapter:

"God never explains to Job why the bad things happened to him. Why do you suppose that is? We have examples in the Bible where God explains why He does or does not do things to people. The main message of the prophets was to explain God's actions if the people didn't repent. God over and over told the kings of Israel and Judah why God will send good or evil upon them. So why didn't He explain why these bad things happened to Job? Perhaps it is because of the second truth about God's sovereignty we discussed: 'God answers to no man, no power or to any other authority'. Job had demanded that God explain Himself and why He had allowed him to suffer when he was blameless. It is one thing for a sovereign God to choose to explain His actions as a measure of grace to His creation. It is another thing for someone to demand Him to defend His actions. The sovereignty of God meant that God did not have to listen and explain Himself to Job. And God, in His sovereignty chose not to answer Job's demands. And Job understood that. This is why Job placed his hands over his mouth and vowed to withdraw His demands against God. In essence, Job realized that he had overstepped his authority."

***

Here is another unedited excerpt from my book, The Sovereignty of God: Chapter Two- Sovereignty: The Potter and the Clay.

How supreme is God's sovereignty over His creation? Consider that the largest star we know of in the universe has a radius 1700 times greater than the radius of our sun and our sun has a radius of 109 times greater than the radius of the earth. We are talking about things so big that we can hardly wrap our finite minds around them. And the nonprofit news organization, The Conversation, estimates that there are 200 billion trillion stars in the universe. I have no clue how big that number is, but when you write it out, it looks like this: 200,000,000,000,000,000,000,000. I still have no clue how big that number really is. To help feeble minds like mine, The Conversation says the number of stars in the universe is 10 times the number of cups of water in all the oceans on the earth.

Okay, so it must be a supremely sovereign God who can speak this massive number of stars into existence, not to mention the planets, moons and asteroids that orbit each of them, correct? It's not just in God's creative power we witness His sovereignty, but it's in His intimate knowledge of His creation that we see His sovereignty.

"He determines the number of the stars; he gives to all of them their names." (Psalm 147:4 ESV).

We struggle to find names for our children, don't we? Yet God knows every one of the stars He made and He has given each of them names, all 200,000,000,000,000,000,000,000+ of them. But that's not all:

"Are not five sparrows sold for two pennies? And not one of them is forgotten before God. Why, even the hairs of your head are all numbered. Fear not; you are of more value than many sparrows." (Luke 12:6-7 ESV).

Jesus, who is God the creator, tells us that He knows every sparrow He has created and He even knows every single strand of hair on every person He has ever created. I have no clue how many billions of souls that God has created since Adam and Eve, but His infinite mind knows every hair stand that He created on each of them.

My whole point in saying all of this is that when we speak of God's sovereignty, we are speaking of things that we will hardly be able to wrap our minds around. God is so far above and beyond us, that our finite minds will never be able to fully understand His infinite nature. And this observation alone should be enough for us to acknowledge and submit to His sovereignty.

But there's more...

***

I just finished the book of Malachi in my daily Bible reading. It will take you less than 15 minutes to read, and I would recommend that each person read it and see how relevant the message is for us today. In it, God speaks to people who have lost their fear of Him. They serve Him the way they want to serve Him and have little respect for what He wants.

When Malachi makes accusations, they turn their nose up at every accusation and ask, "When have we done the things you accuse me of doing?

And God answers every one, yet they continue to scoff. Their attitude is that God should be thankful for what they offer Him. They forgot that God is God and they all should have revered Him and do their best for Him. Yet they gave God leftovers and treated Him with disrespect. Listen to these select passages from Malachi:

> "When you offer blind animals in sacrifice, is that not evil? And when you offer those that are lame or sick, is that not evil? Present that to your governor; will he accept you or show you favor? says the LORD of hosts." (Malachi 1:8 ESV).

> "You have wearied the LORD with your words. But you say, "How have we wearied him?" By saying, "Everyone who does evil is good in the sight of the LORD, and he delights in them." Or by asking, "Where is the God of justice?" (Malachi 2:17 ESV).

This goes on throughout the whole book. Israel was a nation who was moving past God and serving Him the way they wanted to serve Him and not the way that He wanted to be served.

> "You have said, 'It is vain to serve God. What is the profit of our keeping his charge or of walking as in mourning before the LORD of hosts?
> And now we call the arrogant blessed. Evildoers not only prosper but they put God to the test and they escape.'" (Malachi 3:14-15 ESV).

To this, God gives warm counsel to the people who love him and live in the midst of a nation of people who are moving past God:

> "Then those who feared the LORD spoke with one another. The LORD paid attention and heard them, and a book of remembrance was written before him of those who feared the LORD and esteemed his name.
> "They shall be mine, says the LORD of hosts, in the day when I make up my treasured possession, and I will spare them as a man spares his son who serves him.
> Then once more you shall see the distinction between the righteous and the wicked, between one who serves God and one who does not serve him." (Malachi 3:16-18 ESV).

May we all be among the faithful who love God and not be led astray by a wicked people who serve God their way and have no regard or respect for the mighty one true God of us all.

***

If Judgment Day were today, would you be ready?
No more meetings, vacations, honey-do lists, or TV shows to finish.
Just you and King Jesus, face to face.
Are you ready?

"Why do you pass judgment on your brother? Or you, why do you despise your brother? For we will all stand before the judgment seat of God;

for it is written, "As I live, says the Lord, every knee shall bow to me, and every tongue shall confess to God."

So then each of us will give an account of himself to God." (Romans 14:10-12 ESV).

***

I just finished the book of Revelation in my daily Bible reading. It's an interesting and captivating book to say the least. I have heard so many interpretations of what all the symbols mean. But if we take a myoptic approach to the book, it will be easy to miss the big picture that gives hope and peace.

This is a book of victory in the face of apparent despair and defeat. It's a book that shows that our God knows everything that is happening, and if we suffer for our faith, God will even out the score for those who persevere.

It's a book that says evil may have its day in the sun, but recompense is coming from a sovereign and powerful God. It's a book that says when we suffer anything for standing by our faith in the one true and living God, the Conqueror will see and remember us.

It is a book that reminds us that the multitude around us may worship the beast, but in the end, there is no power in numbers when the final victory is won. It is a book that reminds us that the suffering and pain we may experience for the cause of Jesus is nothing compared to the reward and joy that await us.

It is a book that reminds us that victory is a foregone conclusion and we just need to remain faithful and let it all play out. It is a book that reminds us that no one will slip through the cracks in the end; whether for good or evil, the perfect and merciful Judge will stand face to face with everyone who He has ever created.

The book of Revelation reminds us that we are on the front lines of a great battle with enemies who will hate us, but our Protector hasn't forgotten us. We will one day experience His glory and His power. It is a book that reminds us that those who boast in their evil and deny God today will fear Him when they see Him face to face in His power and glory.

> "Behold, I am coming soon, bringing my recompense with me, to repay each one for what he has done. I am the Alpha and the Omega, the first and the last, the beginning and the end." Blessed are those who wash their robes, so that they may have the right to the tree of life and that they may enter the city by the gates." (Revelation 22:12-14 ESV).

***

"And it was so."

I'm in Genesis in my daily Bible reading, and as I focus on the creation account, I read where God said that something was to be made. After He spoke, we see the phrase, "And it was so."

So much is wrapped up in this phrase. It shows God's power and the obedience of everything that comes from His mouth. Everything but man. It's interesting that with His crowning creation, God can speak to us, and most often, it is not so.

Sometimes, when we see what separates us and the rest of creation, we focus on things like, "Behold, it was very good." or this part of creation is made in the image of God. But the dark side of this creation shows that we are the only part of creation where God can use the power of His word to tell us something, and we can respond by not making it so.

Our free will is both a blessing and a curse. It's a blessing in that we are granted a gift of limited sovereignty that the rest of creation does not have. But it's a curse, because it gives us the ability to do harm to ourselves and not fulfill the purpose that God intends for us.

But in His love and patience for us, God grants us forgiveness when we humble ourselves and repent before His Son's throne. When God says something to us, and we refuse to let it be so, we can connect with His blood and turn the "not so" of His word into "And it was so" for our lives.

The great theme of redemption is that we can move from rebellion against our Creator to living in harmony with His powerful word. It's true that God lets us rebel against Him, but in His long suffering and love, He gives us a way to return to the relationship with Him that we were created to have.

By His grace and strength, rebellion can turn into "And it was so" for His

Word in our lives.

***

In my daily Bible reading, I am well into Genesis. In Chapter 13, we read about the tension between Lot and his uncle Abraham. God had blessed both men with riches and livestock. God's blessings for the men were so great, that the land could not support them both. This led to strife between Abraham's men and Lot's men.

> "Then Abram said to Lot, "Let there be no strife between you and me, and between your herdsmen and my herdsmen, for we are kinsmen. Is not the whole land before you? Separate yourself from me. If you take the left hand, then I will go to the right, or if you take the right hand, then I will go to the left." (Genesis 13:8-9 ESV).

We learn some things about Abraham in how he handled this situation. First, he was a man of peace and looked for ways to live in peace with others. As Christians, that should be the type of people we should be as well (Romans 12:18). But too often, we fight for what is due us and for our claim. This wasn't so with Abraham.

We also see that he was a man who trusted in the Lord and not in himself. Abraham was the patriarch and could have chosen the best land for himself and sent Lot to the inferior land. But Abraham knew that it didn't matter which way he went, because in the end, God would provide. Friends, this is the epitome of faith. Abraham struggled with this concept regarding his heir, but in this case, he knew his destiny was in God's hands. This allowed him to go to the right or to the left and leave his future in God's hands, and not in his own hands.

In the end, Abraham and Lot's choice was moot at best. First, God said to him that it didn't matter which way Lot went, He was giving it all to Abraham.

> "The LORD said to Abram, after Lot had separated from him, "Lift up your eyes and look from the place where you are, northward and southward and eastward and westward, for all the land that you see I will give to you and to your offspring forever." (Genesis 13:14-15 ESV).

Second, the choices we often make are choices based on selfishness, and not on faith. Lot chose what looked good to him and it cost him dearly. The land he chose was under a death sentence. Perhaps a little due diligence would have let him know of the evil that lurked in this Eden that lay before his eyes.

In the end, Lot made decisions based on carnal appeal and not on spiritual appeal. Abraham, on the other hand, made his decision based on spiritual principles of peace and deference to others, and not on carnal, selfish reasons, and God rewarded him for it.

When we are faced with decisions like these, how many times do we look at things from a spiritual perspective versus jumping at a decision based on carnal considerations only? Do we pray for the wisdom in choosing what is best in God's eyes, for the way we can best please and glorify Him? If we truly do this, then we can have every expectation that the Lord will be with us in making the decision that is best for us. It may not be the decision we like, but the Lord can take the apparent loss we experience from making a prudent decision and turning it into a tremendous blessing.

This is what living by faith looks like.

**

When I think of what I can do for God, I quickly realize that there really isn't anything I can offer that He needs. It is the most lopsided relationship that I am in. I get up each day and pray that He gives me and my family our daily bread, because I have learned never to take the basic necessities for granted.

I pray that He gives me my daily allotment of wisdom because I realize that without Him, I have nothing of value to offer anyone I meet. I pray that He opens my eyes to ways that I can serve Him so that I may hear the words of His dear Son say to me, "Well done, My good and faithful servant."

No matter how many words I may write, or conversations I may have, or how many people I may baptize, in the end, I feel privileged that God has allowed me to have any stewardship He sees fit to bestow upon me. And when all my work is done, I pray that people may not see me in my work, but that they see Jesus and Jesus only.

I never want to boast, but in Jesus. I never want glory; I want my King to get all the glory. I never want praise; I want the Lord of lords and King of kings to get all the praise. I Never want honor; I want He and He alone to get all the honor. The one verse that brings me joy and contentment is this:

> "So you also, when you have done all that you were commanded, say, 'We are unworthy servants; we have only done what was our duty.'" (Luke 17:10 ESV).

When I think of all that I can do for God, it is not in my abilities that I focus, but in His stewardship that He in His grace will bestow upon me. And whatever that is, it is with humble thanks that He finds me worthy enough to serve and do what is only my duty.

***

I am reading about Joseph in Genesis for my daily Bible reading. Sometimes we focus on his rise to tremendous power and glory and forget the years of his fall and struggles. He was hated, sold, accused and forgotten, all while remaining faithful to God.

It reminds me of the importance of not becoming too myopic with my life. It is my tendency to see good and see God, and see evil and think that God has forgotten me. But there are great lessons for me in the pit of Joseph's life that are just as important as the lessons I learn from his pinnacle.

When good happens to me, it is right to see God in that; but when I am suffering, or things are a struggle, it's just as important to see God in that, too. God never promised a life of ease, but He has promised to walk with me when things get difficult. God was with Joseph in the pit and the prison as well as when he was on the throne.

I want to develop Joseph's steadfast faithfulness in the times of trials that help me move to the times of deliverance.

> "But the LORD was with Joseph and showed him steadfast love and gave him favor in the sight of the keeper of the prison." (Genesis 39:21 ESV).

***

What Will Precipitate The Return Of Jesus?

Is it me, or does the chatter in the world regarding the second coming of Jesus seem to be intensifying? I don't know; I'm over 50 years old and I guess I remember people predicting the end-time events even then. One year after I was born, Hal Lindsey came out with his best-selling book, *The Late Great Planet Earth*, where he looked at what he viewed as biblical prophecies that would point to the beginning of the end.

Men have been doing this for centuries, and if the Father withholds His Son from returning, they will be predicting Jesus' return for centuries from now. But here's the reality: One day, someone may be right in their prediction. Not because they know anything, but because someone just may pick a date from the carousel of prophets who may just get lucky. Here is what we know for certain:

> "But concerning that day and hour no one knows, not even the angels of heaven, nor the Son, but the Father only." (Matthew 24:36 ESV).

The day of the end will be chosen by the Father, and the Father only. The problem with man, is that we want to know everything we can about the end, so we grasp at any verse and make it say what we want it to say. Some read the Bible and see the rapture, a time of tribulation and the battle between Jesus and His army vs Satan and his army, where Satan will be defeated and Jesus will reign over the earth for 1000 years on a throne in Israel.

Others think that the 1000 years (literal or figurative) of plenty and prosperity for the Kingdom of God on earth will immediately precede the coming of Jesus. Still, others do not believe that there is a 1000-year reign of Jesus on earth, but that Jesus began to reign when He ascended to His Father and will continue to reign on the throne of David.

These are very high-level views, and to be fair, people believe in nuanced versions of these basic views, so it would be unfair to push people into one of these broad views. But my point is that there seems to be something in man that wants to figure out that which only the Father knows, namely, how can we know when Jesus will return?

The problem with trying to figure out hints of when Jesus will return, is that the whole basis of "end times prophecies" forget one important and consistent teaching of Jesus regarding His promised return: Namely, when it happens, it will come as a thief in the night, with no warning:

> "Behold, I am coming like a thief! Blessed is the one who stays awake,

keeping his garments on, that he may not go about naked and be seen exposed!" (Revelation 16:15 ESV).

And

"But know this, that if the master of the house had known in what part of the night the thief was coming, he would have stayed awake and would not have let his house be broken into.
Therefore you also must be ready, for the Son of Man is coming at an hour you do not expect." (Matthew 24:43-44 ESV).

And

"For you yourselves are fully aware that the day of the Lord will come like a thief in the night." (1 Thessalonians 5:2 ESV).

As the Lord says in Matthew 24, since we don't know when He will return, we need to be ready. And that's the point. Once the end times events start, and Jesus does return, only those who are ready and watching will be prepared. There will be no death-bed confessions; there will be no opportunities to follow Him. Only those who are waiting and watching will be found prepared for His return.

Perhaps the Father has chosen a fixed date, and when that date gets here, He will send His Son. Or perhaps the Father has a condition chosen and once that condition is met, He will send His Son back. I know some wonder if He is waiting until there is no one left to repent and that's when He will send His Son back, much like it was in the days of Noah.

Speculating what will precipitate the return of Jesus is just that... speculation. The truth is that only one being knows when this event will happen, and He's not telling. So where does that leave us? It means that we will need to be ready for His return now. As much as I would love to believe in a rapture where I would have the chance for a "do-over" if I were left behind, I do not see any evidence of people getting a do-over during a tribulation period.

What I see is that Jesus is waiting for His Father to say, "Go, get Your bride." And when that happens, we need to be His bride and we need to be waiting and watching for our Bridegroom's return:

"Let us rejoice and exult and give him the glory, for the marriage of the Lamb has come, and his Bride has made herself ready;
it was granted her to clothe herself with fine linen, bright and pure"-- for the fine linen is the righteous deeds of the saints.
And the angel said to me, "Write this: Blessed are those who are

invited to the marriage supper of the Lamb." And he said to me, "These are the true words of God." (Revelation 19:7-9 ESV).

So, we will never know what the events are that will precipitate the return of Jesus. What we do know is that the return is imminent. He is returning someday, and when He does, it will be as a thief in the night. Only those who are found watching and waiting, as a bride adorned for her Bridegroom, will be taken home with Him. And there will be no second chances. We only have the here and now to prepare for eternity with Him. Let's be ready when the Father says to our Bridegroom, "Go, and bring your bride home."

"For I feel a divine jealousy for you, since I betrothed you to one husband, to present you as a pure virgin to Christ. But I am afraid that as the serpent deceived Eve by his cunning, your thoughts will be led astray from a sincere and pure devotion to Christ." (2 Corinthians 11:2-3 ESV).

***

So, if we mess up in our walk with Jesus, we have a choice to make.

We can either give up because we feel that we just can't do it, so why try?

Or we can brush ourselves off, get back up and put our hand back into the hand of Jesus.

We'd do anything to help up our own children when they fall, making sure they don't give up.

How much more is the perfect Father of us all waiting for us, with His hands outstretched, for us to get back up and keep moving forward?

If we walk away from the Lord, then it's our choice. God is patient enough to work with us as long as it takes for us to overcome sin through His grace, as long as we are willing, and we don't give up.

"fear not, for I am with you; be not dismayed, for I am your God; I will strengthen you, I will help you, I will uphold you with my righteous right hand." (Isaiah 41:10 ESV).

***

Genesis 44 is a chapter of repentance. It's a chapter that shows growth and a willingness to do what is right, even if that means you will suffer for it. Let me set the stage...

Joseph was hated by his brothers, and they sacrificed him by selling him into slavery. They presented his blood-soaked coat of many colors to their father who concluded that a wild animal had killed Joseph. Decades later, a famine hit the land, and the family heard that the only place that had food was Egypt. So, the boys went to buy food. Little did they know that their brother, Joseph, was the leader of Egypt, second only to Pharaoh himself.

On their second trip to buy more food, they have Joseph's younger brother with them. Joseph tests the brothers, who still do not recognize that he is Joseph, by putting his personal cup into Benjamin's sack and then sending his men out to find the planted stolen goods.

When Joseph's official overtakes them and makes the charge of theft against them, they become indignant and tell the official that if one of them has the cup, that brother would die and the rest would become slaves in Egypt. But the official says that only the guilty would be punished.

Of course, the cup was found in Benjamin's sack. And here is where we see the repentance and change of heart. Would these brother's sacrifice their younger brother and leave him in Egyptian slavery as they had done Joseph, saving themselves by sacrificing another brother? The official gave them every chance to do this by telling them that all but Benjamin were free to go. What did the brother's do?

> "Then they tore their clothes, and every man loaded his donkey, and they returned to the city." (Genesis 44:13 ESV).

They all went back together, demonstrating that they would not commit the same sin that they committed with Joseph. They did what was right, even though it might cost each of them their lives or their freedom. Verse 13 is a microcosm of the wonderful journey of repentance and redemption that we see in the family of Joseph.

No matter what our past, there is room for the Word of God to transform us into something better than what we are. The past can be just that- the past- if we let the Word into our heart and pave the way for repentance and change in our lives.

Do you feel burdened by a sin that weighs you down? Release it through a true repentance and be set free by the power of Jesus' Word in you. It can change you and make you someone that He wants you to be. None of us have to be held captive by sin or our past. We see it in the brothers of Joseph, and the same truth can be ours today.

"So Jesus said to the Jews who had believed him, "If you abide in my word, you are truly my disciples, and you will know the truth, and the truth will set you free." (John 8:31-32 ESV).

***

I believe in the power of prayer. I believe it can accomplish tremendous things.

Recently, I have been on a productivity spree like none other in my life.

I purchased and assembled patio furniture, lights, and I am looking at starting some new yard and landscaping projects.

I have coordinated a number of purchase returns and replacements.

I have helped to proactively take care of Ryder to ensure that his mother is uninterrupted during both illnesses and times of intense work scheduled.

I have taken care of extended family needs that came up unexpectedly.

The last few weeks of my life have been the most productive of my life, and I am still moving forward in a strong way with more future plans.

At first, I felt proud of myself for this new-found energy and productivity. But yesterday, when I was in the car with my wife, something hit me hard, because this is so unlike me. I turned to my wife and asked in all seriousness…

"Have you been saying any specific prayers about me lately?"

I believe in the power of prayer, even if the prayers are from someone else that may impact me in answer to their prayers.

I never did get a straight answer from my wife, but I'm not complaining. I'm enjoying this new-found productivity!

***

Have you ever wondered why God made the universe so massive? With 200 billion trillion (200,000,000,000,000,000,000,000) estimated stars, it hurts our head just trying to think about such a large number.

And with the distance in space from one end of the universe to the other end so expansive that we will never be able to travel or explore even a minute part of it, why so big?

"The heavens declare the glory of God, and the sky above proclaims his handiwork." (Psalm 19:1b ESV).

God created something so grand for His own glory. If He is the Creator, how can anyone walk away from any other conclusion but that He is a mighty and powerful Being full of glory? And to accentuate this, the Psalmist says,

> "He determines the number of the stars; he gives to all of them their names." (Psalm 147:4 ESV).

Every single one of them. All 200 billion trillion of them.
Yet, our Creator knows this as well:

> "Are not five sparrows sold for two pennies? And not one of them is forgotten before God. Why, even the hairs of your head are all numbered. Fear not; you are of more value than many sparrows." (Luke 12:6-7 ESV).

So, if God knows every star in the massive universe He created, how wonderful and glorious is it that He is immensely interested in this small blue speck of a planet where He pours out His grace upon the insignificantly small being that He created in His image?

> "When I look at your heavens, the work of your fingers, the moon and the stars, which you have set in place, what is man that you are mindful of him, and the son of man that you care for him?" (Psalm 8:3-4 ESV).

And that is the most glorious thing about God in my humble opinion. He created a mind-blowing, massive universe for His glory and still is intimately aware of me and every hair He made on my body.
That is my God!

***

Today's post is a little different from most. It's more of an admonition than an encouraging post. And I fully expect many people not to agree with me on the premise, but it's something I feel compelled to share.

According to the Atlantic (June 23rd, 2014), an Ohio State University research study found that men think of sex on average 19 times a day. While some of those thoughts may be wholesome thoughts between a man and woman in marriage, it's not a stretch to conclude that many of those thoughts are of an impure nature.

While other studies found different results, it's obvious that men think about sex a lot, and research is bearing out that this isn't only a male problem. If we are not careful, we can accept these behaviors as natural and just part of how we are made.

But the truth is that God did not make us to sin. Jesus says,

> "You have heard that it was said, 'You shall not commit adultery.' But I say to you that everyone who looks at a woman with lustful intent has already committed adultery with her in his heart." (Matthew 5:27-28 ESV).

Lust begins in the heart. It's part of these "19 times a day" thoughts. It's not natural or the way we were made. It is a learned behavior. The Proverbs say "For as he thinketh in his heart, so is he: (Proverbs 23:7a KJV). So if we are thinking things we shouldn't be thinking about 19 times a day, then it is because we have put those building blocks of thoughts into our hearts that we shouldn't be putting into our hearts.

Rather, we need to be putting the building blocks of pure things into our hearts. What we watch, what we listen to, what we read, what we say, where we go... all of these things will put in the raw material that will determine what we think about 19 times a day.

> "Finally, brothers, whatever is true, whatever is honorable, whatever is just, whatever is pure, whatever is lovely, whatever is commendable, if there is any excellence, if there is anything worthy of praise, think about these things." (Philippians 4:8 ESV).

I wonder what the people in the days of Noah chose to put into their hearts? Whatever it was, it had a devastating result that brought about judgment upon them from the Lord:

> "The LORD saw that the wickedness of man was great in the earth, and that every intention of the thoughts of his heart was only evil continually." (Genesis 6:5 ESV).

Before we get too comfortable saying that thinking about sex 19 times a day is just natural, let's remember that we will only think about what we put in our hearts. Whether it is good or evil, it is only natural to think about what we choose to consume in our hearts and minds.

***

Happy Father's Day to my Dad. He instilled a faith in me that didn't just teach me the family religion but he taught me how to seek after God. When I went out on my own and struggled with God, the lessons he taught me kept me grounded in what was important.

I hope that one day my own children will look at me the same way I look at my father.

Happy Father's Day, Dad. I love you more than you will ever know. Thank you for giving me bread and fish when I was going after going after serpents and stones.

***

If you want to get the most out of the book of Job, take the time to read it straight through in one sitting. If you jump in the middle of a speech given by a main character, you may walk away with the wrong message.

Job is adamant about his innocence and tries to make sense of his circumstances without sinning against God. However, he is harsh against his friends and at times he is very sarcastic. Without reading through the book, it would be easy to miss these touches of sarcasm and accusations.

Job is a man who is wrestling with his worldview that is being shattered by his current circumstances. And his friends are not making it easy by trying to get him to admit to fault in something that he knows he isn't guilty of.

Have you felt this way before? Are you struggling with something that is testing the way you think about how the world works, especially a world where you know that God is sovereign?

If so, why not set aside a couple of hours and read Job in a way that you may never have read it before? You may be surprised at the insights you might walk away with.

***

Thought Question: Do you have a standard that you bring to the Bible, and as long as the Bible fits your standard, you follow the Bible,

Or do you learn the standard of the Bible, then apply your beliefs and practices to the Holy standard?

This small distinction in words makes all the difference in our lives.

***

Jesus Is God

Perhaps we talk about the deity of Jesus in a casual, theoretical fashion, tucking the phrase in the back of our minds as we come to an agreement on a statement of doctrine. We say that Jesus is God; He is deity. But do we really know what we are saying? Do we understand the implications of that statement? Better yet, do we understand how that truth, by nature, puts us all-in as followers of Jesus?

First, let's establish that the Bible does, indeed, claim that the man Jesus, who walked the earth and performed miracles, was more than a mighty prophet of God. Listen to what the inspired writers of the Bible say about the nature of who Jesus is:

> "I give them eternal life, and they will never perish, and no one will snatch them out of my hand.
> My Father, who has given them to me, is greater than all, and no one is able to snatch them out of the Father's hand.
> I and the Father are one." (John 10:28-30 ESV).

And

> "Have this mind among yourselves, which is yours in Christ Jesus, who, though he was in the form of God, did not count equality with God a thing to be grasped," (Philippians 2:5-6 ESV).

And

> "For in him the whole fullness of deity dwells bodily, and you have been filled in him, who is the head of all rule and authority." (Colossians 2:9-10 ESV).

And

> "In the beginning was the Word, and the Word was with God, and the Word was God." (John 1:1 ESV).

All of these verses, and many more, let you walk away with no other conclusion than the Man who lived on the earth 2000 years ago is called God by those who wrote the New Testament. And the contemporaries of Jesus understood His claim to deity. Here are a few passages that show that His claim was put out for all to see:

"The Jews answered him, "It is not for a good work that we are going to stone you but for blasphemy, because you, being a man, make yourself God." (John 10:33 ESV).

And

"This was why the Jews were seeking all the more to kill him, because not only was he breaking the Sabbath, but he was even calling God his own Father, making himself equal with God." (John 5:18 ESV).

Whether we believe the claim or not, it is there. The Bible claims that Jesus, son of Mary and Joseph, was indeed the Son of God. It claims that He existed as God before man, that He was our Creator, and that He left heaven to become one of His creation so that He could visit us, understand us, die for us to redeem us back to the Father, and serve as our perpetual High Priest.

If Jesus is not God, then we are all guilty of the vilest and most evil blasphemy of all time. We have stripped what only belongs to God and we have set it upon the creation. That's the way that the Jews saw it. That's how Paul saw it until Jesus revealed Himself to the apostle. That's how Jesus' own family viewed it until they saw their risen Brother.

On the other hand, if Jesus is our Creator Who spoke everything into existence, then that leaves us only one possible choice to make. If He is God, then we must hunger and thirst after His words and do everything to submit to Him. Not because we like or agree with His teachings; not because He was a powerful and persuasive teacher; and not because we agree with the worldview He invites us to live in.

The only choice we can make if Jesus is the Creator is to fall to our knees, realize He is our Potter and we are His clay, and live every moment letting Him fashion us into the servants He wants us to be. Our choice becomes binary, stark, and unambiguous: Either we accept the will of our Creator who visited us 2000 years ago, or we reject Him and wait to face Him on the Day of Judgment for our rejection.

But if He is God, then we have an amazing life in store if we accept Him and follow Him with all of our life, soul, and mind. For He is above nature. He is supernatural, and our relationship with Him is one based on supernatural existence. In Him, all things are possible that are impossible without Him. In Him, He gives us the grace and power to overcome sin that is impossible to do if we live only a natural life. In Him, we have the ability to overcome all obstacles that the Devil and the world place before us, not in our own strength, but because He does the impossible lifting for us.

If we wholly commit to Jesus, we are committing to more than a great prophet; we are committing to the Son of God, the sovereign Creator of His universe. But the choice is binary. Either He is God or He is not God. There is no middle ground. We must place our spiritual stake in the ground and take a stand. We must either be all-in or we will be all-out.

I boldly confess before you that I believe that Jesus is my Creator and my God. I believe He came to earth to die for my sins. I believe that He is my Potter and I am His clay. I believe His words, and His words alone have within them eternal life. I believe I will kneel before Him in judgment one day.

> "for I know whom I have believed, and I am convinced that he is able to guard until that day what has been entrusted to me." (2 Timothy 1:12b ESV).

What about you?

***

I don't have to figure out everything about God.
I just have to have faith in what He says,
I have to believe He can do all things,
I need to believe that He will reward me for seeking Him,
and I have to understand that He knows all the things I do not, nor cannot know.

> "And without faith it is impossible to please him, for whoever would draw near to God must believe that he exists and that he rewards those who seek him." (Hebrews 11:6 ESV).

***

I've just been summoned for jury duty. I've been summoned before but never chosen to serve. It's not something I relish, but it is a civic duty I take seriously.

My biggest concern is in seeking justice and what is right. Putting away my personal inclinations to consider what is just.

I fear God in this role because He expects those who judge to represent His justice. If I am chosen to serve, please pray for wisdom that I will seek righteousness, fairness, and justice.

> "You shall do no injustice in court. You shall not be partial to the poor or defer to the great, but in righteousness shall you judge your neighbor."

(Leviticus 19:15 ESV).

***

Moses was one of the greatest prophets and leaders of Israel. He had a special relationship with God, and God defended him vigorously against those who challenged this humble man.

But Moses wasn't perfect. In one instance, he did not uphold God as holy before the congregation and it cost him the experience of entering the promised land. His whole life's work for forty years was to lead people to their inheritance, but in His grace, God did allow Moses to see the land he had worked so hard to lead the people to.

> "The LORD said to Moses, "Go up into this mountain of Abarim and see the land that I have given to the people of Israel. When you have seen it, you also shall be gathered to your people, as your brother Aaron was," (Numbers 27:12-13 ESV).

That made me think about God doing a similar thing for us today. In a show of grace, God allows us to use powerful telescopes that rotate around the Earth to see parts of His universe that we may never have an opportunity to visit ourselves.

In a sense, through these powerful telescopes, we can peer across the expanse of space, distances that we have no way of traversing (at least now), and peer into His glorious creation. We see stars, galaxies, black holes, pulsars, supernovas, exoplanets, and so much more await our discovery.

Thanks be to God who has given us this magnificent mountain top view into the expanse of His wondrous creation.

***

In my daily Bible reading, I am in the book of Leviticus. It's tempting to rush past all the rules and laws given to the priest to get to the action and inspirational parts of the Old Testament. But there are some important things we learn when we spend time reading about all the rules and rituals that went into the instructions found in Leviticus.

In this book, the people learn about sin and the importance of repentance and atonement. Even in the Old Testament dispensation, God gave an avenue for His grace and His forgiveness.

In the book, the people learn that their sin was so bad, that it cost another living being its blood as atonement. Sin never was something that could be taken away without blood and a sacrifice of the living.

In this book, we see that a sacrifice for the sin which separates man from God can turn away God's wrath in a way prescribed by God. Going all the way back to Cain, we see that God always prescribed how to deal with sin. It was never left to us to decide how to do that.

And in the book of Leviticus, we see the love that God has for man. What seems like a litany of rules and regulations is, in reality, the path by which sinful man can be reconciled back to a holy and blameless God. God loved His people enough to show them the way back to Him when their sin broke the relationship with Him.

And all of this pointed to the perfect and eternal sacrifice that God made on our behalf. When the blood of bulls and goats could not be the perfect sacrifice that could save us, God Himself became man for the purpose of offering His life as a sacrifice once and for all. This sacrifice was made with holy blood from a blameless God. It serves the spiritual needs of man forever as the enduring sacrifice.

But we learned the importance of this blood sacrifice in Leviticus and we learned just how important that atonement for sin is to our God. When man did all he could humanly do, God Himself stepped in to provide the perfect sacrifice for us.

> "But when Christ had offered for all time a single sacrifice for sins, he sat down at the right hand of God, waiting from that time until his enemies should be made a footstool for his feet. For by a single offering he has perfected for all time those who are being sanctified." (Hebrews 10:12-14 ESV).

***

Love Like Jesus Loves

Satan will do everything he can to distract us from staying focused on the Lord. And many things he uses are not evil things in and of themselves.

He may throw in a political victory or a political defeat to have us focus an inordinate amount of time cheering or worrying.

He may help us see other people, made in the image of our God, as our mortal enemies because they hold a different political view than we profess. Perhaps we even forget that Jesus died for them, too, because He loved these capitalists or socialists as much as he loved us.

Satan may take a sports team and cause us to dwell on the mistakes or shortcomings of players and coaches, forgetting that it's just a game, and stir up anger or hatred in our hearts against men and women made in God's image.

We witness violence and hate speech, either against us, or by people who believe the way we do against those to whom we disagree. It's easy to have compassion for people who believe the way we believe and feel justified when people with whom we disagree suffer. But those with whom we agree and those with whom we disagree are all made in the image of God.

Satan is a master at helping us feel justified in our hate by getting us to vilify others and forget that we are all made in God's image and that King Jesus loved them and died for them just as He died for us.

The next time someone does something reprehensible, hate what they are doing, but look at them as one of God's created children that He loves. He has no pleasure in destroying them. He wants more than anything for the reprehensible to come to repentance.

If God is longing for evil men and women to come to repentance where He will graciously remember their evil acts no more, then shouldn't we see the violent, the profane, the irreverent people in our society the same way?

We say, "Hate the sin and love the sinner", but that is often easier said than done. However, that is exactly what Jesus did for you and me. He hated our sins, but He loved us. If we can see people who do and say things we detest, and still love them, it will open us to be the stewards that God wants us to be.

So, when we witness people doing and saying things we detest, let God work in our hearts to help us see them as He sees them, rather than bow before Satan to see them as the devil would have us see them.

> "Have I any pleasure in the death of the wicked, declares the Lord GOD, and not rather that he should turn from his way and live?" (Ezekiel 18:23 ESV).

> "Be merciful, even as your Father is merciful." (Luke 6:36 ESV).

***

I am finishing the book of Leviticus in my daily Bible reading. This is a book where God creates a religion for His people. The rules and rituals cover everything that the people and the priests must do in detail from the sacrifices to how they are to remain holy and clean.

The amazing thing about this book is that it taught people who didn't know how to worship or act in a way pleasing to God. This detail of worship and ritual usually evolved over decades and centuries. But the Israelites didn't develop this worship over time; God gave them the details from the beginning.

Sometimes our eyes glaze over these rules and rituals and we totally miss the awesome intervention of the Lord in which He delivered a complete way to worship to a people with no experience worshiping Him this way.

God taught the people how to worship, how to be holy, and how to revere Him. The next time you read this dry book of rules and regulations, remember that it was written to people who had no clue how to worship God until He revealed to them in detail what He wanted.

The book of Leviticus is tangible evidence of the love and providence of God.

***

I was reading the book of Numbers where God would lead the people in the wilderness by resting a cloud over the tabernacle. When the cloud rested, the people camped, but when the cloud lifted, it was counted as a command of the Lord to break camp and move.

> "At the command of the LORD the people of Israel set out, and at the command of the LORD they camped. As long as the cloud rested over the tabernacle, they remained in camp.
>
> Even when the cloud continued over the tabernacle many days, the people of Israel kept the charge of the LORD and did not set out.
>
> Sometimes the cloud was a few days over the tabernacle, and according to the command of the LORD they remained in camp; then according to the command of the LORD they set out.
>
> And sometimes the cloud remained from evening until morning. And when the cloud lifted in the morning, they set out, or if it continued for a day and a night, when the cloud lifted they set out." (Numbers 9:18-21 ESV).

For forty years, they camped when God said to camp and they moved when God said to move. Sometimes they were only a day at camp, sometimes they were there perhaps over a month.

I wonder if they got tired of moving and desired to put down roots and stay in a particular place? That's the way we think, sometimes, isn't it?

The Lord leads us through this world toward our heavenly home and often we long to set down roots here. But we need to have the mind of the Israelites in the wilderness. We move where the Lord leads. We don't put down roots here, but we sojourn as a pilgrim until Jesus leads us home.

We need to enjoy the long periods of time where peace and rest are given by God, but when we find ourselves moving, we need to have faith in God that He will lead us to safety when He wants us to travel with Him.

Perhaps, we pick up and move from a job that is causing us to lose our focus that belongs on God. Perhaps we have to cut ties with our friends and companions who are poor influences in our lives. Perhaps we have to leave behind habits and ruts that have caused us to fall into complacency.

Following the Lord's lead isn't always about calling Mayflower, packing up our belongings, and moving to another location. It could be, but more often for us, it is moving away from the parts of our lives that put distance between us and the Lord.

So, as the cloud of the Lord starts to move us in another direction, we have the same choice that the Israelites had in Numbers. We can follow the Lord's lead or we can stay behind and grow deeper roots. But the deeper roots we grow, the harder it will eventually be to follow the Lord's lead.

Soon, we may find that the Lord has moved to safety without us while we have stayed behind with deep roots, satisfied with the life we have built without Him.

***

Here is another unedited excerpt from my upcoming book, The Sovereignty of God…

> "Then his wife said to him, "Do you still hold fast your integrity? Curse God and die."
> "But he said to her, "You speak as one of the foolish women would speak. Shall we receive good from God, and shall we not receive evil?" In all this Job did not sin with his lips." (Job 2:9-10 ESV).

Satan must have been giddy with joy when Mrs. Job gave her husband this advice. The accuser of the brethren did know human nature well. I am too afraid to think of how I would have reacted if I was in Job's situation, because to my shame, I have said a lot worse when faced with a lot less. And though Mrs. Job was wrong and sinful in urging her husband to curse God and die, I understand why she did it. That doesn't mean that she was justified or that her sinful comment should be overlooked. But you can understand when a grief-stricken mother of ten who lost her children, lost her means of livelihood, and has a husband who is hanging on to life by a thread is grief-stricken. And when we are face to face with grief-stricken people, aren't we quick to give grace and slow to condemn? But you have to appreciate Job's mindset, don't you? This is a mindset that can only be where it is if you understand the sovereignty of your Creator Who gives and takes away as He pleases:

> "But he said to her, "You speak as one of the foolish women would speak. Shall we receive good from God, and shall we not receive evil?" In all this Job did not sin with his lips." (Job 2:10 ESV).

So, Job wins. God wins. Satan loses. But it is not over. May I propose an inference as to why this suffering still plays out in forty more chapters? We ask ourselves, why is it that Job has to continue to endure suffering? Let me be clear that I do not know because God does not say. But there are a couple of reasons that may be true, or it may be a reason that we will never know. That said, perhaps God is giving Satan time to wear down Job in order to find a victory over a weakened Job. We have all been there before, haven't we? We face a new challenge with strength and resolve, but as time drags on with no relief in sight, we start to lose faith.

> "Therefore we must pay much closer attention to what we have heard, lest we drift away from it." (Hebrews 2:1 ESV).

Few things cause us to drift away more than when we have to endure trials. Perhaps this is what Satan was angling for. Or, perhaps God knew that Job and his friends, who we are about to meet, needed to learn a lesson about His sovereignty that they didn't know. It seemed that they had made a couple of assumptions about God that were not true and that led them to some false ideas about who God was which was a challenge to His sovereignty. Maybe God was going to take this terrible thing that Satan had incited Him to do against Job and glorify His name and His sovereignty in a way that only this circumstance could accomplish. Whether or not this is God's purpose in allowing the suffering to continue, it was certainly a result as we see in the next 40 chapters. This is why I say that the book of Job is more a book on the sovereignty of God than it is a book on suffering.

***

In Luke 12, Jesus tells the story of the rich man who planned to take his excess produce, build bigger barns to store it, and take it easy for the rest of his life. The problem is that the rich man never considered God in all his plans. Jesus said to him:

> "But God said to him, 'Fool! This night your soul is required of you, and the things you have prepared, whose will they be?'" (Luke 12:20 ESV).

This is more than a prophet saying that God said this. This is Jesus, God Himself, saying what HE said to the rich man.

This is what we call a primary source. In essence, Jesus said, "I said to him, 'Fool, tonight I am taking your soul...'"

When Jesus gives us warnings, He's not speaking as simply a messenger of God. These are His words that will judge us on the last day (John 12:48).

The people who heard Jesus preach realized that He was speaking as someone different from the scribes. He had authority behind His word. This is something we always need to remember too. When we read the words of Jesus, we are reading the words of God Himself.

> "And they were astonished at his teaching, for he taught them as one who had authority, and not as the scribes." (Mark 1:22 ESV).

***

Yesterday, we looked at how Jesus spoke as one with authority. He is God and when He told the rich man in Luke 12 that God said this very night his soul would be required of him, it was Jesus, our God, who said that to the rich man.

And in His sermon on the mount, Jesus says this:

> "But if God so clothes the grass of the field, which today is alive and tomorrow is thrown into the oven, will he not much more clothe you, O you of little faith?" (Matthew 6:30 ESV).

Again, when you realize Who is saying this, it brings even more comfort to us. Jesus says that God loves us so much more than the grass of the field that He clothes. And Jesus, being God, is giving us insight into His very heart.

In essence, Jesus looks out over His creation listening to Him on the mountainside, and tells them, "I take care of my grass that I created and you, my children, are worth so much more to Me than the grass. If I take care of the grass, how much more do you think that I will take care of you?"

Every time we read where Jesus gives insight into how God feels toward us, we need to understand that He is giving us a personal glimpse into His own heart. What a wonderful God and Savior we have Who tells us so plainly how much He loves us and how He feels when we forget about Him.

***

Jesus, Our Bridegroom

When we talk about weddings, we talk about them steeped within our culture. Reciting vows, lighting a unity candle, and exchanging rings are all part of many American weddings. And each culture has its own traditions with symbolism that tells a story that often only those in the culture understand.

I submit to you that the wedding talk in the New Testament is steeped in symbolism that would have made perfect sense to the people who heard Jesus teach on it, while many of us may miss the amazing nuances He is teaching. Over the last few months, I have done a deep dive into studying the first-century Jewish wedding rituals and what I learned will make me never read the words of Jesus the same way again. I am convinced that many who read this will walk away and look at the relationship we have with Jesus in an amazing new light.

Let's start off by explaining the Jewish wedding customs in the first century. This is a summation and not a detailed exposition. There is so much that could be said on this that it could easily fill an entire book. But for our purposes, we can look at the Jewish wedding done in three phases. And as we highlight these three phases, I am convinced that many will draw the same conclusions that I drew without me saying a word. And when you do, your knees will buckle and your heart will skip a beat.

From a high level, the Jewish wedding would happen in three distinct phases: First, a man and a woman would be pledged together and a legal contract was written. Then, the betrothal phase would happen. Finally, the wedding itself would happen, the marriage would be consummated and the man and woman would live as husband and wife in the same house as one.

In the first phase, a man and a woman would be legally bound to each other via a legal contract. This could happen by the man and woman themselves or this could be an arranged marriage by the parents of the groom and bride. The groom or the groom's father would pay the agreed-upon price by the father of the bride and the two would legally be considered married. However, the bride would return to her father's house and the groom would return to his father's house. Then, the next phase of the wedding would begin- the betrothal.

During the betrothal, the woman would live in purity and prepare to become a wife. This period would often last a year or so, though sometimes longer and sometimes shorter. If it was an arranged marriage between two young children, this period would be much longer. In any case, the bride was expected to give evidence of her purity. At any time, the marriage could be legally annulled at this stage if the bride showed any impurity. Joseph and Mary were betrothed when Mary was pregnant with Jesus and Joseph had decided to end the marriage in this phase until an angel visited him to ensure that Mary had no impurity.

But the groom had responsibilities during the betrothal period as well. He would go back to his father's house and begin to build a room onto the family home for he and his new bride. During the betrothal, the father of the groom would keep check on the purity of the bride and the preparation of his son to ready himself to become a husband and to carry out all the responsibilities of a husband. And it was the father of the groom- not the groom or the father of the bride- who made the final determination that all was ready for the marriage to enter its final stage. This is why at least 9 months to a year or more was given in this betrothal period while his son made his preparations.

And the father of the groom didn't discuss this time with his son. When he made the decision, it would come as a "thief in the night." Sound familiar? And at the time of his choosing, the father of the groom would go to his son and say. "It's time. Go get your bride." This would lead to the final stage of the Jewish wedding custom. The groom would gather his friends and they would lead a procession down the streets (usually at night), where he and his friends would shout their intentions along the way. And the prepared bride would finally see her groom return to her to take her to her new home. She would have been prepared and waiting for this very thing to happen during the whole betrothal period.

The groom would then take her to his father's home (usually) where they would have a small ceremony and then a wedding feast, to be attended by all friends and family, that may have lasted for days. When it was all over, the bride and groom moved into the room that the groom had prepared for his bride and they would live as one forever.

Knowing that, does it give a new understanding of the passages in the New Testament that talk about Jesus being our groom and the church being His bride? Consider,

> "Husbands, love your wives, as Christ loved the church and gave himself up for her, that he might sanctify her, having cleansed her by the washing of water with the word, so that he might present the church to himself in splendor, without spot or wrinkle or any such thing, that she might be holy and without blemish." (Ephesians 5:25-27 ESV).

When Jesus talks about the church being His bride, it is more than an allegory. It is a marriage in the fullness of the term, much more even than the physical marriage between a man and woman on earth. Jesus paid the price- His own blood- given by the Father of the Groom, our heavenly Father. And Jesus did it all to ensure that His bride, the church, would remain pure during the betrothal period.

Today, we are in this betrothal period. For the Father of the Groom loved the world that He paid the price for the bride by giving His only begotten Son. That was His part of signing the marriage document. And when we are baptized into Christ, this is our part of signing this marriage document and entering into a relationship with Jesus:

> "having been buried with him in baptism, in which you were also raised with him through faith in the powerful working of God, who raised him from the dead. And you, who were dead in your trespasses and the uncircumcision of your flesh, God made alive together with him, having forgiven us all our trespasses, by canceling the record of debt that stood against us with its legal demands. This he set aside, nailing it to the cross." (Colossians 2:12-14 ESV).

And so, by His grace, our Bridegroom is giving us everything we need to remain pure and ready for His return to claim us and take us home. Do you remember what he said to His disciples before He was crucified, resurrected, and ascended into heaven?

> "Let not your hearts be troubled. Believe in God; believe also in me. In my Father's house are many rooms. If it were not so, would I have told you that I go to prepare a place for you? And if I go and prepare a place for you, I will come again and will take you to myself, that where I am you may be also." (John 14:1-3 ESV).

This statement would have had tremendous meaning for the people of His day. This is what the bridegrooms did during the betrothal periods- they prepared a room in their fathers' houses for their brides. This is exactly what Jesus says He's doing for us at this very moment. And when the time comes, He will bring us to this home He has prepared for us. And when will that be:

> "But concerning that day and hour no one knows, not even the angels of heaven, nor the Son, but the Father only." (Matthew 24:36 ESV).

Sometimes we spend so much time trying to figure out how Jesus, who is God and knows everything, can not know the time of His return that we miss the wonderful, marvelous point that He is making. Just like the weddings that the people knew well, the time of His return would happen when His Father says to Him, "It's time; go get your bride!" And when that happens, Jesus will return with a shout and with an entourage to claim His bride, the church!

Knowing this, we should strive to keep ourselves pure and undefiled as we await the return of our bridegroom. We should be ready and waiting when we hear His shout and see Him come to claim His bride. And we should never act in a foolish way to take our eyes off the prize before us or not live each day in preparation for the coming of our Bridegroom. We've just scratched the surface of the verses that teach, beyond a shadow of a doubt, that we are in our betrothal period awaiting the return of our Bridegroom to take us home. Let's not be found impure or unprepared when He returns.

> "Then the kingdom of heaven will be like ten virgins who took their lamps and went to meet the bridegroom. Five of them were foolish, and five were wise. For when the foolish took their lamps, they took no oil with them, but the wise took flasks of oil with their lamps.
>
> As the bridegroom was delayed, they all became drowsy and slept. But at midnight there was a cry, 'Here is the bridegroom! Come out to meet him.'
>
> Then all those virgins rose and trimmed their lamps. And the foolish said to the wise, 'Give us some of your oil, for our lamps are going out.' But the wise answered, saying, 'Since there will not be enough for us and for you, go rather to the dealers and buy for yourselves.'
>
> And while they were going to buy, the bridegroom came, and those who were ready went in with him to the marriage feast, and the door was shut. Afterward the other virgins came also, saying, 'Lord, lord, open to us.'
>
> But he answered, 'Truly, I say to you, I do not know you.' Watch therefore, for you know neither the day nor the hour." (Matthew 25:1-13 ESV).

***

I am convinced that very few men who lived were like Job. Here was a man who served, feared, and loved God regardless of his circumstances. In his steadfastness, he never forgot who God was. He may have faltered a bit when he demanded that God explain Himself, but he never once sinned against God by blaming Him for evil.

Job knew he hadn't sinned against the Lord and asked the Lord to make it known if he had sinned in a way he wasn't aware of. And when pressed by his friends to confess to a sin that he hadn't committed, Job held to his integrity.

In the end, he never cursed God to his face as Satan suggested he would do and as his wife counseled him to do. That is why Job is mentioned in rare company. He stayed true to his faith in spite of being stripped of possessions, family, honor, and health.

> "Son of man, when a land sins against me by acting faithlessly, and I stretch out my hand against it and break its supply of bread and send famine upon it, and cut off from it man and beast, even if these three men, Noah, Daniel, and Job, were in it, they would deliver but their own lives by their righteousness, declares the Lord GOD." (Ezekiel 14:13-14 ESV).

This is the highest testimony that the Lord has given to a man. Before we curse God for the suffering we endure, let's remember this testimony and strive to always glorify God and not sin against Him with our lips. In our most challenging days, the Lord will give us this strength by His grace if we turn to Him and seek this strength.

***

Are we to think that God hates us because we will spend eternity in hell if we do not accept Him? Why will He let us suffer forever if we reject Him?

It's not that He is vindictive and allows us to be tortured if we reject him. It's actually that He loves us so tremendously that He's provided a way to escape that condemnation. He knows what awaits us if we do not embrace the safety and refuge found only in Him.

So, we are all deserving of hell but He said, "No!" And He made the ultimate sacrifice for us by dying for our sins.

If we end up in hell, it's not because God is vindictive or hateful. He's done everything so we can choose life. And there is no doubt that His heart is broken for everyone made in His image who suffers needlessly.

Hell is so needless. We have been given a lifeline. No one has to end up there. You, me... anyone. He came to save, not condemn. If we are condemned, it's because, and only because, we refused salvation.

> "For God did not send his Son into the world to condemn the world, but in order that the world might be saved through him." (John 3:17 ESV).

***

God is so far above us and there is none like Him.

When a man is clean and touches something unclean, he becomes unclean.

But when Jesus, who is clean, touches an unclean man, the man becomes clean.

What a wonderful Savior we have!

"And Jesus stretched out his hand and touched him, saying, "I will; be clean." And immediately his leprosy was cleansed." (Matthew 8:3 ESV).

And to us…

"that he might sanctify her, having cleansed her by the washing of water with the word, so that he might present the church to himself in splendor, without spot or wrinkle or any such thing, that she might be holy and without blemish." (Ephesians 5:26-27 ESV).

***

The five didn't kill.
The five didn't lie.
The five didn't take advantage of the weak and innocent.
The five didn't take drugs or get drunk.
The five didn't commit fornication or use the Lord's name in vain.
Yet the five missed it all.
What was the thing that caused them to miss Jesus?

"And while they were going to buy, the bridegroom came, and those who were ready went in with him to the marriage feast, and the door was shut. Afterward the other virgins came also, saying, 'Lord, lord, open to us.' But he answered, 'Truly, I say to you, I do not know you.' Watch therefore, for you know neither the day nor the hour." (Matthew 25:10-13 ESV).

The five just didn't prepare for Jesus.
Are you ready today to see Him?

***

I am reading Numbers in my daily Bible reading. In it, we see the importance of the unclean person being cleansed through water and blood.

It seems that water and blood have always been cleansing agents by God. God cleansed the unclean in the Mosaic law with water and blood.

God cleansed the earth with water via the flood of Noah by killing all land-dwelling flesh, sacrificing them in the cleansing.

And we are cleansed in the water of baptism as commanded by the Lord, coming into contact with the cleansing blood of Jesus that was sacrificed for us.

It isn't ritual washing that saves us, because there is no power in the water. It is in the obedience to God in a good conscience that saves us.

Are we against obedience to God so much that we scoff at His command to be baptized and tell Him that we will not obey for salvation; rather He MUST save us while we do not obey?

Water and blood have always been God's agents of cleansing. And so it is when God came to earth and said this:

> "Go into all the world and proclaim the gospel to the whole creation. Whoever believes and is baptized will be saved, but whoever does not believe will be condemned." (Mark 16:15b-16 ESV).

And decades later, before he died, His apostle Peter tells us this:

> "Baptism, which corresponds to this, now saves you, not as a removal of dirt from the body but as an appeal to God for a good conscience, through the resurrection of Jesus Christ," (1 Peter 3:21 ESV).

I know that many have had it drilled into our heads that baptism has nothing to do with salvation. I agree that water has no power to save…

But obedience through baptism as an appeal to God for a good conscience is what saves us. That is how we connect with the saving blood of Jesus that washes away our sins.

I prayerfully ask you to consider listening to Jesus and Peter who ask for our obedience to the Holy word of Jesus rather than men who teach us to ignore the words of Jesus and His apostles.

> "Do you not know that all of us who have been baptized into Christ Jesus were baptized into his death? We were buried therefore with him by baptism into death, in order that, just as Christ was raised from the dead

by the glory of the Father, we too might walk in newness of life. For if we have been united with him in a death like his, we shall certainly be united with him in a resurrection like his." (Romans 6:3-5 ESV).

***

If we see Jesus tomorrow, will what we did today be worth it?

***

Have you ever thought much about this verse?

"Jesus Christ is the same yesterday and today and forever." (Hebrews 13:8 ESV).

This tells us something really amazing about our God.

1. He has no reason to change- What do I mean? Well, why do we often change? Isn't it because something new comes along that causes us to rethink our position? But Jesus is all-knowing. There is never any new piece of information that will cause Him to reevaluate things.

2. He is trustworthy- We often change our stances or commitments. But we can put our trust in Jesus because He is 100% dependable. He won't be swayed because of a bad day or second thoughts.

3. His character is predictable- If we want to know what Jesus is like today and what He will be like tomorrow, then we can spend time in His word to see how He was yesterday. Sometimes people never know what they will get with us. We can almost be like two different people depending on which side of the bed we get up on in the morning. But Jesus is predictable and we can rest easy knowing that the Jesus we read about is the same one we serve now.

This is what makes Jesus our perfect hope, our perfect anchor, and our perfect shelter in the storms of life.

***

Under the Old Covenant, we needed a reminder of our sins and the need for atonement. This reminder happened in the sacrifices themselves.

Under our Law of Grace, Jesus offered His blood once and for all. But we still need a reminder of the atonement Jesus made once and for all for our sins.

We remember this great sacrifice every first day of the week as He instructed.

> "And he took bread, and when he had given thanks, he broke it and gave it to them, saying, "This is my body, which is given for you. Do this in remembrance of me."
> And likewise the cup after they had eaten, saying, "This cup that is poured out for you is the new covenant in my blood." (Luke 22:19-20 ESV).

We have a much more perfect sacrifice and we must never let that memory grow cold in our hearts.

***

We must give each other the benefit of the doubt when we can ascribe either good or evil to each other. Why? Because we do not know the hearts of men.

But God never gives us the benefit of the doubt. Surprised? You shouldn't be. He never gives us the benefit of the doubt because there is never a doubt when He looks into our hearts.

> "If you say, "Behold, we did not know this," does not he who weighs the heart perceive it? Does not he who keeps watch over your soul know it, and will he not repay man according to his work?" (Proverbs 24:12 ESV).

***

Am I crazy or do you get the idea that the theory of relativity and quantum physics is child's play to God?

> "who alone stretched out the heavens and trampled the waves of the sea;" (Job 9:8 ESV).

> "Where is the way to the dwelling of light, and where is the place of darkness, that you may take it to its territory and that you may discern the

paths to its home?" (Job 38:19-20 ESV).

"What is the way to the place where the light is distributed, or where the east wind is scattered upon the earth?" (Job 38:24 ESV).

"It is he who sits above the circle of the earth, and its inhabitants are like grasshoppers; who stretches out the heavens like a curtain, and spreads them like a tent to dwell in;" (Isaiah 40:22 ESV).

"He stretches out the north over the void and hangs the earth on nothing." (Job 26:7 ESV).

"And God said, "Let there be light," and there was light." (Genesis 1:3 ESV).

***

I fear that we have settled with the knowledge we have now and we have lost the zeal to continue searching God's word, putting to test our beliefs and spiritual assumptions. May we never grow weary in testing every belief we have against the Word of God, no matter what those beliefs are.

"Now these Jews were more noble than those in Thessalonica; they received the word with all eagerness, examining the Scriptures daily to see if these things were so." (Acts 17:11 ESV).

***

"Righteousness exalts a nation, but sin is a reproach to any people." (Proverbs 14:34 ESV).

***

I am in Deuteronomy in my daily Bible reading. Moses is prepping the people to go into the land before he exits and turns the leadership over to Joshua. Two verses jumped out to me that I want to meditate on today and I thought I'd share them with you.

The first is when he recounted the days when the people feared God and were humbled in his presence. God had this to say to them:

> "Oh that they had such a heart as this always, to fear me and to keep all my commandments, that it might go well with them and with their descendants forever!" (Deuteronomy 5:29 ESV).

What a wonderful place to be. I believe that the same holds true for us today. If we fear Him and keep His commandments, all will go well with us. God has no pleasure in bringing judgment. He longs that we obey so that it only goes well with us.

And I also read this:

> "And the LORD commanded us to do all these statutes, to fear the LORD our God, for our good always, that he might preserve us alive, as we are this day." (Deuteronomy 6:24 ESV).

Again, God tells the people that He has left His word for their benefit. Following the word of God is always for our good. And to us, this is where we have to put away our will and do the will of the Father. We must have faith in God that when we do His will, even when it seems hard or when we might suffer for it, it will always be ultimately for our good.

The world offers us a choice that removes God and urges us to enjoy the pleasures of sin for a season. Let us all fear God and obey him so that it might go well with us forever.

***

I have it on good authority that it's very possible that the Lord may be returning in the next 24 hours...

***

Finding Joy When We're Late To The Party

Often, when we jump into a new commitment, we feel overwhelmed and very inadequate compared to the people who have been doing things for a long, long time. And that feeling can cause us to question whether we have it in us to stick with the commitment we made. We feel like we're late to the party and perhaps we're not cut out to do the things that we see others doing so effortlessly and successfully.

And when we think about our spiritual lives, this can easily be something we wrestle with. We make a commitment to serve Jesus and we are on top of the world with every expectation that God will help us in our new walk with Him. But then we start to make mistakes or struggle with understanding passages that everyone else seems to take as the milk of the Word. Or we try to share our faith and we end up offending the people we are trying to save.

Soon, we can get to the place where we grow timid in our faith because we just can't see ourselves ever catching up to where other people are in their faith. We feel like a failure or wonder if we have what it takes to be like the strong men and women of faith we admire so much, and we start to wonder if maybe we are too late to the party. If you have struggled with thoughts like these, then let me walk you through something pretty amazing about the apostle Matthew. Hopefully, his experience can give us all the confidence found in Jesus when we see how this apostle, late to the party, ended up leaving a big mark for the cause of his King.

Matthew was a tax collector, hated by the Jews and used by the Romans. He was among a small group of people and probably felt that he had no true home. But he wrote some of the most iconic and memorable words about our King. Here is a quick summary of what this tax collector contributed to the world:

- **Genealogy and Birth of Jesus**: Matthew tells us about the lineage of King Jesus and about His virgin birth. He tells us about the wise men who visited and worshiped Him as an infant. We read of the massacre of the babies by Herod who tried to stop this King found in prophecy.
- **John the Baptist**: Matthew also tells us about the cousin of Jesus sent to prepare the way for His coming and we get to see His cousin baptizing Him to fulfill all righteousness. Matthew gives us a glimpse of the Trinity, together as the obedient Son, the voice of the Father, and the Spirit in the form of a Dove.
- **The Temptation**: Matthew also tells us about the temptation of Jesus by Satan in the wilderness. We witness an epic battle as Satan gives all that he has to tempt Jesus to sin.
- **Launch of Jesus' Ministry**: Matthew then shows us when Jesus starts His ministry and calls His early disciples. These early men are there from the beginning, right with Jesus as it all begins. They witness the growth in the popularity of the Son of God.

- **Sermon on the Mount**: And in a feat not matched elsewhere, Matthew records one of the most well-known and well-quoted sermons of all time. Matthew records the beloved beatitudes and shows how the Messiah teaches, not like a scribe, but as one who has authority, and how this amazes all the people who hear Him.
- **Miracles of Jesus**: Matthew then shows that this Preacher is more than just a powerful speaker; Jesus can do amazing things. Things like cleansing a leper or healing a gentile's servant who was paralyzed. Matthew shows us that Jesus could even perform miracles over great distances.
- **Power of Jesus Over All**: Matthew is the one who shows just how powerful Jesus is. He calms the storm with a rebuke and it obeys; He casts out demons and they obey His voice, and then Matthew shows that the power of God in Him confirmed that this Messiah could even forgive sins.

That takes us into the 9th chapter of his book. After the chapter starts with the healing of the paralytic and forgiving him of his sin, Matthew writes about something that seems so nondescript that we may be tempted to read right past it with little thought. Nine chapters into his book, we read this verse:

"As Jesus passed on from there, he saw a man called Matthew sitting at the tax booth, and he said to him, "Follow me." And he rose and followed him." (Matthew 9:9 ESV).

Did you catch that? The man who gives us some of the most beloved things about our King didn't even join the Savior as an apostle until after all of these things we read about were already done. In a sense, Matthew was late to the party, wasn't he? Whether or not he personally witnessed many of the things we read about is not known, but he was not a called apostle when they occurred.

I wonder if Matthew felt any overwhelming feelings of inadequacies as he fell in next to people like Peter, James, and John who had been witnesses of the things from the early ministry of Jesus. I wonder if he ever worried if he had what it took to walk in the shoes of the men who were called before him.

I suppose that human nature could have caused him to become frozen in his inadequacies, but Matthew had one very important blessing that allowed him to not only walk with the Messiah but do so as a man late to the party; one who was able to leave an indelible mark on the Kingdom of Christ with his faith and by writing a letter to the Jews in defense of the Savior. This blessing is the same blessing that we have today. He was blessed by walking hand in hand with the Creator of the universe.

The next time you feel the cold grip of inadequacy tighten around you, lean on the same Savior that Matthew leaned on. It doesn't matter how late we are to the party or how much others in the Kingdom are already doing when we arrive, Jesus will have meaningful work for each of us to do.

The next time we are worried because we are late to the party, look at the wonderful things that Matthew did for the Kingdom even though it was a third of the way through his letter before the Lord called to him and he followed. When we answer Jesus' call, we are never truly late to His party.

***

I am finishing the books of Moses and something struck me. Human nature has not changed much. We look at the people who sinned in the wilderness and condemn them for their unbelief and stubbornness. But often, we are guilty of the very same thing in other ways and never see it. For example:

- When God punished the people for fearing the giants in the land, He pronounced the judgment of wandering in the wilderness for 40 years. But some people decided to go out and fight, even though Moses warned that God wouldn't be with them. But they went anyway and died. How many times do we do what we want to do, even when the Lord warns against it, thinking that we can still do things our way and God will accept us?
- Speaking of the people who spied out the land, some feared the people in the land more than they feared God and they succumbed to the fear rather than putting trust in God. Boy, is this one for us to heed today. Our society is full of giants willing to persecute us for believing the wrong thing about morality and sin; we live in a time where we must call evil good and we must call good evil; we must kill innocent lives and protect the guilty over the victim that God says we should protect; we must pervert justice rather than administer it. Listen, do we fear the giants in our land who insist we engage in this sin, or do we stand with the few who say, "Do not be in dread or afraid of them" as Joshua told his people?
- Are we a people of gratitude or are we like the people who wandered in the wilderness complaining about everything to the Lord? Rather than being thankful for the good that God gives us, do we complain about what we don't have? Rather than be content with the homes and clothes we are blessed with, do we

complain to the Lord about not having what we desire? Are we thankful for the job that we have, or do we despise the blessing of the Lord because we are not in the job that pays more or in the one we want to be in? Are we doing a lot more complaining to the Lord or a lot more thanking? There is nothing wrong with bringing our desires to the Lord as long as we do it with an attitude of thankfulness and not one of complaint.

Human nature doesn't change much, does it? Let us all be careful not to fall into the same condemnation of unbelief that the Israelites fell into when in the wilderness. It's a lot easier to do than we think. And we know how the Lord responded to them when they did. Do we really believe that God will overlook our sin if we do the same?

***

Don't you love when you have one of those experiences where you get a specific answer to a specific prayer and you know that there is no other conclusion but that the Lord answered you?

It was too specific to be a coincidence.

It was too timely to be by chance.

It's a reminder that there is a God in heaven and He can do all things. Nothing is impossible for Him.

I had one of those experiences today and I still have chills thinking about it. Not in His answer to my prayer, but that the God of heaven actually listened to me.

These are the confirmations of faith that you treasure in your heart.

***

While we get up, eat breakfast, and get ready for the day,
Angels are praising King Jesus around His throne at this very moment.
As we speak to our spouses and children this morning,
In heaven, creation listens to the voice of God speaking to them.
As we cope with pain and loss,
Saints who have gone on before live in the presence of Jesus having all tears wiped away by His fingers.
As we begin to deal with those who hate and persecute us,
The sovereign God over all stays His hand in longsuffering before

bringing His righteous judgment.

As we look at our calendars for upcoming appointments and vacation plans,

The Father sees the date He will say to His Son, "It's time... Go bring home your bride."

"So we are always of good courage. We know that while we are at home in the body we are away from the Lord, for we walk by faith, not by sight." (2 Corinthians 5:6-7 ESV).

***

Man makes idols to serve.
God makes man to serve Him.
Man carries his idols from place to place.
God carries us where we need to go.
Man prays to an idol with no eyes and no ears.
God hears and sees everything, even the things we do in secret.
We have this choice:
Create a god to serve and do for him what he is incapable of doing for himself,
Or serve the Creator of all and praise Him for doing for us what we are incapable of doing for ourselves.

"Bel bows down; Nebo stoops; their idols are on beasts and livestock; these things you carry are borne as burdens on weary beasts.

They stoop; they bow down together; they cannot save the burden, but themselves go into captivity.

"Listen to me, O house of Jacob, all the remnant of the house of Israel, who have been borne by me from before your birth, carried from the womb; even to your old age I am he, and to gray hairs I will carry you. I have made, and I will bear; I will carry and will save.

"To whom will you liken me and make me equal, and compare me, that we may be alike?

Those who lavish gold from the purse, and weigh out silver in the scales, hire a goldsmith, and he makes it into a god; then they fall down and worship!

They lift it to their shoulders, they carry it, they set it in its place, and it stands there; it cannot move from its place.

If one cries to it, it does not answer or save him from his trouble.

"Remember this and stand firm, recall it to mind, you transgressors, remember the former things of old; for I am God, and there is no other;

I am God, and there is none like me, declaring the end from the beginning and from ancient times things not yet done, saying, 'My counsel shall stand, and I will accomplish all my purpose,' (Isaiah 46:1-10 ESV).

***

If we're honest, don't we sometimes feel a sense of dread, wondering if we understand the Will of the Lord correctly?

Sometimes, aren't we tempted to wonder if we will meet Jesus on the Day of Judgment and find out that we were wrong in our understanding of His Words?

While we need to have a healthy respect for seeking God's Word, having finished the book of Deuteronomy, I take comfort in this one thing:

As long as we seek the Word with our heart, God has placed it where we can find it.

Our problem comes when we quit seeking it or ignore what we know to be true.

Rather than worry about our inability to understand His Will, we need to place our faith in Him and His ability to make His Word known to all who diligently seek it.

Listen to the comforting worlds that Moses leaves the children of Israel about this very thing:

> "For this commandment that I command you today is not too hard for you, neither is it far off.
>
> It is not in heaven, that you should say, 'Who will ascend to heaven for us and bring it to us, that we may hear it and do it?'
>
> Neither is it beyond the sea, that you should say, 'Who will go over the sea for us and bring it to us, that we may hear it and do it?'
>
> But the word is very near you. It is in your mouth and in your heart, so that you can do it." (Deuteronomy 30:11-14 ESV).

What I need to remind myself is that rather than putting all the weight on my shoulders alone for finding and understanding God's will for me,

I need to place my faith in Him that He will give me success in finding and knowing His Will for me. I just need to diligently seek it. That's my part.

And if I do this, then my God will reward me for my diligence.

Yes, I need to learn to place more faith in Him and less in myself.

> "And without faith it is impossible to please him, for whoever would

draw near to God must believe that he exists and that he rewards those who seek him." (Hebrews 11:6 ESV).

***

In the Beginning Was The Word

We read John 1:1 and we focus on Jesus being God. He's eternal. He embodies everything that is God. And John begins his Gospel this way to show that Jesus was more than a prophet; more than a great teacher; that this Messiah was even more than the promise of a man who God would tap to be a Super-Judge for Israel. John sets the stage to show that Jesus was God Himself, coming to earth to do for man what man cannot do for Himself.

"In the beginning was the Word, and the Word was with God, and the Word was God." (John 1:1 ESV).

And later, John says this…

"And the Word became flesh and dwelt among us, and we have seen his glory, glory as of the only Son from the Father, full of grace and truth." (John 1:14 ESV).

But rather than focus on His deity, I want us to think about the fact that Jesus is called the Word. This is such a powerful lesson for us to comprehend. The Word is the very communication from our Creator to us. It is the special revelation that God gives to man to show that man is special to God. The Word is what sets man apart from all of creation.

And the Word is eternal. "In the beginning." (Vs. 1). And the Word was not only with God, but He was God. We see that Jesus played an important role, not just in the beginning of the first century when He came to earth, but as the eternal Word, He was there from the first utterance of "Let there be light." Verse 10 even says that the world was made through Him.

When God said to Adam, "Don't eat the forbidden fruit," this was the Word that was there at the beginning. When God told Cain to "rule over sin," it was the eternal Word. When God spoke to Noah and told him to build the ark, it was the Word that existed from the beginning. When God spoke to Abraham and the patriarchs, it was the eternal Word.

When God spoke through Moses and the prophets, when He spoke through donkeys, and even through dead Samuel, it was the eternal Word who spoke. He spoke face-to-face with people, through visions, and through dreams. But in every case, it was the Word of God Who spoke.

John is setting the stage for a radical and amazing revelation. Jesus wasn't merely a man who God spoke through, He was the Word. He was the revelation of God to man. And when John writes of the ministry, death, and resurrection of Jesus from Nazareth, the author wants us to understand that no other speaker ever arose like Him. And people witnessed this special truth about Jesus. They might not be able to understand it, but they saw it:

> "The officers then came to the chief priests and Pharisees, who said to them, "Why did you not bring him?" The officers answered, "No one ever spoke like this man!" (John 7:45-46 ESV).

And

> "And they were astonished at his teaching, for he taught them as one who had authority, and not as the scribes." (Mark 1:22 ESV).

John begins His Gospel with a line in the sand. He shows that Jesus is God. And as God, He is the eternal Word to man. And up until the time when God came to earth, He spoke to man in different ways and manners. But during the 33 years He was on earth, God spoke to man himself, with His own physical mouth.

When we read that Jesus is the Word, we need to understand that He was more than the Word at the moment of His birth as a man; He was the Word then, and before, and forever more. That is why the Hebrew writer says,

> "Long ago, at many times and in many ways, God spoke to our fathers by the prophets, but in these last days he has spoken to us by his Son, whom he appointed the heir of all things, through whom also he created the world." (Hebrews 1:1-2 ESV).

And our God, the Word Who existed from the beginning, became flesh and dwelt among us. And He loved us enough to visit us and speak His Words to us Himself, to ears we heard with and into hearts that caused us to say, "No one ever spoke like this man."

Open your Bible and read it daily. When you do, you get the wonderful, marvelous, privilege of hearing Jesus speak to you today. His Words have power and will change your life. His Words can transform you into a new creature. His Words can save your soul. This is the eternal Word Who always existed with God, as God.

> "In the beginning was the Word, and the Word was with God, and the

Word was God." (John 1:1 ESV).

***

I just read about the crossing of the Jordan as Joshua led the new generation of Israelites into the promised land. It had been about 40 years since the crossing of the Red Sea and the only people alive who witnessed the Red Sea crossing were Joshua, Caleb, and a few people who were very young when it happened and were too young to be among those condemned to fall in the wilderness.

So, most people were witnessing this event for the first time, or at least for the first time since being young children. Perhaps Joshua and Caleb were the only ones with vivid memories of the original crossing. Even though it happened over 40 years ago, something like that would stay fresh in your mind.

I'd like to think that Joshua and Caleb were standing side-by-side when this happened. Two men of God who were beaming ear-to-ear with a smile that brought back powerful memories. And together, they could enjoy the wonder on the faces of this new generation as they experienced the mighty power of their God.

Have you had a similar experience? Parents, have you seen the joy and wonder on the faces of your children as they experience for the first time God's action in their life? An answered prayer, the gift of wisdom just when they needed it, comfort when all seems lost?

When we see the younger generation getting to experience the joys and marvels of being children of the living God, I imagine we experience a lot of what Joshua and Caleb must have experienced during the second crossing. These are the unifying experiences that unite multigenerational cultures under one Faith.

When you get the blessings of experiencing these moments, enjoy them and give praise to God.

> "and as soon as those bearing the ark had come as far as the Jordan, and the feet of the priests bearing the ark were dipped in the brink of the water (now the Jordan overflows all its banks throughout the time of harvest),
>
> the waters coming down from above stood and rose up in a heap very far away, at Adam, the city that is beside Zarethan, and those flowing down toward the Sea of the Arabah, the Salt Sea, were completely cut off. And the people passed over opposite Jericho." (Joshua 3:15-16 ESV).

***

Now this blows my mind. Abraham was born 2 years after Noah died.

Shem, Noah's son whom Abraham descended from, was alive during most of Abraham's life.

Shem died when Abraham was 150 years old, just 25 years before Abraham died.

Think about that.

While Shem, a person saved by God on the ark, was still alive, man had so quickly fallen away from God.

When Joshua was about to die, he said this…

"And Joshua said to all the people, "Thus says the Lord, the God of Israel, 'Long ago, your fathers lived beyond the Euphrates, Terah, the father of Abraham and of Nahor; and they served other gods." (Joshua 24:2 ESV).

It's hard to believe, but while the son of Noah, Abraham's forefather, was still alive, people had already forgotten God and His power.

It's not surprising that after Joshua, there arose a generation that didn't know God.

We learn from Shem that it doesn't take long for generations to stop seeking after the Old Paths.

Unfortunately, it's all too easy to underestimate the importance of bringing up our children in the nurture and admonition of the Lord, isn't it?

***

How smart is it to ignore the God who created you and will judge you by His words on the last day?

I don't get it.

***

Have you seen some of the images from the JWST? They are amazing and demonstrate just how much the heavens declare the glory of God. The smarter man becomes, the more God allows us to see how great He is.

***

Wherever you travel, you can see the glory of God.

Whatever the weather, whatever the season, whatever the environment, you can see God's glory.

His glory is everywhere. If we have an open heart, He will continually amaze us.

If we remain willingly ignorant, then we will miss out of some of the most amazing moments of life.

Open your heart and be amazed by God.

"For his invisible attributes, namely, his eternal power and divine nature, have been clearly perceived, ever since the creation of the world, in the things that have been made. So they are without excuse.

For although they knew God, they did not honor him as God or give thanks to him, but they became futile in their thinking, and their foolish hearts were darkened." (Romans 1:20-21 ESV).

***

There is joy in serving the Lord. But that joy happens when we want to serve the Lord, not when we do it grudgingly.

When we serve out of compulsion alone, we are missing the inherent joy that serving the Lord brings.

When we refuse to give over our will fully to His, then we serve with resentment and a secret desire to be doing what our heart really wants to do. This can be a most dreary place to be.

But when we desire to serve Him and we seek every opportunity to do so, then our joy is pure and absolute. When we seek to serve God eagerly, we are filled with anticipation and gratification every day.

And best yet, when our desire and joy line up with our service to King Jesus, the Father Himself will look upon us and bestow His honor upon us.

Our selfless service pays two priceless benefits. It gives us joy that cannot be taken away and it brings honor from the One who created us.

The journey to lose self in Jesus is a wonderful journey to make that transforms us into the image of our Master, and one that truly brings honor when the carnal man sees only dishonor.

"If anyone serves me, he must follow me; and where I am, there will my servant be also. If anyone serves me, the Father will honor him." (John 12:26 ESV).

***

The day is coming when everyone will want to be like those who serve Jesus; when everyone will confess Jesus as Lord; when there will be no one left to resist Him as Lord and King.

Sadly, for most, on that day it will be too late.

Be among the few today who will be among the ones most envied on that day.

***

Taking A Vacation From God

We all have our own definition of what makes a good vacation. For some of us, we look forward to peace and quiet, a time to recharge and relax from a life of bustle and grind, sitting on a beach and reading a good book. For others, we look for adventure and thrill, perhaps ziplining, wilderness hiking, or mountain climbing. Still, others look for ways to pursue their passions like writing a book, traveling the globe, or learning a new hobby.

To each his own, right? But one thing vacations have in common is that they are a break from the norm to do what we really want to do when we don't have the time or resources to do those things all the time. Vacations can spotlight our passions and give us a glimpse of what motivates our hearts.

And vacations are, by nature, a temporary respite. When they are done, we return to the routines of life that make up our day-to-day existence. We treasure these respites and plan for them often to help recharge and renew ourselves.

I wonder if the love and need for vacations sometimes unconsciously makes its way into our service to God. Perhaps, we feel from time to time that we need a break from watching and waiting on the Lord. Or perhaps we think we need those "what happens in Vegas, stays in Vegas" moments. Do we look for those times where we can drop our guard just a little, let our hair down, and have a little fun?

Do we sometimes think that we need a vacation from God?

This is an interesting question to think about before we give a quick answer, whether "yes" or "no." For some, a life of following Jesus is full of tremendous sacrifices that intersect with our health and livelihood. If this is us, perhaps we long for a "vacation" from the sacrifices we must make daily just to gain respite for a moment before we go back to the daily service to our Lord and King.

Most would understand this desire for respite, for a "vacation" as we use this word.

For others, perhaps we have one eye on the Kingdom and another eye on the world. We look with anticipation for the reward that King Jesus will bring, but we still look longingly at the pleasure of sin that we gave up or the sins that call to us through our friends and acquaintances. If this is the "vacation" from God that we are contemplating, then we need to beware of this enticement.

Listen to the words of Jesus when He tells the parable of the servant who decided to take a vacation from his duty while the Master was away:

> "But if that wicked servant says to himself, 'My master is delayed,' and begins to beat his fellow servants and eats and drinks with drunkards,
>
> the master of that servant will come on a day when he does not expect him and at an hour he does not know and will cut him in pieces and put him with the hypocrites.
>
> In that place there will be weeping and gnashing of teeth." (Matthew 24:48-51 ESV).

The danger in "vacation thinking" when it comes to serving the Lord is a dangerous thing to engage in. It presupposes three things that can cause us to stumble in our walk with the Lord.

First, it shines a light on our evil motives. If we look for a chance to take a break from living a life that the Lord wants us to live, it exposes our desires to be doing something that the Lord forbids us to do. This goes right to the motives of the heart.

Second, it exposes our incomplete understanding of servanthood. Being a servant is a life-long endeavor, not something we do like an employee who punches a time clock and is on his own time when not "on the clock." When we are servants of King Jesus, there is never a time we are not on the clock for Him.

Third, it demonstrates that we still haven't learned what true joy we have in a life fully devoted to Jesus. When we are all-in for Him, then we need not go elsewhere for what we think the pleasures of sin for a season will bring to us. There is no need for a vacation from serving King Jesus because it is in Him that we will find contentment, refreshment, and renewal each day.

And yet, perhaps we all yearn for the respites that come with sacrifice. We pray for an easing of the physical pain that assaults our health or the health of a loved one that is brought about specifically because of our decision to follow King Jesus. Or perhaps we pray for ease from the pain brought about when our families are broken because we made the choice to follow Jesus.

Sometimes, it is okay to desire a respite, or vacation, from the consequences of our decision to serve King Jesus. But this is not the same thing that Jesus talks about with the wicked servant who took a vacation from serving the master while the master was away.

We are followers of Jesus 24/7. There is never a time that we take a vacation from serving. That's why Jesus gave many admonitions like this, an admonition that we need to remember when we are tempted to take a vacation from serving the Lord:

> "Therefore, stay awake, for you do not know on what day your Lord is coming.
> But know this, that if the master of the house had known in what part of the night the thief was coming, he would have stayed awake and would not have let his house be broken into.
> Therefore you also must be ready, for the Son of Man is coming at an hour you do not expect." (Matthew 24:42-44 ESV).

***

When we look at pictures from the James Webb Space Telescope, it's easy to see how we can get a Ph.D. in astrophysics.

When we see bacteria through an electron microscope, we understand how we can get a Ph.D. in microbiology.

When we study the depths of the seas, there is enough material to get a Ph.D. in oceanography.

When we study how the complex body operates at the cellular level, we can get our Ph.D. in biochemistry.

In all these disciplines, we see evidence of God in His complex yet wonderfully knitted together creation.

We can spend a lifetime studying any detail of God's creation and hardly scratch the surface of what He has spoken into existence.

The more intelligent we become, the more we learn that with God, indeed, the half hasn't been told.

***

I'm not convinced that the Lord is expecting grand actions on our part to be considered His faithful steward.

More often than not, He's expecting us to say something that may only help one person on their walk with Him, rather than something that moves the masses.

Our legacy in His eyes is just as powerful when we help a handful of nameless people than when we leave behind an army of followers who will remember our name.

> "And whoever gives one of these little ones even a cup of cold water because he is a disciple, truly, I say to you, he will by no means lose his reward." (Matthew 10:42 ESV).

***

Paul was a fantastic servant of Jesus, but listen to what he says here:

> "Not that I have already obtained this or am already perfect, but I press on to make it my own, because Christ Jesus has made me his own." (Philippians 3:12 ESV).

When I read this, I can have one of two reactions.

First, I can think, "If Paul is struggling to be complete in Jesus, then I have no chance of being the servant I need to be in Jesus." We think this because we realize that Paul is an amazing Christian that has done more than most of us will even be called to do.

Or

Second, I can think, "I praise God for showing me that if Paul is still striving to be complete, then I should show myself some grace for continuing to strive to be complete in Jesus." Paul is an example that God does not expect perfection; He just expects us to move toward perfection.

I will never be perfect, but I can always move toward perfection with God's grace. When I fall, I get back up and keep moving forward. God's hand will always lift me up when I reach for it.

I leave God when I decide to quit getting up and moving forward; it is never that God leaves me.

Let's never forget to keep pressing on, regardless of how many times we stumble and fall.

***

I wonder if we spend too much time looking for things that divide and not enough time looking for things that unite.

***

Something stunning and sad just hit me. I was reading Job, and God said this to Satan:

> "And the LORD said to Satan, "Behold, all that he has is in your hand. Only against him do not stretch out your hand." So Satan went out from the presence of the LORD." (Job 1:12 ESV).

And

> "And the LORD said to Satan, "Behold, he is in your hand; only spare his life." (Job 2:6 ESV).

We readily believe that God is sovereign, and even Satan has to listen to Him when God sets boundaries. Think about that. Satan hates God, and he hates the children of God. Does anyone really believe that if he could do it, he'd kill Job when it became apparent that Job wouldn't curse God and die as he predicted?

But Satan couldn't harm Job beyond the boundaries God placed on him. So, why is this stunning and sad to me?

When God places boundaries on the most evil creature, the creature must obey.

But when God places boundaries on me, I can look at God and thumb my nose at Him and say, "No!"

When God says not to kill, I can kill.

When God said not to lie, I can lie.

When God says I need to be baptized, I can refuse.

When God says not to forsake the assembly of the saints, I can miss the church's assembly anyway.

When God says to help those who are in need, I can keep what He has blessed me with to use for myself.

In short, when the sovereign Creator gives me boundaries, I can choose to stay within His boundaries or brazenly ignore His restrictions and commands.

Not even Satan can do that. And God has a special place reserved in judgment for this evil creature.

Shouldn't we be careful about rebelling against God when even Satan must stay within the boundaries God imposes upon him?

> "Then he will say to those on his left, 'Depart from me, you cursed, into the eternal fire prepared for the devil and his angels." (Matthew 25:41 ESV).

***

Jesus healed the blind, the deaf, and the mute.

Can you imagine what it must have been like for people who saw their parents for the first time?

Can you imagine what it must have been like for those who heard and understood what their children sounded like for the first time, having never learned the language before?

Can you imagine what it must have been like for those who spoke perfect Hebrew without having to attend any speech therapy sessions?

It must have been an overwhelming experience for these people. But think about what these events must have been like through the eyes of Jesus.

Our Lord created each of these people to have a perfect working body, yet sin broke His perfect creation and ushered in disease and death.

It must have pained Him to see a sea of humanity with broken bodies. But for a few He chose, He could experience the awe they felt when they saw for the first time, heard for the first time, spoke for the first time.

I wonder if He felt overwhelming joy as He experienced His creation made whole when He fixed their damaged bodies and brought people closer to the state they were meant to live.

I must admit that when Jesus gives me my perfect body, free of death and disease, I will probably feel overwhelmed as I realize I will no longer ache, suffer, or grow tired.

But I imagine that Jesus will feel more joy than the sea of people with new, perfect, spiritual bodies as He witnesses the awe we experience when we are given these bodies.

He will be the happy parent who lives vicariously through us as we receive the ultimate gift of a body prepared for eternity.

When Jesus healed the blind, the deaf, and the mute, it was a small foretaste of what awaits all who call upon His name.

And as overwhelming as it will be for us, I doubt we will ever be able to appreciate what the joy will be like for the One who restores to us what our existence was intended to be in His presence.

"But our citizenship is in heaven, and from it we await a Savior, the Lord Jesus Christ,
who will transform our lowly body to be like his glorious body, by the power that enables him even to subject all things to himself." (Philippians 3:20-21 ESV).

***

I don't think any of us will be prepared for the awe we'll experience the first time we see Jesus sitting on His throne.

***

We have staked everything on this one fact:

"For I have come down from heaven, not to do my own will but the will of him who sent me." (John 6:38 ESV).

Jesus was more than a prophet of God. He existed before He was born, in heaven as God.
He was the God of Israel.
He created the world.
He was the God of the Old Testament.
And He came down from heaven.
Jesus gives us no wiggle room.
We are either all-in, accepting Him as God,
Or we must reject Him as a blasphemer.
Most Jews today reject Him as an evil blasphemer.
He said that He came down from heaven.
If we believe that, we must be all-in for Him.
For if He did come down from heaven, then He is the One to whom we must submit,
The One whom we must believe,
The One whom we must worship,
The One whom we must have faith in.
Jesus cut off all other possibilities about Him.
He is either God, or He is an evil, blasphemous liar.
I confess Him as my Lord and God.

What about you?

***

You remember Lazarus, right? Jesus raised him from the dead.

From Luke 16, we know that when we die, we are carried to Abraham's bosom by angels.

Lazarus made that trip with angels before the Lord raised him from the dead.

I bet he had a unique sense of excitement as he grew closer to the second time he died, knowing from experience that angels were waiting to carry him away again.

I can only imagine how awesome that will be.

The second time he made that trip, Lazarus didn't have to imagine- he knew.

These are the things that comfort me.

***

Be Salt In A Wicked Land

In the Sermon on the Mount, Jesus teaches a lesson on Kingdom living. At the beginning of the sermon, He teaches the importance of being salt and light. Light represents the influence that followers of Jesus have on the world. We are seen, not for our glory, but for the glory of God to be seen in us.

And salt serves two functions for the servants of Jesus, both functions to the glory of Jesus through us. The first, like light, is an influencing function. We should live holy and righteous lives so that the evil world in which we live is palatable to God. Without the seasoning effect of our salt, there is often nothing good in a society void of God.

And because of this, our salt acts as a preservative in the evil societies in which we live. How many times have we seen where God was willing to spare the many because of the obedience of the few? God was ready to spare the cities of Sodom and Gomorrah for the goodness of only ten people. And in Genesis 15, God tells Abraham that He is not giving him his inheritance because the iniquity of the Amorites is not full. We can see over and over in Scripture where the righteous lives of the few preserved the many before the Lord.

Here is what Jesus says in the sermon on the mount:

> "You are the salt of the earth, but if salt has lost its taste, how shall its saltiness be restored? It is no longer good for anything except to be thrown out and trampled under people's feet." (Matthew 5:13 ESV).

Sometimes, when we look at the evil where we live, it's easy to grow despondent. In our own lifetime, we have seen a marked departure by our society from Kingdom living principles that many of us grew up with. I fear that this trend will only get worse as we begin our wholesale abandonment of God and as our society turns toward idols we create to replace God.

As this abandonment continues to march forward, it is all the more important that we remember the words of Jesus. We are still the salt of the earth. There has never been a more important time for us to remember the value of our preserving effect on the society in which we live.

How long this preservation will last is anyone's guess. It is up to the sovereign God to determine when our society becomes so distasteful in the mouth of God that not even our salt will be enough to preserve it. This is when we need to remember that no matter what happens, we are citizens of a heavenly Kingdom. And the darker our world becomes, the more it loses its flavor, then the more pronounced our influence will be seen and felt on it.

When all around us sin; when society calls good evil and calls evil good; when we make the innocent victims and uphold the hands of the guilty; when society spews vile thoughts and persecutes holy thinking; our salt will be all the more important.

It's easier to be salty when all around us think like salt. But as we find ourselves in an ever-shrinking group who live like salt, we will have to make an even more conscious decision each day to live up to the Master's expectation for us to be the salt of the earth. Let's set it in our hearts now to be the world's salt that preserves our evil society through our influence upon it for as long as we can. And when the iniquities of our society become full, let us continue to be the salt and the light in a world in which our godly influence will be seen all the more in increasingly starker contrast.

As we think about our salt, let's remember the words of Paul to the young preacher Titus:

> "For the grace of God has appeared, bringing salvation for all people,
> training us to renounce ungodliness and worldly passions, and to live self-controlled, upright, and godly lives in the present age,
> waiting for our blessed hope, the appearing of the glory of our great God and Savior Jesus Christ," (Titus 2:11-13 ESV)."

***

Why do I have peace in my assurance of my salvation?
Because I know that my salvation is not something I earn.
It is a gift of grace given by God.
My salvation cannot be taken away from me.
It is a gift that is mine to accept or reject, but once I accept it, Jesus will keep it sure,
I will continue to walk with God, and accept His help as I need it.
But I sleep a peaceful sleep because no matter what happens in my life, my gift of salvation is sure.
My faith is in His promises, which is why I have blessed assurance.

> "which is why I suffer as I do. But I am not ashamed, for I know whom I have believed, and I am convinced that he is able to guard until that day what has been entrusted to me." (2 Timothy 1:12 ESV).

***

We all need a friend who we can be vulnerable with. Someone who will not judge or condemn, but will speak the truth we need to hear, no matter how hard it may be to hear.

Someone we can bring things we wrestle with and be a sounding board for us. Someone who can give us a different perspective when we we start to see things with blinders on.

We need that person who will allow us to vent and still love us, show our frustration and still respect us.

We need that friend who has a long memory when it comes to the good things about us and a short memory when it comes to our areas of imperfections.

We need that friend who will support us yet not excuse our inexcusable behavior. We need that friend who helps us become more of who Jesus wants us to be and not one who helps us descend away from what Jesus expects from us.

This is an amazing and rare friend. But to have one, I must first be willing to be one.

> "Love is patient and kind; love does not envy or boast; it is not arrogant or rude.

It does not insist on its own way; it is not irritable or resentful; it does not rejoice at wrongdoing, but rejoices with the truth.

Love bears all things, believes all things, hopes all things, endures all things. Love never ends." (1 Corinthians 13:4-8a ESV).

***

This thought just sent shivers up my spine:
God is patient... until He isn't.

***

I'm reading the book of Judges in my daily Bible reading. However, there is a sad message that is a recurring theme.

Even when God sends a savior, man will easily forget God and return to his own way.

But there is also another message that is easily forgotten.

Though many forget God when He sends a savior and returns to his own way, there will always be a remnant who looks at the Lord's salvation and remain humble at His strength and provision.

These people are peppered throughout the book of Judges and are often not the judges themselves.

Not much has changed today. The Father has sent the ultimate Savior to save us from our sins, yet we often do what the children of Israel did in the book of Judges.

Though we want salvation, we want to live our own way more. So we are willing to take salvation from the Lord, but we are not willing to turn to Him fully.

But as we learn from Judges, unless we return fully to the Lord after receiving His salvation,

Our way and our rejection of God will only lead to one place- back to the slavery and domination of sin.

What do we learn from the Israelites in the book of Judges? That we can't have it both ways: We cannot accept salvation from God and continue to walk in the way that causes us to be lost.

"For if we go on sinning deliberately after receiving the knowledge of the truth, there no longer remains a sacrifice for sins, but a fearful expectation of judgment, and a fury of fire that will consume the adversaries." (Hebrews 10:26-27 ESV).

**

If you want to be godly, surround yourself with godly people.
If you want to be a servant, surround yourself with servants.
If you want to be a better Bible student, surround yourself with people who study the Bible.
If you want to attend church more, surround yourself with people who go to church.

"Iron sharpens iron, and one man sharpens another." (Proverbs 27:17 ESV).

**

He Knew.
From the beginning when Adam and Eve sinned, He knew.
He knew that His heel would be bruised. That He would be the seed of woman Who would suffer to save them and their descendants.
In Matthew 16, Jesus asked the disciples who they thought He was. Peter answered, "You are the Messiah, the Son of God."
It is no coincidence that Jesus tells them the following after this confession:

"From that time Jesus began to show his disciples that he must go to Jerusalem and suffer many things from the elders and chief priests and scribes, and be killed, and on the third day be raised." (Matthew 16:21 ESV).

He knew, and He was preparing them to know.
His heel was about to be bruised and when it was, it was not because He was beaten by man or by Satan.
Again, He showed them that He knew.
This time, in the next chapter, Matthew records Jesus' transfiguration on the mountain. After His identity as God's Son was again revealed, He told them the Son of Man would certainly suffer at the hands of evil men.
He Knew.
And the last time that Matthew tells us that Jesus knew, it was on the way

to Jerusalem, just before His sacrifice:

> "And as Jesus was going up to Jerusalem, he took the twelve disciples aside, and on the way he said to them, "See, we are going up to Jerusalem.
> And the Son of Man will be delivered over to the chief priests and scribes, and they will condemn him to death and deliver him over to the Gentiles to be mocked and flogged and crucified, and he will be raised on the third day." (Matthew 20:17-19 ESV).

He knew.

When we remember His death every first day of the week, we remember that His enemies didn't overcome Him through death, but that He, through death, overcame sin and Satan.

He knew.

***

The Drip Drip Drip of Satan

When we live the Christian life, we have an enemy who wants us to fail with all his might. Satan doesn't care much about us or our happiness. His main focus is on hurting God. And since He cannot do anything to God personally, he chooses to attack God where it really hurts- in what He loves.

So, Satan will come at us in any way he can. And we are not ignorant of his devices, are we? Often, it's not the big attacks that we fall victim to; rather, it's the drip, drip drip of the temptations we face day after day that wear us down. We fight and we pray and we hold his attacks at bay with the help of Jesus, and then one day we give in. And when we do, Satan is just as thrilled with the fall as he would be if we failed in one massive attack.

But we have a Savior who is ready to serve as our High Priest and take away the sin when we stumble after we succumb to the drip, drip, drip that Satan brings to us. Still, part of our growth as Christians is to learn to do better with the never-ending small daily assaults that Satan brings to us. That means that we need to prepare for these day-after-day assaults that the enemy sends our way.

We have an example of someone who had to deal with this drip, drip, drip of temptation in Genesis 39. Joseph was a young, handsome man who found himself a slave to the second most powerful man in the world. Potiphar was the Captain of the Guard to the Egyptian Pharaoh, a very powerful position. But Joseph was also a servant of the one true God. And God was with

Joseph, even in slavery. And because God was with him, everything Joseph did caused Potiphar to prosper.

But Potiphar was married to an evil and sexually perverse woman who wanted to have her way with Joseph. Joseph resisted and told her that he couldn't sin against her husband or against God. So, he fought the temptation and won... at least for a moment.

Then the drip, drip, drip came:

> "And as she spoke to Joseph day after day, he would not listen to her, to lie beside her or to be with her." (Genesis 39:10 ESV).

Did you see that? The temptress didn't give up but came at Joseph day after day. Can you imagine what it must have been like for Joseph to have to deal with this every day? Of course, you can. How many of us have to deal with our own "day by day" temptations? How many times do we wake up knowing we will have to steel ourselves against the same volley of attacks that we faced yesterday, the day before, and the day before that? This is a common device that Satan often uses as he attempts to wear us down or catch us in a moment of weakness.

And yet, Joseph found his strength in the same place we will find ours. In God. God will walk with us and give us the power to overcome sin, even the drip, drip, drip temptations that we face every day. And if we do stumble, John reminds us that we still have help:

> "If we confess our sins, he is faithful and just to forgive us our sins and to cleanse us from all unrighteousness." (1 John 1:9 ESV).

And lest we are too hard on ourselves, let's remember that this drip, drip, drip device that Satan uses so effectively was even used on our Savior. When Satan tried to get Jesus to sin in the wilderness, Jesus fought every temptation successfully. And when it was over, Satan fled... but he'd be back.

> "And when the devil had ended every temptation, he departed from him until an opportune time." (Luke 4:13 ESV).

"Until an opportune time."
Drip, drip, drip.
So, my friends, we are in good company when we experience the day-after-day temptations that we have to constantly prepare ourselves to endure. And as we do, let me leave you with these three truths to hold on to.

1. These temptations have been shared by many others before us. Indeed, there is no temptation we face that is not common to man. And if this is true,

then it means that others have resisted, as Joseph did, and so can we.

2. God will be there when we face them. Our Savior will not allow the drip, drip, drip that Satan uses to wear on us so much, that we will not have the ability to resist. In fact, God will actively stop Satan when he starts to put a burden upon us too heavy for us to bear.

3. God will always give us a way of escape to help us bear the temptations. With Joseph, it was through the door and into the street without his coat.

God gives us everything that we need to fight against all the temptations that Satan will use to try to get us to fall. But we have a backup plan from our God. If, in spite of all that He gives us to be successful, we still give into the temptation, then He is ready to forgive us of the sin. If we are willing to confess and repent, then He is willing to snatch defeat from the jaws of Satan and still make us victorious.

What a wonderful Savior we serve. If we continue to walk with Him, then He will continue to keep us safe from the evil one. Even when the evil one continues to drip, drip, drip upon us day after day.

> "No temptation has overtaken you that is not common to man. God is faithful, and he will not let you be tempted beyond your ability, but with the temptation he will also provide the way of escape, that you may be able to endure it." (1 Corinthians 10:13 ESV).

***

I had a wonderful surprise in the mail Monday. Mark Roberts sent me a signed copy of his book, "Romans for Everyone" in his "Coffee and the Bible Series." Yesterday, I picked it up and started to read it, intending to read about a chapter a day and get through it in a couple of weeks.

Well, Mark wrote the book in a way that made it hard to put down. Imagine that… a religious book written on Romans that made you want to read just one more chapter before putting it down. It was almost like reading a good novel that you wanted to keep reading, only this was not a story or a piece of fiction.

Well, I made it through a third of the book before calling it a night. It's made me want to go back and read the entire book of Romans in one sitting. But here is what pulled me into the book. Mark set the context for the church that existed in Rome. The church started as most had. Jews were the first converts, followed by Gentiles. But there came a time when the emperor Claudius expelled the Jews from Rome, including Christian Jews. Among them were Aquila and Priscilla, who Paul met in Corinth. But under Nero, the Jews were later allowed to return to Rome.

But for 5 to 7 years, the church continued to exist and grow with only Gentiles. No Jews or their experiences as God's people to influence them. Gentiles took up the responsibilities to fill the leadership roles and continue spreading the Gospel to other Gentiles in the city. By the time the Jews were able to return, they undoubtedly stepped into a congregation much different from the one they had left. This would naturally cause tension between the Jews who wanted to return things to the way they were before they left, and the Gentile who probably thought they were doing just fine.

So, Paul begins his letter to a divided church. And the Spirit leads him to begin his letter to them with a strong case for unity. Only this appeal to unity is probably something they least expected to hear. We are all sinners, Jews and Gentiles. We all have fallen short of the glory of God. No one can look at anything we have done and claim to be superior in the eyes of God. We are all worthy of condemnation in the eyes of God.

That is the basis of unity that Paul starts with as he begins his letter. But he also says that we all have been justified through the same faith in Jesus, both Jews and Gentiles. We were all given the same gift of grace that took both Jews and Gentiles, who were worthy of death in God's eyes, and had their faith counted to them as righteousness because of the blood of Jesus.

This is the basis of unity that Paul begins his letter to this predominantly Gentile church that had a large Jewish membership infused back into it. As I said, I am a third of a way through Mark's book, and I am eager to finish it. I want to thank Mark for his gift, and so far, I highly recommend it to anyone who might be intimidated by Romans.

And Mark, I took your advice and read your book with a simple cup of coffee- a few cups to be precise.

***

I love this thought. When the book named after him started, Job was a wealthy man. He was so rich that the text tells us that he was the greatest of all the people of the east:

> "There were born to him seven sons and three daughters. He possessed 7,000 sheep, 3,000 camels, 500 yoke of oxen, and 500 female donkeys, and very many servants, so that this man was the greatest of all the people of the east." (Job 1:2-3 ESV).

Now, I'm not going to talk about his suffering, bankruptcy, the loss of all his children, or the challenge Satan put to God that brought about his hardships. But when the book was over, God doubled his blessings:

> "And the LORD blessed the latter days of Job more than his beginning. And he had 14,000 sheep, 6,000 camels, 1,000 yoke of oxen, and 1,000 female donkeys. He had also seven sons and three daughters." (Job 42:12-13 ESV).

Until recently, I always wondered why God didn't double his number of children. In the end, he had just as many children as he had at the beginning. But then I realized that God did, indeed, double his children.

You see, when Job lost his sheep, his camels, his oxen, and his donkeys, they were gone forever. So when He rewarded Job, he doubled the blessings He had given him before his ordeal.

But the ten children who died in the tornado were never lost. Job knew where they were. And when Job died an old man, full of days, and when the last of his second set of children died, Job was reunited in the presence of God and the angels with all of his children; all 14 sons and 6 daughters.

We all need to ensure that we don't get so caught up in the here and now that we neglect the age to come. Job reminds us that it may seem like we lose in this life, but in the next life, we will have treasures that pale what this world offers.

***

God has put man on the earth with everything we need to know Him, spiritual things, and eternity. I am afraid that sometimes we are tempted to buy into the things that man- "who God has given over to exchanged the truth about God for a lie and worshiped and served the creature rather than the Creator"- what these men teach.

Not only has God given us His special revelation so that we know His mind and what His will is for us, but he also has taught us about Him in His creation. For the heavens declare the glory of God. And as the Ecclesiastes writer says, He has also set eternity in our hearts.

We are spiritual creatures living in a physical world. We, by nature, seek after Him. He has made Himself easy to find if we seek with a pure heart. But once we reject the things of God- His nature, His attributes, His sovereignty over us and over all things- then we will follow a path away from Him and take His revealed will and conform it to us, rather than conforming us to His will.

God has created us to know Him, through what we can observe about Him and what we can read about Him. Many are no longer looking for Him.

Let us be careful to the voices we are listening to, whether the voices of men who have been given over to exchange the truth of God for a lie, or to the testimony of His creation and His revealed word.

> "He has made everything beautiful in its time. Also, he has put eternity into man's heart, yet so that he cannot find out what God has done from the beginning to the end." (Ecclesiastes 3:11 ESV).

> "The heavens declare the glory of God, and the sky above proclaims his handiwork." (Psalm 19:1b ESV).

> "Long ago, at many times and in many ways, God spoke to our fathers by the prophets, but in these last days he has spoken to us by his Son, whom he appointed the heir of all things, through whom also he created the world." (Hebrews 1:1-2 ESV).

***

Before I use my hands to do things I shouldn't do, I need to think about the hands of Jesus that were pierced on the cross for me.
Before I use my feet to take me to places I know I shouldn't go, I need to think about the nail that was driven through the feet of Jesus on the cross for me.
Before I use my mind to think about sinful things like impure sexual thoughts, hate, and envy, I need to think about the crown of thorns placed upon Jesus' head as His enemies prepared to kill Him on the cross.
Before I pull things close to my bosom and choose what I hold dear to me, I need to think about the spear that was thrust into Jesus' side by a Roman soldier when He finished the will of God upon the cross.
Before I do anything, I need to think about what Jesus did for me on the cross and let His sacrifice for me dictate what I do, where I go, what I think, and what I embrace.

> "but God shows his love for us in that while we were still sinners, Christ died for us." (Romans 5:8 ESV).

***

The best I can tell, it was roughly 2000 years from creation to Abraham.

It was roughly 2000 years from Abraham to Jesus.
It's been roughly 2000 years since Jesus to us today.
Now, I know we cannot predict the timing of the second coming of Jesus. It will be like a thief in the night.
But it will happen.
It's been 2000 years since the promise of the return of Jesus.
It may happen today or it may be another 2000 years before our King returns.
The big question is not, "When will Jesus return?"
But
"Am I ready if He comes today?"

> "And when he had said these things, as they were looking on, he was lifted up, and a cloud took him out of their sight.
>
> And while they were gazing into heaven as he went, behold, two men stood by them in white robes,
>
> and said, "Men of Galilee, why do you stand looking into heaven? This Jesus, who was taken up from you into heaven, will come in the same way as you saw him go into heaven." (Acts 1:9-11 ESV).

***

Only A Step Between Me And Death

As I finish 1 Samuel in my daily Bible reading, I find it intriguing that David faced many hardships while Saul pursued him. He was a man who stared death at every corner. Yet David put his trust in the Lord. When Saul pursued, he trusted God. Listen to how David describes his situation to his friend, Jonathan, Saul's son:

> "But David vowed again, saying, "Your father knows well that I have found favor in your eyes, and he thinks, 'Do not let Jonathan know this, lest he be grieved.' But truly, as the LORD lives and as your soul lives, there is but a step between me and death." (1 Samuel 20:3 ESV).

Have you felt this way at times? "There is but a step between me and death?" Perhaps not literally, but we all have felt the grip of adversity squeeze around us as it seems that there is but a step between us and disaster.

Yet David put his trust in the Lord and let the Lord lead him through the valleys of death that he walked through. It even got to a point where David had to find refuge in the midst of the enemies of God's people to keep away from Saul. But even in the midst of the enemies, God was with David.

God does not promise immediate deliverance to us when we call upon Him, but He does promise His strengthening hand and His presence as He walks with us during times of trial. Look at all the ways that the Lord preserved David as he fled the presence of Saul:

- God spared David from taking revenge upon foolish Nabal in 1 Samuel 25 through the wise council of Abigail.
- God kept David from dying at the hands of the Philistines in 1 Samuel 27.
- When God passed judgment upon Saul and was going to deliver his family and the army of Israel into the hands of the Philistines, God ensured that David was distracted with his own mission so he would not be forced to lift his hand against the Lord's anointed or to fight against the Lord when judgment was carried out by God against Saul (1 Samuel 30).
- And when David's men thought about stoning him when the enemies took their wives and children, God strengthened David, kept all their families alive, and delivered a tremendous victory by David's hand.

We read about all these things and think how encouraging and uplifting this must have been for David to witness the presence and deliverance of the Lord in all these ways. But when we feel that there is only a step between us and death, sometimes we must see the deliverance of the Lord in hindsight to truly appreciate it.

But when we experience adversity in real-time, we often fight feelings of hopelessness, discouragement, depression, and uncertainty. These are natural responses to intense trials. We don't have to get far into the Psalms to see that these are some of the same feelings that David wrestled with as well,

But in the midst of these overwhelming struggles, David never forgot God and allowed God to shoulder his burdens. And sometimes David had to wake up day after day for years before God finally removed his adversity. Yet, these moments were not a waste for David.

It was during the times of wrestling with adversity that David learned how to trust in the Lord. During these times when there was a step between David and death, David learned how to be the king that God was raising him up to be.

I am convinced that God never allows His children to suffer adversity for no reason. We may never understand what the reasons are, but they are there and this is where our trust in the Lord comes in. Whether it is to produce patience or to prepare us for another phase in our service to Him, all suffering is profitable to us in some way.

And this is sometimes tough to believe, especially when we are in the midst of walking with God in the valley of the shadow of death. Yet our faith is seen when we believe God but we can't see the reasons; when we trust Him as we step into the precipice and not see where our feet will fall.

It's not a fun place to be when there is only a step between us and death, but God lives fully in that step. That is what David learned and it shaped him into one of the greatest servants that we ever read about. And if we see God in the step between us and death, then we will be transformed in ways we can hardly imagine.

What a wonderful God we serve who never leaves or forsakes us, even in the step between us and death.

***

I'm in 2 Samuel, reading how God is giving David victories over his enemies.

No matter what his enemies do or how many times they gang up on David, God gives David the victory.

And with the victories come spoils. And much of those spoils go into storage to build the Temple of God.

Isn't it amazing how much God does for us and how little things are left up to us?

God expects us to live faithfully, but He will give us the increase. He is always the source of every good blessing.

***

If Jesus returned in the next 5 minutes, would you be full of regret, or would you be found watching and waiting?

You still have time to prepare for His return.

"Watch therefore, for you know neither the day nor the hour." (Matthew 25:13 ESV).

***

Don't you just feel good after coming home from spending time with God's people?

***

David had a bad day.

A really bad day.

In 2 Samuel 15, we read about his son, Absalom, attempting to take his throne away.

Some may understand Absalom's actions. He killed his oldest half-brother because his brother violated his sister, Tamar.

When David heard about this despicable act, he became angry but did nothing.

I wonder how events might have changed if David had been the father he should have been concerning the sins of his son.

But as Nathan had decreed from God, the sword would not depart from David's house because David had murdered Uriah, Bathsheba's husband, and took his wife to be his own wife.

And so, David's sins opened the door to this rebellion. God would not stop it.

Even when we repent and turn back to the Lord, we may have to walk with the Lord through the consequences of our sins.

We need to be careful not to equate consequences to guilt, for when the Lord forgives, He forgives completely.

When sin causes us to have a bad day, we need to draw all the closer to God and let Him walk with us in that day, and not let the consequences we may have to face be the stumbling block that shipwrecks our faith.

God delivered David from the hand of Absalom, but not until after David had to endure many tears before his deliverance.

***

Suggestion to consider for the day:
First, let us glorify King Jesus by serving someone today.
Then, let us bring petitions for ourselves before His throne.

"And the King will answer them, 'Truly, I say to you, as you did it to one of the least of these my brothers, you did it to me.'" (Matthew 25:40 ESV).

***

I am really trying to live by the philosophy of assuming the best in people and not the worst; giving them the benefit of the doubt even with the slightest evidence it's warranted. That changes the internal battles we often fight in our minds.

"Love bears all things, believes all things, hopes all things, endures all things." (1 Corinthians 13:7 ESV).

***

The Feeding of the Multitudes

In the Gospels, we read about the feeding of the 5000 and the 4000 in various accounts (5000 men plus women and children in Matthew 14 and the 4000 men plus women and children in the next chapter). We see this as a miracle showing Jesus's power as God over matter. But what is interesting to me is that this miracle wasn't simply to show that He was from God, but that He was God. And feeding multitudes is something that Jesus has been doing since He created man.

As Creator, Jesus has been taking care of His creation since He put Adam and Eve into the Garden of Eden. Do you remember what He said to Adam?

"And the LORD God commanded the man, saying, "You may surely eat of every tree of the garden, but of the tree of the knowledge of good and evil you shall not eat, for in the day that you eat of it you shall surely die." (Genesis 2:16-17 ESV).

Jesus claimed the name I AM in John 8:58, which tells us that He was the God we read about in the Old Testament. The people took up stones to kill Him because of this claim. But if Jesus was telling the truth, we see many times that the Father fed the multitudes through Him. We see Him feeding the millions of Israelites in the wilderness with manna from heaven for forty years. Is it any wonder that when He became flesh that He said this:

"I am the bread of life. Your fathers ate the manna in the wilderness, and they died. This is the bread that comes down from heaven, so that one may eat of it and not die. I am the living bread that came down from heaven. If anyone eats of this bread, he will live forever. And the bread that I will give for the life of the world is my flesh." (John 6:48-51 ESV).

God gave manna from heaven so that people might have the nourishment they needed. When the Father gave them manna, it sustained them but did not give them eternal life. In Jesus, the Father sends the only bread that can give eternal life, and that bread is Jesus Himself.

Jesus sustained a physical nation in the wilderness, and now He sustains a spiritual Kingdom by offering Himself for us to partake. We must fully feast upon Jesus to have this eternal life that manna could never provide man. The miracle of feeding the 5000 and the 4000 demonstrated that there will always be abundance and life in His presence. He is the source of all nourishment that we will ever need.

If we turn to Jesus in this wicked and perverse world, He will sustain us. He will nourish us. He will do more than give our bodies the calories it needs to survive; He will sustain our spirit and give us life beyond this physical existence. He is the Word incarnate, and His Word has life. It is not merely a great literary work but the inspired Word of the incarnate God. We find Jesus in the Word because He is the Word.

The multitude Jesus feeds today is far greater than when He sustained a nation in the wilderness or when He put man in Eden. Today, we can partake of the food that sustains us eternally. We partake of the food that will cause us to never die. No other food can do that. Only in Jesus can we find the Bread that will let us live forever.

And when He comes in Judgment and takes us home to be with Him, He will continue to provide the nourishment we need for life. He has prepared for us a place in heaven with Him. Listen to what He has done for us, what is waiting if we remain faithful:

> "Then the angel showed me the river of the water of life, bright as crystal, flowing from the throne of God and of the Lamb through the middle of the street of the city; also, on either side of the river, the tree of life with its twelve kinds of fruit, yielding its fruit each month. The leaves of the tree were for the healing of the nations. No longer will there be anything accursed, but the throne of God and of the Lamb will be in it, and his servants will worship him." (Revelation 22:1-3 ESV).

Jesus has always fed the multitudes. He did it the day He put man in Eden, and He does it today. And when He brings an end to the earth, He will continue to nourish us so that we may never die. The feeding of the 5000 and the 4000 was an amazing miracle to show His divinity, but that miracle hardly scratches the surface of what He is doing for you and me today and what He has in store for us in heaven.

***

I must fight the danger of putting God in a box. He is so far beyond me, He transcends even my wildest imagination of who He is and what He can do.

***

Random Thought:
I bet if there was a bonafide faith healer who could heal every illness, a hospital would soon choose not to make him welcome in their facility.

Given the choice of achieving their mission of healing all who need healing and going out of business, my gut says they would choose to keep illness around in order to keep the money flowing in rather than having people be healed and no longer need their services.

That made me think… Do I have lofty missions of mercy that I profess until I figure out that true service means that I must give up myself and fully live for others?

We all need to be certain that we are ready to live up to the biblical principles we espouse when we realize that doing so will mean a seismic shift in how we live life.

Are we ready to be the people of God when the rubber hits the road?

> "I appeal to you therefore, brothers, by the mercies of God, to present your bodies as a living sacrifice, holy and acceptable to God, which is your spiritual worship. Do not be conformed to this world, but be transformed by the renewal of your mind, that by testing you may discern what is the will of God, what is good and acceptable and perfect." (Romans 12:1-2 ESV).

***

I asked God for wisdom and He let me suffer to learn lessons I could learn no other way.

I asked God for wealth and He took away money so I could see clearly the true riches He has blessed me with.

I asked God for boldness and He allowed enemies to rise up against me to teach me how to be bold.

I asked God for relief and He sent me someone who needed a cup of cold water to serve so that I might focus less on my need for relief as I provided relief for another who needed it more than me.

I may ask God for what I think I need at the moment, but in His wisdom, He will always answer my prayers in the way that only an omniscient God can answer.

> "Three times I pleaded with the Lord about this, that it should leave me. But he said to me, "My grace is sufficient for you, for my power is made perfect in weakness." Therefore I will boast all the more gladly of my weaknesses, so that the power of Christ may rest upon me." (2 Corinthians 12:8-9 ESV).

***

If tonight is the night that the Lord returns, let's meet up at the River of Life after the Judgment and walk together to the throne of Jesus to worship Him.

> "And he who was seated on the throne said, "Behold, I am making all things new." Also he said, "Write this down, for these words are trustworthy and true."

And he said to me, "It is done! I am the Alpha and the Omega, the beginning and the end. To the thirsty I will give from the spring of the water of life without payment." (Revelation 21:5-6 ESV).

***

Chapter 1 Excerpt: What Is Sovereignty?

Note: Here is an excerpt from my upcoming book, The Sovereignty of God. It is raw and unedited to its final form, but I thought I'd give you another peek at where this book aims to take you.

I have some good news and some bad news for you. The good news is that we will look at God and His sovereignty in light of this definition and hopefully walk away with such a rich and deep understanding of this amazing attribute of God that it will literally change our lives and the way we approach each day. I believe that the more we understand God's sovereignty, the easier it will be to align our will to His will, and the easier it will become to live the way God wants His children to live. Living in the sovereignty of God is how we find the strength to conquer the sins we have struggled with over and over. Understanding God's sovereignty is the first step in bringing ourselves into subjection to Him and living fully in His grace. If you are like me, what you learn from His word about His sovereignty will be life-changing.

And here is the bad news. God is God. That means He is above us, and there are some things about Him we may never be capable of figuring out or understanding…

> "For my thoughts are not your thoughts, neither are your ways my ways, declares the LORD. For as the heavens are higher than the earth, so are my ways higher than your ways and my thoughts than your thoughts." (Isaiah 55:8-9 ESV).

What this means for our study is that as powerful as this lesson on sovereignty is or as life-changing as I believe it will be, it will not scratch the surface of the true nature of God's sovereignty. It is simply far beyond our human ability to fully comprehend. That said, I am excited to dive into what we can know about His sovereignty. What the Spirit has revealed is life-changing for us who choose to understand and apply what we learn.

We talked about sovereignty being a continuum. At one end we have limited sovereignty and at the other end, we have absolute sovereignty. In this book, we will explore the extreme to which sovereignty can exist; perfect sovereignty in all its power and glory. Sovereignty in which there is no lack or no imperfection. When we talk about God's supreme power, we are talking about the only supreme power. There is simply no greater power that exists. When we talk about God not being controlled by any external power, we are talking about Him being exempt from the control of any existing power. When we talk about His controlling influence, we are talking about an influence so powerful it can perform the impossible in our lives.

By now, you probably have many Bible verses running through your head that demonstrate the sovereignty of God. No doubt, we will examine many of them in this book. But what I am most excited about is the, "So what?" of this study because this is where the power to transform us will come. Consider these questions...

How can living in the sovereignty of God help me conquer through my battle to overcome sin and temptation?

How can bowing the knee daily to a sovereign God equip me to persevere through any trial?

How does my free will intersect with the sovereignty of God?

How will the sovereignty of God change the way I look at suffering and unanswered prayers?

How will God's sovereignty realign the way I look at my fellow man who is created in His image?

How will the sovereignty of God cause me to reevaluate my role as a steward of God?

This is just a taste of what awaits us as we dive into this study. But it all begins with having a clear understanding of what we are talking about. The definitions and aspects of sovereignty that we discussed in this chapter are a great starting point. In the next chapter, we will look at the claims that the Scriptures make about God's sovereignty.

***

The older I get, the more evidence I see that my body is decaying. The more pain I feel, the slower I move and the more I have to rest.

But I have confidence that the I am closer each day to receiving that eternal body made to go without sleep, never hunger or thirst and will never again know pain.

I wake up each day with the knowledge that I am one day closer to having the new body that will prepare me for the eternal praise and worship I will give my God.

> "They shall hunger no more, neither thirst anymore; the sun shall not strike them, nor any scorching heat. For the Lamb in the midst of the throne will be their shepherd, and he will guide them to springs of living water, and God will wipe away every tear from their eyes." (Revelation 7:16-17 ESV).

***

Where I live, it's cloudy outside. I went out to check the mail and looked into the clouds. It reminded me of the verses I am thinking about which will be the focus of my next "Tuesdays With Tony" post:

> "And Jesus said, "I am, and you will see the Son of Man seated at the right hand of Power, and coming with the clouds of heaven." (Mark 14:62 ESV).

"Coming with the clouds of heaven..." This is a description of divinity as seen in Daniel :

> "I saw in the night visions, and behold, with the clouds of heaven there came one like a son of man, and he came to the Ancient of Days and was presented before him." (Daniel 7:13 ESV).

So as I looked up into the clouds, I thought to myself, "I am looking at the scene in which Jesus, the Son of Man, will return in His glory.
The next time you see the clouds, imagine Jesus returning with them. You will never look at a cloudy day the same again.

***

> "But the day of the Lord
> will
> come like a thief, and then the heavens
> will
> pass away with a roar, and the heavenly bodies
> will
> be burned up and dissolved,
> and the earth and the works that are done on it
> will
> be exposed." (2 Peter 3:10 ESV).

Question: What are you waiting for?

> "Since all these things are thus to be dissolved, what sort of people ought you to be in lives of holiness and godliness," (2 Peter 3:11 ESV).

***

Jesus, what have I sacrificed for You?
Jesus, what have I suffered for You?
Jesus, what have I given up for You?
Jesus, what I have laid down for You?
Please, Jesus, help me see what I have done, but more importantly, what I can still do for You.
Help me trim my lamp so I can be found ready when You return.

"Let us rejoice and exult and give him the glory, for the marriage of the Lamb has come, and his Bride has made herself ready;" (Revelation 19:7 ESV).

***

Jesus, Son of Man

For most of my life, I have heard sermons about the explanations of two titles that are used for Jesus in the New Testament. One is the Son of God and the other is the Son of Man. What I heard about these titles is that the title Son of Man illustrates Jesus' humanity and the title Son of God illustrates His divinity. But as you view these two titles through the lens of the Jewish reader, I am not sure that these two definitions are as cut and dry as we have made them out to be.

For sure, when the title, Son of God, is placed upon Jesus, it is given a literal meaning since He was the only begotten Son of God. But when the Jewish audience heard this term, they were used to this term also being used for a man. Adam was called the Son of God (Luke 3:38) as was Solomon (1 Chronicles 28:6). Even Israel itself is called the firstborn son of God (Exodus 4:22).

But what really seemed to upset the Jewish leaders is when Jesus called Himself the Son of Man. This is when they would tear their clothes and hurl the accusation of blasphemy at Him, saying He was worthy of death. Why was this such an anathema to them? Well, as you look at the term Son of Man through their lens, it quickly becomes apparent why this term troubled them so much and may shed light on how we have maybe overlooked the significance of this term when we make our quick definition that this simply represents His humanity.

In the Old Testament, the term Son of Man is used in two ways. First is the way we traditionally think of it. Ezekiel is called the Son of Man throughout the book to emphasize his humanity and his distance from the divinity and perfection of God. Son of Man is, indeed, a focus of man's humanity. But in Daniel, we see a different application of the term Son of Man. I believe that it's through this lens that the term applied to Jesus caused the Jews to feel Jesus was blaspheming when He called Himself the Son of

Man:

> "I saw in the night visions, and behold, with the clouds of heaven there came one like a son of man, and he came to the Ancient of Days and was presented before him. And to him was given dominion and glory and a kingdom, that all peoples, nations, and languages should serve him; his dominion is an everlasting dominion, which shall not pass away, and his kingdom one that shall not be destroyed." (Daniel 7:13-14 ESV).

Notice what Daniel saw about the one like the Son of Man. First, he was with the clouds of heaven. This was an image reserved for God alone according to Deuteronomy 33:27. Yet this was ascribed to the one like the Son of Man. Then, whoever this Son of Man was, He was presented to God, the Ancient of Days in heaven. When this son of man was presented to who I believe is God the Father, He was given an eternal kingdom and He would receive power to rule alongside the Ancient of Days. He would receive service in heaven that only belonged to God.

When Jesus came to earth and used the title Son of Man, which Son of Man is He ascribing to Himself? The Son of Man in Ezekiel or the Son of Man who Daniel saw? Which Son of Man do you think the Jewish people thought Jesus was ascribing to Himself when they tore their clothes and accused Him of blasphemy? To answer this, let's look at the earliest Gospel written: Mark. This was written perhaps 3 or so decades after Jesus died, which gives us insight into how the earliest Christians viewed Jesus. Some scholars say that the divinity of Jesus was attributed to Jesus centuries after He died, but is this what we see in this early Gospel?

In the first instance where Jesus calls Himself the Son of Man, He does so by ascribing attributes that belong to God Himself:

> "And he said to them, "The Sabbath was made for man, not man for the Sabbath. So the Son of Man is lord even of the Sabbath." (Mark 2:27-28 ESV).

The Sabbath observance was given in the Ten Commandments. In this passage, Jesus is making Himself not just Lord of the Sabbath, but Lord over the Law given to Moses. This was a definite attribution to Himself, the Son of Man, that only belongs to God.

Let's look at places where Jesus is given prerogatives belonging to God, Yahweh Himself, in the Gospels. Look at what John the Baptist says about his ministry as it relates to Jesus. When pressed by the Jewish leaders to explain who he is, John replies with:

> "He said, "I am the voice of one crying out in the wilderness, 'Make straight the way of the Lord,' as the prophet Isaiah said." (John 1:23 ESV).

This is a quote from Isaiah 40:3:

> "A voice cries: "In the wilderness prepare the way of the LORD; make straight in the desert a highway for our God." (Isaiah 40:3 ESV).

If you notice in my translation (ESV), you will see the word LORD in all caps in the Isaiah reference. This happens when the name of God, Yahweh, is used. You can see that in John's Gospel, Jesus is inserted where the Old Testament uses Yahweh. Jesus is Yahweh, the name of God.

We don't have to go far in the Gospel of Mark to see the same thing happening. Jesus is inserted in the Gospel where Yahweh was used in the Old Testament. In Mark 4, we see Jesus calming the storm and Mark ascribes to Him that which the Old Testament ascribes to Yahweh:

> "But he was in the stern, asleep on the cushion. And they woke him and said to him, "Teacher, do you not care that we are perishing?" And he awoke and rebuked the wind and said to the sea, "Peace! Be still!" And the wind ceased, and there was a great calm." (Mark 4:38-39 ESV).

Look at what the Old Testament says about this very thing:

> "For he commanded and raised the stormy wind, which lifted up the waves of the sea. They mounted up to heaven; they went down to the depths; their courage melted away in their evil plight; they reeled and staggered like drunken men and were at their wits' end. Then they cried to the LORD in their trouble, and he delivered them from their distress." (Psalm 107:25-28 ESV).

Verse 28 says that the LORD, Yahweh, delivered them when they cried out in their distress. Mark says Jesus delivered them from the stormy sea. Even the earliest Gospel plugged Jesus into the things specifically written about Yahweh.

And then we get to the climax of Mark's Gospel in Mark 14:62 where all of this comes to a focal point. Jesus Himself takes on the attributes of Yahweh and it pushes the Jewish leaders over the edge, and He does it by taking the title, Son of Man. In doing so, He confirms the attributes of deity that the disciples ascribed to Him. When the High Priest asks Him point blank if He is the Christ, the Son of the Blessed, here is how Jesus answers:

"And Jesus said, "I am, and you will see the Son of Man seated at the right hand of Power, and coming with the clouds of heaven." (Mark 14:62 ESV). Within this one answer, Jesus claims three times that He is Yahweh:

1. I AM. This is who God said Moses should tell Israel was sending him to free them from Egyptian bondage.

2. You will see the Son of Man Seated at the right hand of Power. Only God is seated on His throne. For man to claim this position of authority is paramount to blasphemy.

3. You will see The Son of Man coming in the clouds. Again, this is a reference back to how Daniel saw the Son of Man. Only God comes in the clouds. Jesus was attesting that He was not only the Son of Man in humanity but that He was the one like the Son of Man in Daniel who would share a throne with God and reign in heaven at the side of the Ancient of Days.

There was no doubt that the earliest Christians understood Jesus to be Yahweh, God, having all attributes of God. And thus, He was worthy to be worshiped as God. Is this what the Jews thought when Jesus called Himself the Son of Man? I believe the text leaves no doubt that they understood fully what this meant:

"And the high priest tore his garments and said, "What further witnesses do we need? You have heard his blasphemy. What is your decision?" And they all condemned him as deserving death." (Mark 14:63-64 ESV).

Jesus was the Son of God, But He was also the Son of Man. When we read this title, let's not be too quick to say that the title Son of Man only represents His humanity. Through the lens of the Jews, they knew that this title meant He was claiming much more, as were His disciples.

And so they nailed Him to the cross for claiming to be the Son of Man.

**

I love rainbows. Few things cause us to grab a camera faster than seeing a full rainbow so we can share it with our friends. As Christians, we know the deep theology behind the rainbow, don't we?

After the Flood, God set His bow in the sky as a sign of the covenant to man He made to never again destroy the world by water.

Scientists will tell us that the bow is a natural phenomenon caused by the refraction of light as it hits drops of water. They're right, but we believe that this is how God set the bow in the sky.

So when we see the bow and marvel at its beauty, let's not forget why God set it in the sky. The bow is an ongoing, visible gift from God that we can witness even today, representing His promise to us. The bow reminds us that God is not forgetful.

4000 plus years later, God continues to send His bow to us. 4000 years later, we still get to witness a visible sign of His covenant to us.

The next time you see a bow, enjoy its beauty, but don't forget to say "Thank You" to our God who still keeps His covenant with us.

> "I have set my bow in the cloud, and it shall be a sign of the covenant between me and the earth. When I bring clouds over the earth and the bow is seen in the clouds, I will remember my covenant that is between me and you and every living creature of all flesh. And the waters shall never again become a flood to destroy all flesh." (Genesis 9:13-15 ESV).

***

Here's a peek at the contents of my upcoming book, The Sovereignty of God:

Introduction
Chapter 1: What Is Sovereignty?
Chapter 2: Sovereignty: The Potter and the Clay
Chapter 3: Fundamental Attributes of Sovereignty
Chapter 4: God's Sovereignty and Man's Free Will
Chapter 5: God's Sovereignty Seen In Job
Chapter 6: God's Sovereignty Seen In Daniel 4
Chapter 7: Ways God Accomplishes His Purposes
Chapter 8: Foreknowledge And God's Sovereignty
Chapter 9: Prayers, Providence, Miracles, and the Sovereignty of God
Chapter 10: What Will I Do With The Sovereignty Of God?

***

Awesome quote from Ken Weliever during his lesson at our Legacy Weekend tonight:

"Next time the devil reminds you of your past, you remind him of his future!"

Amen!

***

In 2 Kings 6, we read a few short verses that contain an amazing miracle from God. The chapter starts with the prophets of the Lord building a larger dwelling for themselves. As one of them was cutting a log, the axe head came off the handle and fell into the water.

> "But as one was felling a log, his axe head fell into the water, and he cried out, "Alas, my master! It was borrowed." Then the man of God said, "Where did it fall?" When he showed him the place, he cut off a stick and threw it in there and made the iron float. And he said, "Take it up." So he reached out his hand and took it." (2 Kings 6:5-7 ESV).

Elisha, the man of God, performed a miracle and did the impossible, causing the iron axe head to float. That should teach us a valuable lesson.

Nothing is impossible for God.

When we have a need, let's not spend time trying to determine if the need is too big for God. If God can make an iron axe head float in water, isn't there nothing that He can't do for us if it is His will to accomplish it for us?

When we find ourselves praised by those in the world, let's remember Him from Whom all blessings flow.

It's much too easy to confuse God's blessings with our own greatness.

The same God who raises us up for His glory can also bring us down for His glory.

When we find favor in the eyes of others, let us thank God and use that favor to His glory.

"And David became greater and greater, for the Lord of hosts was with him." (1 Chronicles 11:9 ESV).

"The Lord was with Joseph, and he became a successful man, and he was in the house of his Egyptian master." (Genesis 39:2 ESV).

"And God gave Daniel favor and compassion in the sight of the chief of the eunuchs," (Daniel 1:9 ESV).

***

I'm in 1 Chronicles 22 in my daily Bible reading. In this chapter, King David prepares material for the building of the Temple that Solomon, his son, will build.

He then charges Solomon with the task of building the Temple, showing His son all that he has prepared for the Temple. David ends with instructions to Solomon to be faithful to the Lord.

When we distill 1 Chronicles 22 (also chapter 28) down to its simplest message, isn't it that fathers should spend their life preparing their children to serve the Lord and work to prepare all we can for their success in serving God?

Fathers, what have we done to prepare for our children's successful service to the Lord?

Have we had our one-on-one conversations with them, encouraging them to serve God all of their lives showing them how to be a successful servant to God when we are gone?

***

I started 2 Chronicles in my daily Bible reading. In chapter 6, Solomon is dedicating the Temple.

In one part of the dedication, Solomon pleads with God to listen to the hearts of the people when they cry out to Him in prayer.

When we pray to God, what is really in our hearts? Do we pray one thing with our lips and another with our hearts?

Let's not be deceived. God will not be swayed by our lips when our hearts speak to Him something different.

In humble honesty, let us come before the Lord with pure hearts and pure lips. This is what our great God longs from us.

"whatever prayer, whatever plea is made by any man or by all your people Israel, each knowing his own affliction and his own sorrow and stretching out his hands toward this house, then hear from heaven your dwelling place and forgive and render to each whose heart you know, according to all his ways, for you, you only, know the hearts of the children of mankind, that they may fear you and walk in your ways all the days that they live in the land that you gave to our fathers." (2 Chronicles 6:29-31 ESV).

***

God is not looking for a way to extend His judgment upon you,
He is eagerly looking for a way to extend His grace upon you.
Submit to God in your walk with His Son so He will extend His goodness and not His judgment.

"O Jerusalem, Jerusalem, the city that kills the prophets and stones those who are sent to it! How often would I have gathered your children together as a hen gathers her brood under her wings, and you were not willing!" (Matthew 23:37 ESV).

***

Jordan Shouse is speaking on living an authentic life instead of a fake life.
Integrity demands we don't put on a show and portray ourselves differently from who we are.
If we are not the person who we want people to think we are, don't pretend to be. Rather become the person we want to be.
If we want people to see us as righteous, then be righteous. Don't pretend to be righteous.

***

Presidents deliver gaffes.
Queens die.
Governors have one set of rules for themselves and another for everyone else.
But..
King Jesus' words transforms and saves.

King Jesus conquered death for us.

King Jesus never changes and treats everyone equally.

When you have to grab the Tums when men spin the world out of control, remember that King Jesus is trustworthy, dependable, and predictable.

In the end, King Jesus is Lord of lords and King of kings.

When the world seems to burn around us, we sleep well because we find comfort in the Lord.

If you want peace, then submit to the only One who can give you true peace in the midst of a world plagued with distress, frustration, stress, and agitation.

***

Do we double down in sin? This is what king Ahaz did. Even some of the most evil kings, like Manassas, humbled themselves when God brought them low, but not Ahaz.

If we cannot humble ourselves before the Lord, but double down in our sins, it's a dangerous sign that we may be much closer to the point of no return in our relationship with God.

May we never reach the point that instead of humble repentance, we double down in our sins before Him.

"In the time of his distress he became yet more faithless to the LORD—this same King Ahaz.

> For he sacrificed to the gods of Damascus that had defeated him and said, "Because the gods of the kings of Syria helped them, I will sacrifice to them that they may help me." But they were the ruin of him and of all Israel." (2 Chronicles 28:22-23 ESV).

***

As I read through Ezra, it's a rather exciting book as you read it through in one reading. No matter what man tried to do to alter God's purpose, in the end, God ensured that His will was done concerning the rebuilding of the Temple.

But that didn't mean the Jews didn't have to face opposition, discouragement, or threats that put fear in them. But in light of all this, God was still able to accomplish His will.

What a great God we serve Who doesn't need man's consent or

cooperation to accomplish His purposes.

> "and this house was finished on the third day of the month of Adar, in the sixth year of the reign of Darius the king." (Ezra 6:15 ESV).

***

So, I recently prayed for patience and God gave me stressful situations that tested my patience.

I spoke without thinking and acted from a disposition of anger.

My cause was just, at least in my mind, but somewhere in the midst of taking someone to the proverbial woodshed, it dawned on me that God was trying to give me what I had asked Him for.

Coming to that realization changed everything for me. I began to ask myself, how would Jesus respond if He were in my situation (yeah, I know, WWJD).

But thinking through that yielded some humbling thoughts. I do not believe He'd have a tongue as sharp as mine.

I don't believe He'd let anger fester and replay someone else's actions in His mind over and over, triggering Himself through a corrosive self-talk.

I think He'd be looking for ways to extend grace when grace wasn't due.

At first, I thought about how much I failed this opportunity to learn patience, but then I realized that part of learning patience is being able to recognize, in the moment, where you are lacking so you can make godly adjustments.

So, I applied what I learned, humbled myself, and not only repaired the damage my anger-filled tongue had caused, but I was able to calm my inner storm and mend a relationship with a fellow man who is also made in God's image.

My takeaway… My walk with Jesus isn't about getting it right all the time; rather, it's about getting back up when I fall and keep walking with Him.

He has proven to be a faithful Friend and Master who has the patience with me that I seek to have with others.

***

In Nehemiah 9, the people of Israel listened to their past recounted to them where God would save them, and then they would fall back into sin only to repeat the pattern of salvation and falling away over and over.

Too often, when we experience the consequences of our sins, we want to reach out and blame someone else for our consequences. Many times, the person we blame is God.

But listen to how the Levites characterized God and the people:

> "Yet you have been righteous in all that has come upon us, for you have dealt faithfully and we have acted wickedly." (Nehemiah 9:33 ESV).

When we act wickedly and suffer the consequences, can we humble ourselves and say to God, "You have dealt faithfully and we have acted wickedly."

Or do we lash out at God and say to Him, "I have dealt faithfully and You have acted wickedly."

We may not say it with our lips, but is this what our hearts are saying?

The first step in reconciliation with God is to recognize our condition so we can approach our God with a humble heart and He will forgive and create a new heart in us.

***

Asking for patience is easy...
Developing patience takes dedication and hard work.

***

So, Boaz was Ruth's redeemer. Under the law, a man could sell his inheritance in hard times, but he never lost the claim on the land.

In hard times of famine, Ruth's family sold their land with the hopes of redeeming it when times were better. But Ruth's husband and male children died before they could redeem their land.

When Ruth returned home, she had no means to redeem their land back to their family. So, Boaz stepped up as a close relative and redeemed her family's land on her behalf.

Boaz certainly lived one of the greatest love stories ever written because it was far more than romantic love. He showed grace by redeeming this family's inheritance for them.

When we lost our inheritance to the Garden of Eden, it took a redeemer to step in on our behalf to redeem by grace what we could not redeem for ourselves.

Jesus redeemed us and restored our place with God when we had no other hope.

"Blessed be the God and Father of our Lord Jesus Christ! According to his great mercy, he has caused us to be born again to a living hope through the resurrection of Jesus Christ from the dead,
to an inheritance that is imperishable, undefiled, and unfading, kept in heaven for you,
who by God's power are being guarded through faith for a salvation ready to be revealed in the last time." (1 Peter 1:3-5 ESV).

***

Today, we worship the King together. And perhaps, if it is His time, we may even get to see Him in the clouds this afternoon.
Are you ready?

***

Rickie Jenkins is preaching about how we view suffering. Joseph is a wonderful example of someone who looked at the evil in his life and saw the good that God could work through it.

***

This morning, we have all been given the gift of God's long-suffering. We woke up to a new day, not to live according to our desires, but to glorify Him. What will you do with this gift of long-suffering today?

"But you, O Lord, are a God merciful and gracious, slow to anger and abounding in steadfast love and faithfulness." (Psalm 86:15 ESV).

***

"Salvation is from God. Works are out of gratitude, not in order to earn

or deserve a thing."
Thanks, Kris Emerson.

***

Gentiles Who Sought Jesus

When Jesus came to earth, He did so for a specific purpose. He came to fulfill the Law of Moses and to preach to the children of Israel. As He told the Canaanite woman,

> "I was sent only to the lost sheep of the house of Israel." (Matthew 15:24b ESV).

And

> "Do not think that I have come to abolish the Law or the Prophets; I have not come to abolish them but to fulfill them." (Matthew 5:17 ESV).

Yet, while on earth, even some Gentiles could not keep away from Him. They came, seeking His help and humbling themselves with even more faith than was found in all of Israel (Luke 7:9). Why is this such an amazing thing to consider?

First, you see Jesus' love for all men and women. When He looked into the eyes of the Gentile, He didn't see race. He saw the child He had created, looking into His eyes, needing help that only their Creator could give them.

And He loved them. While His mission was first to the children He had chosen as a sanctified people to Himself, He came bearing a mystery. When His disciples saw racial distinction, Jesus saw one humanity made from one blood; the blood He created for all men to share. He saw Jews and Gentiles alike whom He created in His own image.

And here was the mystery that He knew which no one else knew at the time:

> "This mystery is that the Gentiles are fellow heirs, members of the same body, and partakers of the promise in Christ Jesus through the gospel." (Ephesians 3:6 ESV).

And even when Jesus came first to the Jews, He could not turn away His creation among the Gentiles when they humbly sought their Creator's help.

From His beginning on earth, Gentile wise men sought Him at His birth (Matthew 2).

In Luke 7, we read about the Roman Centurion who humbled himself before this Jewish preacher so his servant might be healed. This is when Jesus said, "I tell you, not even in Israel have I found such faith."

In Luke 8, Jesus travels to a Gentile region to cast demons out of a Gentile. Until Jesus came, everyone feared him. But when Jesus set him free, this man asked to go with Jesus. The Lord had different plans for him and sent him away proclaiming what He had done for this Gentile.

And then in Matthew 15, there was the Canaanite woman who had a daughter who was oppressed by demons. When everyone wanted to send her away, her persistence made her humble before the Lord. Jesus granted her request, saying, "O woman, great is your faith! Be it done for you as you desire."

When all of Israel anticipated the coming of the Jewish Messiah, our Lord had a mystery that only He knew. He gave tidbits of this mystery, but it went right over the heads of the sons of Israel:

> "I tell you, many will come from east and west and recline at table with Abraham, Isaac, and Jacob in the kingdom of heaven," (Matthew 8:11 ESV).

I loved that Jesus loved the Gentiles. Even though He came to the sons of Abraham first, Gentiles were never forgotten by the Lord. They were never an afterthought. Gentiles were as much part of His plan as were the Jews.

How does this affect me? I'm a Gentile. I was part of the mystery that the Son of Man brought into the world with Him. When John and Jesus both told the Jews that God could raise up children of Abraham from the stones, He did one better. He raised up children of Abraham from Gentiles:

> "Know then that it is those of faith who are the sons of Abraham. And the Scripture, foreseeing that God would justify the Gentiles by faith, preached the gospel beforehand to Abraham, saying, "In you shall all the nations be blessed." (Galatians 3:7-8 ESV).

My God came first to the Jews, but He always knew the Gentiles. And today, just like the Centurion, the demon-possessed man, and the Canaanite women, we Gentiles can receive grace from Him today.

Today, we can dine with Him at His table; we can be the children of Abraham by faith, and we can be a royal priesthood. What a magnificent, wonderful mystery our Lord brought with Him to earth!

***

So, one of my weaknesses is letting the news trigger me, making my tongue sharp and filling my heart with bitterness. But I have found a remedy... Turn off the TV, change the channel, or turn off the radio.

It's amazing how well it works when you stay away from things that tempt or corrupt you.

Fleeing evil is much easier than fighting it. At least that's my experience.

***

I hope we understand that we don't have to like the way God expresses His sovereignty, but we must honor and respect it. And just like our Lord, in His most trying moment, we must say of God's sovereignty, "Not My will, but Yours be done. "

***

I don't think we can truly understand or appreciate God's grace until we understand and appreciate God's sovereignty.

God's sovereignty shows us that He can require anything He wishes from us, and we have no grounds to challenge His requirements.

God's sovereignty demonstrates His supremacy in our lives and demands consequences when we violate His will.

God's sovereignty, by nature, means that we cannot choose our own way but we must abide in His way.

God's grace shows us that even though we deserve death because we have rebelled against our sovereign God, He can choose to provide a way for us to avoid the wages of sin due us.

He didn't have to do that.

We didn't deserve it.

This is His gift to us.

***

You know, I really appreciate our elders at Campbell Road. They labor without drawing attention to themselves, serving us for the glory of King Jesus.

They bring our names before His throne.

They call, send letters, and ensure we don't fall through the cracks.

They don't approach us with accusations, but in sincerity, seek to see if we need anything.

They are supportive and sacrifice whatever time we need to help us through anything we may be going through.

I bet I'll never know how many times Jesus has heard my name in prayers from their lips.

They are not perfect, but they are selfless.

They are men, but they serve with strength and wisdom given to them by the Spirit.

They deserve more than my love and sincere respect, but this is what I can offer.

I will give them grace when they watch over my soul, and believe all things, giving them the benefit of the doubt.

To my six pastors, thank you for your selfless service as you watch over my soul.

***

Mark White: "Is our service to God restricted to what we do within the church building a couple of times a week?

The church building is where we come to learn about God and worship Him. When we go home, we go home to serve Him."

***

I was reading about the birth of Jesus. The learned men had been studying the Scriptures for signs of when the Messiah would come.

They knew He would be born in Bethlehem.

They knew He'd be a descendant of David.

They knew He'd be a great leader who would redeem the people of God.

These learned men fully expected to be the ones who would see the Messiah when He came.

But when Jesus was born, Angels didn't appear to them to announce the wonderful message of peace on earth.

They appeared to simple shepherds and a star led Gentile wise men to the promised infant Messiah.

When the Father announced the birth of His only begotten Son, He didn't throw a lavish party with a "Who's Who" guest list of attendees.

He invited the very ones who would one day follow His Son and dine with Him at His table in the Kingdom.

He invited the poor and humble to celebrate His Son's birth. He invited the Gentiles to see His only begotten Son.

Whoever we are, whatever our lot, no matter how poor or wretched we are, King Jesus still looks for people just like us.

He entered the world by celebrating with the same people He opens His Kingdom to today.

What a wonderful God who gives us a seat at His table by offering us such marvelous grace.

***

A King Who Can Forgive Anything

In Matthew 18, the tax collector writes something about Jesus that may have struck him as more amazing than perhaps it initially struck the other apostles. It began with a question from Peter:

> "Then Peter came up and said to him, "Lord, how often will my brother sin against me, and I forgive him? As many as seven times?" (Matthew 18:21 ESV).

As Jesus begins to teach an amazing lesson on grace and expectation, listen to how the tax collector records Jesus' response:

> "Jesus said to him, "I do not say to you seven times, but seventy-seven times." (Matthew 18:22 ESV).

As Peter struggles to quantify forgiveness and expectations, Jesus responds by telling the apostles that we don't make accounts of wrong. We don't balance the ledger. There is no time when our duty is fulfilled before we are justified in withholding forgiveness.

What would happen if Matthew had employed these principles in his tax booth? As a tax collector, his job was to ensure what was due was collected. Forgiveness could perhaps be extended as the exception to the rule, but here, Jesus seemed to be teaching that forgiveness was the rule. To put a fine point on it, Jesus gives them a parable.

> "Therefore the kingdom of heaven may be compared to a king who wished to settle accounts with his servants. When he began to settle, one was brought to him who owed him ten thousand talents. And since he could not pay, his master ordered him to be sold, with his wife and children and all that he had, and payment to be made. So the servant fell on his knees, imploring him, 'Have patience with me, and I will pay you everything.'" (Matthew 18:23-26 ESV).

Jesus tells of a man who owed the king 10,000 talents. My Bible has a footnote that a talent was equivalent to 20 years' wages. That means that this man owed the king 200,000 years' worth of wages. When he couldn't pay, the king ordered that he and his family be sold to pay off the debt owed to him. But the man pleaded with the king for patience and he would pay all.

Really? 200,000 years of labor? This debt was insurmountable. You know the story. The king had compassion for the man and forgave him of his debt. (vs. 27). All of it. All 10,000 talents. All 200,000 years' worth of wages. This was a far cry from Peter's 7 times forgiveness. It makes me wonder what was the biggest debt the tax collector ever extended to anyone. I can see why the Holy Spirit chose Matthew to record this parable.

The rest of the story is what we usually focus on when we teach the lesson of this parable. We need to forgive others if we want the forgiveness of our Father. What we owe Him is far more than what others owe us. God's forgiveness of us is heavily influenced by the mercy and grace in forgiveness we extend to others.

These are the main lessons that Jesus wants us to walk away with. But I want us to see something amazing we perhaps gloss over as a truth that should cause us to drop to our knees in worship and awe for our great God. It's a lesson about the King. It's a lesson I'm convinced Mathew picked up on immediately, perhaps before any other apostles picked up on it.

The King could forgive 10,000 talents. Have you thought about that? 10,000 is not an insignificant amount for most people. If someone owed us something that would bankrupt us if they didn't pay us back, it would be much different than if they owed us something we could forgive and still move on in life having forgiven.

The king had this kind of wealth. He was full of forgiveness because he had the capacity to forgive anything without it bankrupting him. Jesus was telling us that God had this kind of forgiveness. There is no debt we have against God He cannot forgive. We have done Him no wrong which will cause Him to look at His ledger on the Day of Judgment and say, "Wow, what you have done is more than I can overlook. You were just too bad. You have done too much wrong for me to forgive."

And it is the Judge of mankind who teaches this. Jesus isn't overgeneralizing because He is the one who will be wronged and will settle accounts on the Day of Judgment. His capacity to forgive holds no limits. He is the King who can afford to forgive 200,000 years of debt against Him.

From you.

From me.

From billions and billions of souls whom He created.

He can forgive it all.

And yes, He expects us to show a speck of grace to each other because He gives overflowing grace to each of us. We forgive each other, not out of obligation, but from the overflowing measure of grace we receive from Him.

I bet Peter never looked at his question about how many times we must forgive each other the same way again. More interestingly to me, I bet Matthew, the tax collector, walked away with an overwhelming appreciation of a great God who has the capacity to forgive any and every debt charged against Him and wipe the balance page clean.

Let us drop to our knees daily to that the Great King for His generous spirit and His infinite capacity to forgive us all our wrongs.

***

Jordan Shouse: "Today, you are closer than you ever have been in your life to meeting Jesus."

How should that cause you to live from this moment on?

***

Praise God, He is sovereign, and there is none like Him!

***

God has inherent authority, power, and ability to do whatever He wants.

***

God answers to no man, no power, or to any other authority.

***

God has the right to make the rules and the power to enforce those rules on whomever He chooses.

***

Man can say "no" to a sovereign God, but not in perpetuity.
There will be a day of reckoning.
In the end, God will prove to be sovereign over all.

***

I am back in Psalms in my daily Bible reading. One I read this morning was Psalm 15. It is a short, five-verse Psalm that will give you thoughts to meditate on all day. In verse one, David begins by asking a question:

"A Psalm of David. O LORD, who shall sojourn in your tent? Who shall dwell on your holy hill?" (Psalm 15:1 ESV).

Isn't this what we all look for? How can we dwell with the Lord, in His presence? In the next four verses, God gives us the answer through the Holy Spirit. I have much to consider after reading these revelations.

"He who walks blamelessly and does what is right and speaks truth in his heart;" (Psalm 15:2 ESV).

Do I seek to be blameless and do what is right? Am I honest in my heart or do I harbor rottenness and uncleanness in my heart? I may fool men, but God reads what is true in my heart. To dwell with Him, I must have a clean heart that is seeking to be blameless before Him.

"who does not slander with his tongue and does no evil to his neighbor, nor takes up a reproach against his friend;" (Psalm 15:3 ESV).

How do I seek to be blameless? By controlling my tongue and actions toward my neighbor. My actions and motives toward others must be pure and in line with our Lord's instructions to love my neighbor as myself. Am I harboring evil toward my brother? If so, I need to make it right so I can dwell in the Lord's presence.

> "in whose eyes a vile person is despised, but who honors those who fear the LORD; who swears to his own hurt and does not change;" (Psalm 15:4 ESV).

Do I rejoice in those who fear the Lord and reject those who do not? In our culture, we are feeling the pressure more and more to delight in the ones who reject God while rejecting those who fear God. We must be careful with whom we cast our lot. To dwell with the Lord, I must stand with the just and reject the unjust.

> "who does not put out his money at interest and does not take a bribe against the innocent. He who does these things shall never be moved." (Psalm 15:5 ESV).

The Psalm ends with the exhortation to treat others fairly and justly. Do I look for ways to mistreat people and take advantage of them or do I sacrifice gain at someone's expense to put them first? If I want to dwell with the Lord, then I will extend justice to all.
I want to dwell with the Lord forever. I have much to meditate on today.

***

Time continues, but God said that one day will be the last.
We fill our calendars, but do we remember to keep the Day of Judgment in mind?
We plan for trips, education, dates, and our career but do we plan for what happens after life on earth?
Enjoy your time on earth that the Lord blesses you with, but remember, it is only here for a vapor.
Don't trade your eternity for the vapor, or mist, that is gone as soon as it appears.

> "yet you do not know what tomorrow will bring. What is your life? For you are a mist that appears for a little time and then vanishes." (James 4:14 ESV).

***

Where do we really put our faith and trust? Do we wish for more mighty ships of war?

Do we seek more technology to create iron domes that can strike down incoming missiles and rockets?

Do we seek greater tanks and weapons? Do we seek more submarines and satellites?

I would trade it all for a leader who humbles his heart before the Lord. It is the Lord where strength is found.

Where do we really put our faith and trust? God can cause the most mighty nation to fall into the hands of the weak; God can lift up a people who have no mighty army.

> "The king is not saved by his great army; a warrior is not delivered by his great strength. The war horse is a false hope for salvation, and by its great might it cannot rescue. Behold, the eye of the LORD is on those who fear him, on those who hope in his steadfast love," (Psalm 33:16-18 ESV).

Where do we really put our faith and trust?

***

As I read through the Psalms, I hear David's plaintiff cry for God to be with him as his enemies seek his life. We know that he refused to lift his hand against the Lord's anointed, even when those around him urged him to kill king Saul on numerous occasions.

Yet, David always left vengeance to God. This is so unlike what we are tempted to do, isn't it? And not just us, but we see even great men falling into the temptation of handling things according to our human ways instead of waiting on the Lord.

Abraham chose to bring about an heir his own way rather than to wait upon the Lord. Saul chose to prepare for the battle against the Amalekites rather than wait for the Lord.

I fear that we often try to fix things with our own power and wisdom rather than wait for the Lord. But David gives us the example of putting our trust in the Lord.

Certainly, we act with prayer and after seeking wisdom. But first, we must drop to our knees to seek God and His deliverance. We must learn to wait upon the Lord before trying to fix our problems without first coming before the Lord and waiting upon Him.

And we must live in wisdom, not doing what is wrong to bring about our deliverance. Our lot is never so bad that we are justified in doing what is wrong to deliver ourselves.

If we feel we must compromise our godly values to deliver ourselves, then let us look to David as our example and wait for the Lord. Our God can deliver us if we only wait for Him in faith.

***

When God makes a promise, is it as though it has happened, or do you have a sense of wishing it really will happen?
Bible hope in God's promises is grounded in expectation, not in wishes.

***

Every day, I try to be more like King Jesus, especially in the way I treat others.
I try to control the words and tone I use with the ones I love the most.
I imagine that if Jesus used the tone with me that I sometimes use with my wife and children, it would be as devastating to me as it is to them.
My wife, children, and family deserve my respect. My King expects no less from me than to give it to them.

***

Today is the Lord's Day. We come together to worship the Son on the throne as He is seated at His Father's right hand.

Before we come to offer Him our gift and kiss the Son, let us make sure that our heart is right before Him.

Let us make sure that we are doing what He has earnestly taught us to do. Remember the poor and weak.

Feed the hungry.

Take care of the children in need.

Will our God accept our gifts if we do not take care of those in need?

Will He listen to our prayers and songs if we close our generous hands to those who have a need?

This Lord's Day, we earnestly seek to offer our great God worship, praise, and honor.

Do we think the One who desires that we love our neighbor will turn a blind eye when we offer our gifts to Him today having closed our hands to those in need?

The King we worship today tells us He will judge us on how we treat those in need.

When we offer worship to our King today, let us do it with a clean hand having opened it to our neighbor in need first.

"Give justice to the weak and the fatherless; maintain the right of the afflicted and the destitute. Rescue the weak and the needy; deliver them from the hand of the wicked." (Psalm 82:3-4 ESV).

***

Rickie Jenkins: "We can't make it through this life sleepwalking spiritually. We must maintain our fervent heart lest we create a rut that becomes our grave."

***

Jordan Shouse: "We are all adopted children of God. There is a lot that makes us different from each other, but there is more that makes us alike."

***

I have gotten into the habit of getting up very early to pray and read my Bible daily.

I have done this for very selfless and very selfish reasons.

My selfless reason is God deserves my first fruits. If I don't give Him my prayers and readings first, I find it hard to fit them into my day otherwise.

Selfishly, I know I will come before God daily, asking for His favor and His providence. I want to ensure I give Him what is due Him before I ask what I need from His hand each day.

***

I am in Psalm in my daily Bible reading. In Psalm 108, David, the most successful conqueror in the history of God's people, understands why he is so successful:

> "Oh grant us help against the foe, for vain is the salvation of man! With God we shall do valiantly; it is he who will tread down our foes." (Psalm 108:12-13 ESV).

David understood that his salvation was not by man's hands. Salvation comes through the Lord.

The sooner we learn this lesson, the more at peace we will be. It is frivolous to try to save ourselves without God. In all things, let us learn to bring our need for deliverance to the One in whom all deliverance comes.

We live in a kingdom ruled by God Himself. Let us not act as the people act who abide in the kingdoms of men. Let us always look to our King for deliverance.

***

Coffee (Or Tea) With Jesus

I am fond of meeting people over coffee. It's an intimate way to visit and get to know someone. You can relax and just chat when you meet over coffee or tea. Unlike formal meetings, coffee and tea meetings have a way of putting people at ease and lowering the walls we get so good at erecting.

When I suggest that we have coffee meetings with Jesus, I am not suggesting that we trivialize our relationship with Him or take a holy relationship and make it too casual. Instead, I suggest that we learn to personalize His word to us and not make it a general message. If we can do this, I believe it can change how we approach His Word and our commitment to Him.

Let's take three expectations that people have struggled with for the last 2000 years since the Holy Spirit has spoken to us in these last days through God's Son (Hebrews 1:2). None of us may be struggling with all of these things, but all of us collectively may be struggling with at least one of these things:

Pornography

Lying

Prayer

Now, we can read the Scriptures and quickly arrive at the truth of how we are to behave with each of these things, right? We have read the Scriptures, and we have heard the sermons. We know the truth, and yet, we still struggle with them. And our society doesn't make it easy on us to overcome these sins, does it? In fact, our society seems to go out of its way to place enticements before us to encourage us to lie, commit sexual sins, and forget to pray. Yet, what does the Bible say?

> "But sexual immorality and all impurity or covetousness must not even be named among you, as is proper among saints. Let there be no filthiness nor foolish talk nor crude joking, which are out of place, but instead let there be thanksgiving." (Ephesians 5:3-4 ESV).

And

> "Therefore, having put away falsehood, let each one of you speak the truth with his neighbor, for we are members one of another." (Ephesians 4:25 ESV).

And

> "do not be anxious about anything, but in everything by prayer and supplication with thanksgiving let your requests be made known to God." (Philippians 4:6 ESV).

These verses scratch the surface of things we learn about Pornography, Lying, and Prayer. But even though the Bible teaches how we are to relate to these things, collectively, we struggle with them, don't we? We try to put away pornography and lying, only to fall into the vice repeatedly. We try to be people who pray without ceasing, but weeks go by, and we can't remember the last time we have spoken to the Lord.

With our fictional coffee meeting with Jesus, He will speak to us about these things. In our mind, let's imagine the Savior seated at the kitchen table, across from us, speaking His words to us as He calls us by name. He's not going to teach general lessons we must learn to apply to ourselves. Instead, He's going to make this personal.

When we have this coffee meeting with Jesus in our hearts, I hope we find that all of His Words are just as personal to us. We can insert our names whenever we read His will for us. We can see Him looking into our eyes as His word, for this moment in time, applies to me and me alone.

What if I hear Jesus tell me, "Tony, I want to talk to you about three things today. Grab a cup of coffee." All of a sudden, what I am about to hear isn't general teachings I need to find a way to make personal; instead, I hear His voice making it personal to me.

"Tony," our Savior says, "I made you for a purpose. I made you to walk with Me and overcome sin. But I see that you're struggling with sexual sins." This language takes the words from the pages of the Bible and makes them personal. I see me in them. I hear Jesus illustrate me in His words.

He goes on, "Tony, I know Satan doesn't make it easy for you, but I am stronger than Him. If you trust Me, I will carry this burden with you and help you overcome it. Tony, this sin is crouching at your door and desiring to overcome you. But you should overcome it. I will give you the grace to rule over it, but you must trust Me and seek My help. I have made you for so much more."

This is what it means to "walk it off the page." It's finding a way to take what the Spirit writes and make it personal to me. Whether I imagine Jesus sitting with me at the table and speaking to me over coffee or not, I need to see me in His words.

He then turns His attention to lying. "Tony, you know my Word is truth, and those who follow me follow truth. Yet, I see you have been struggling with falsehoods. You know that Satan is the father of lies. Yet, I have made you for much more than lying and falsehoods. Lies tear down and destroy. Truth builds up and establishes."

It's much harder to hear the Words of Jesus addressed to me personally. It shows a clear path of accountability that doesn't allow me to hide behind generic teachings. Jesus continues, "Tony, I need you to commit yourself to truth, My truth. I want people to be able to see Me when they see you. You are my representative on earth. I need you to trust that truth will set you free, even when you can't see it at the moment or when fear tempts you to hide behind the lie. Hard truth is designed to refine you and make you better. If you are given to lies, you will never allow yourself to gain the wonderful benefits I have built into truth for you."

I look at Jesus as we sit alone in my kitchen. I know what He says is true. I know He will help me. I know what He expects of me. But I have tried this many times before. It is so hard. I am ashamed of myself and my failures. I don't want to look at Him anymore. I want to go back to generic lessons from the Bible. Making it personal is too painful. It reminds me of just how weak I am.

But Jesus is here to help me. He whispers in my ear, "Tony, I promise never to leave or forsake you." Yes, even His great promises can be personal to me. I find comfort that I am not alone.

"Tony, talk to me. Every day when you get up, let Me start the day with you. You will find it much harder to give in to the sins of pornography and lying if you begin the day in prayer with Me." I know He's right. Not only have I struggled with sins, but I have struggled alone.

"When Satan tempts you, come to Me. Let Me carry that burden with you. If you only ask, I will give you the strength to overcome. Don't worry about overcoming tomorrow or next week. You have enough to think about with today's struggles. Let's tackle this one day at a time."

Our coffee cups are about empty. I know it's time for Him to leave and for me to live up to His expectations for me. And by making His words personal to me, I know the strength and grace He promises are not generic promises. They are promises to me, Tony. I know when I pray to Him, He will be listening to me, Tony. I know when He shoulders burdens, they are not generic but my burdens.

Perhaps imagining Jesus sitting across from you in a personal meeting like this is not your cup of tea. I get that. But however we read His words for us, it is essential that we somehow find a way to hear Him speaking to us personally when we read them. We need to see Him as our Champion Who stands ready to help us in all ways. He is cheering me, Tony, on to succeed. And He is ready to help me succeed in all He asks of me.

"I can do all things through him who strengthens me." (Philippians 4:13 ESV).

**

In a land where we value rugged individualism, we must remember the importance of God in our lives. We can try to lean on our own might and understanding, but in the end, we must understand that without God, we are living a futile life.

Our purpose is found in the understanding that all we do must be with God at the center of our life.

"A Song of Ascents. Of Solomon. Unless the LORD builds the house, those who build it labor in vain. Unless the LORD watches over the city, the watchman stays awake in vain. It is in vain that you rise up early and go late to rest, eating the bread of anxious toil; for he gives to his beloved sleep." (Psalm 127:1-2 ESV).

***

I love the book of Proverbs. Every time I read it, I gain new insights. I love this one in particular; it gives me instruction and wisdom with whom I should choose to keep company:

"Whoever walks with the wise becomes wise, but the companion of fools will suffer harm." (Proverbs 13:20 ESV).

***

What do these verses have in common?

"The sacrifices of God are a broken spirit; a broken and contrite heart, O God, you will not despise." (Psalm 51:17 ESV).

"For godly grief produces a repentance that leads to salvation without regret, whereas worldly grief produces death." (2 Corinthians 7:10 ESV).

"But the tax collector, standing far off, would not even lift up his eyes to heaven, but beat his breast, saying, 'God, be merciful to me, a sinner!' I tell you, this man went down to his house justified, rather than the other. For everyone who exalts himself will be humbled, but the one who humbles himself will be exalted." (Luke 18:13-14 ESV).

In order to repent and ask forgiveness, there must first be a sin against God.

Often, we look at our sins and mistakes and do not give ourselves the grace to forgive. Sometimes, we turn the humility that God seeks in us into humiliation.

We should cry over our sins, but we shouldn't forget that God is pleased when we humble ourselves before Him.

Do not let Satan help us turn our humility into humiliation.

Humility will reconcile us back to God, which is what God is seeking.

Humiliation plays into the devil's hands because it makes us give up on believing that God can get past the sins we have committed against Him.

***

I came across an interesting thought from Solomon in his book of Ecclesiastes. If we read it in isolation, it may be hard for us to understand what it is saying. But if we read the book in a single sitting, perhaps the context of the book's message gives us help:

"Be not overly righteous, and do not make yourself too wise. Why should you destroy yourself? Be not overly wicked, neither be a fool. Why should you die before your time?" (Ecclesiastes 7:16-17 ESV).

Solomon is casting the vanity of all that is under the sun in his book. No matter what we pursue, we all end up the same.

Great knowledge will give us no advantage over simple ones when our time comes to die.

Great riches will not keep us from experiencing the same end the poor man will experience.

Under the sun, all of our pursuits will lead to the same end.

So, when Solomon says do not be overly righteous or too wise, it seems to be in the context of pursuing these things to the neglect of enjoying what the Lord blesses us with while on the earth.

If we pursue righteousness and wisdom while denying the joys we can get from this earth, then we miss out on the totality of blessings that God intends for us while we live in the world He created for us.

It seems that Solomon may be telling us that God wants His children to enjoy a balanced life; one that seeks righteousness and wisdom while not doing so in a way that causes us to miss the joys He intends us to have while we spend our limited days on the earth He created for us.

I don't think that God is telling us that we can be too righteous or wise, but that we need to pursue these things while enjoying the totality of the blessings He has made for us.

In the end, Solomon concludes,

"The end of the matter; all has been heard. Fear God and keep his commandments, for this is the whole duty of man. For God will bring every deed into judgment, with every secret thing, whether good or evil." (Ecclesiastes 12:13-14 ESV).

As we pursue righteousness and wisdom, and as we enjoy the fruits of our labors and the world that God created for us, let us remember that God will hold us accountable for doing all these things while keeping Him first.

***

What angered God in the past angers Him today.
What pleased God in the past pleases Him today.
Let us learn from the lessons of those before us.
Listen to the state of the nation in Judah before God brought judgment to that nation:

"For the look on their faces bears witness against them; they proclaim their sin like Sodom; they do not hide it. Woe to them! For they have brought evil on themselves." (Isaiah 3:9 ESV).

There has never been a more vital time for us to be the salt of the earth and a light in a dark nation.
Let us be careful to be light and salt and not to cast our lot with the wicked.

***

If I have a terminal illness, the doctor may prescribe medication, not to cure my incurable condition, but to deal with the symptoms.

Every time I take my medication, it's a reminder to me that I am sick. I know that the medication is not curing the illness, but it's still there.

The sacrifices in the Old Testament were like that. Every year, during the Day of Atonement, the nation offered sacrifices for sin. But these sacrifices didn't cure the underlying problem:

"But in these sacrifices there is a reminder of sins every year. For it is impossible for the blood of bulls and goats to take away sins." (Hebrews

10:3-4 ESV).

And so, these sacrifices happened over and over and over because they could not cure the underlying sickness of sin.

Just like I am reminded of my illness every time I take my medication, so were the people reminded of their sins every time they sacrificed to the Lord.

But Jesus became the sacrifice that was better than the sacrifices of bulls and goats. His was a perfect sacrifice of His own life and His own blood.

When He died on the cross for our sins, His sacrifice did what the blood of bulls and goats could not do. His sacrifice didn't cover up the sins, but it cured the underlying disease of sin.

Where the sacrifices of bulls and goats were a reminder of sins every year, Jesus died once to remove sins forever, and God says I will remember their sins no more.

> "And by that will we have been sanctified through the offering of the body of Jesus Christ once for all." (Hebrews 10:10 ESV).

***

We all have a past. We all have done things we are ashamed of.

Jesus would have us come to Him so His sacrifice can take away our sins. His Father will remember them no more.

Satan, however, wants us to fixate on what Jesus has removed.

Don't let Satan cause you to remain paralyzed in your past. You don't have to worry about the things you did anymore.

When we come to Jesus, He is good enough and powerful enough to remove the most shameful parts of our lives and replace them with a new, pure, and spotless life with no blemish.

With the help of Jesus, forget the past and keep your eyes fixed on what our King has in store for us.

> "Brothers, I do not consider that I have made it my own. But one thing I do: forgetting what lies behind and straining forward to what lies ahead, I press on toward the goal for the prize of the upward call of God in Christ Jesus." (Philippians 3:13-14 ESV).

***

Do We Think Like The Scoffers?

Peter writes two letters that bear his name. In the second letter, he starts the third chapter like this:

> "This is now the second letter that I am writing to you, beloved. In both of them I am stirring up your sincere mind by way of reminder, that you should remember the predictions of the holy prophets and the commandment of the Lord and Savior through your apostles," (2 Peter 3:1-2 ESV).

The apostle is stirring people to remember what the prophets have predicted by the Spirit and what our Lord has commanded. Peter focused this encouragement on us to stay true to the Word and prepare ourselves to be ready when the Lord returns.

Peter mentions that he knows he is about to die because the Lord Jesus Himself has told him as much:

> "I think it right, as long as I am in this body, to stir you up by way of reminder, since I know that the putting off of my body will be soon, as our Lord Jesus Christ made clear to me. And I will make every effort so that after my departure you may be able at any time to recall these things." (2 Peter 1:13-15 ESV).

And so, the aged apostle pens his second letter by stirring the reader to remember the promises and prophecies we have been taught. We know that Jesus will return and judge all men, great and small. Since this will happen, we need to

> "Make every effort to supplement your faith with virtue, and virtue with knowledge, and knowledge with self-control, and self-control with steadfastness, and steadfastness with godliness, and godliness with brotherly affection, and brotherly affection with love." (2 Peter 1:5b-7 ESV).

But decades had passed since Jesus died. Perhaps some were waiting for the Lord's return year after year and decade after decade, only to think that life would always go on today as it has for centuries past. If life were to continue in perpetuity, then is it so urgent to live a life where we supplement our faith with the things Peter listed above?

And, of course, many will have no intentions of living a life of faith. The more time that passes between the death of Jesus and His promised return, the more ludicrous it seems to them that there will be a second coming at all. These are the people who will scoff at us, as we see when we pick back up with Peter's thoughts in the third chapter:

> "knowing this first of all, that scoffers will come in the last days with scoffing, following their own sinful desires. They will say, "Where is the promise of his coming? For ever since the fathers fell asleep, all things are continuing as they were from the beginning of creation." (2 Peter 3:3-4 ESV).

And the real danger that Peter speaks about is not that we will face these scoffers and be persecuted by them because we hold to the belief that King Jesus will return. Instead, it is the danger that we will start to let their denials and unbeliefs about the Lord's return give us pause.

We start to think, "Will the Lord really return in my lifetime?" Or even more insidious, we ask ourselves, "Will the Lord return at all?"

These are the machinations of the scoffer who mocks and heckles the disciple seeking to make himself ready for the imminent return of King Jesus. These are the taunters and teasers who laugh at the one who trims his lamp as Jesus instructed so he will be ready for the Lord's return.

> "For they deliberately overlook this fact, that the heavens existed long ago, and the earth was formed out of water and through water by the word of God, and that by means of these the world that then existed was deluged with water and perished." (2 Peter 3:5-6 ESV).

There were scoffers in the day of Noah who said the same thing that scoffers say today. But one day, the rain started, and judgment came. In God's longsuffering and grace, the seeds of scoffing often begin to germinate.

> "But do not overlook this one fact, beloved, that with the Lord one day is as a thousand years, and a thousand years as one day. The Lord is not slow to fulfill his promise as some count slowness, but is patient toward you, not wishing that any should perish, but that all should reach repentance." (2 Peter 3:8-9 ESV).

And so, Peter makes his final preparations for us as he prepares for his death. He stirs us to remembrance so we will not heed the scoffers. But more importantly, the aged apostle stresses the importance of not letting the seed of scoffing germinate in our hearts.

It's dangerous to forget King Jesus' promises and believe there is time for me to live my way before I submit to Him. It's dangerous to forget that the earth will one day end, and everything will be burned up.

It's dangerous because it puts us at the risk of not being ready when the Lord returns. But if we let Peter stir us to remembrance and if we prepare for the imminent return of King Jesus, we can ask ourselves, in clarity,

> "Since all these things are thus to be dissolved, what sort of people ought you to be in lives of holiness and godliness, waiting for and hastening the coming of the day of God, because of which the heavens will be set on fire and dissolved, and the heavenly bodies will melt as they burn!" (2 Peter 3:11-12 ESV).

Whether we see Jesus return with our own eyes or leave this life still waiting, let us be ready, and may the seeds of scoffing never invade our hearts.

***

I am in Isaiah in my daily Bible ready. There is so much in my reading to think about, but these verses are the ones I will continue to think about this morning, They speak of God's goodness and power to provide for His people when we see the impossible.

What a mighty, awesome, and wonderful God we serve. No circumstance is too great for God not to deliver. No need is beyond His ability to rescue. Our God can do all that He pleases. What is impossible for man is as nothing to the Lord.

Let these verses cause us to drop to our knees in praise and worship to our God Who can do all things.

> "When the poor and needy seek water, and there is none, and their tongue is parched with thirst, I the LORD will answer them; I the God of Israel will not forsake them.
>
> I will open rivers on the bare heights, and fountains in the midst of the valleys. I will make the wilderness a pool of water, and the dry land springs of water.
>
> I will put in the wilderness the cedar, the acacia, the myrtle, and the olive. I will set in the desert the cypress, the plane and the pine together,
>
> that they may see and know, may consider and understand together, that the hand of the LORD has done this, the Holy One of Israel has created it." (Isaiah 41:17-20 ESV).

***

Human reason is a wonderful gift that God has given to His image bearers, but if we are not careful, it can cause us to lose the wonder and awe that we should have in a God who can do things we can never begin to imagine.

"Now to him who is able to do far more abundantly than all that we ask or think, according to the power at work within us," (Ephesians 3:20 ESV).

***

When King Jesus returns, I would love to witness a sea of kneeling servants bowing in His presence before being lifted in the air to meet Him.

"For the Lord himself will descend from heaven with a cry of command, with the voice of an archangel, and with the sound of the trumpet of God. And the dead in Christ will rise first.
Then we who are alive, who are left, will be caught up together with them in the clouds to meet the Lord in the air, and so we will always be with the Lord.
Therefore encourage one another with these words." (1 Thessalonians 4:16-18 ESV).

***

What a dangerous place to be, either as an individual or as a nation. May we always bow before the eyes Who see all:

"You felt secure in your wickedness; you said, "No one sees me"; your wisdom and your knowledge led you astray, and you said in your heart, "I am, and there is no one besides me." (Isaiah 47:10 ESV).

***

It will be too late to prepare for the Lord's return when we hear the trumpets sound and see the clouds part for the King. We must be ready when all is peaceful and typical.

We must be ready when the moment is just like it is this morning.

***

Say your prayers.
Forgive your brother.
Read your Bible.
Help the poor and needy.
Jesus didn't come today,
But tomorrow will be one day closer to His return.
Good night, all.

***

"Is not this the fast that I choose: to loose the bonds of wickedness, to undo the straps of the yoke, to let the oppressed go free, and to break every yoke?

Is it not to share your bread with the hungry and bring the homeless poor into your house; when you see the naked, to cover him, and not to hide yourself from your own flesh?

Then shall your light break forth like the dawn, and your healing shall spring up speedily; your righteousness shall go before you; the glory of the LORD shall be your rear guard.

Then you shall call, and the LORD will answer; you shall cry, and he will say, 'Here I am.' If you take away the yoke from your midst, the pointing of the finger, and speaking wickedness,

if you pour yourself out for the hungry and satisfy the desire of the afflicted, then shall your light rise in the darkness and your gloom be as the noonday.

And the LORD will guide you continually and satisfy your desire in scorched places and make your bones strong; and you shall be like a watered garden, like a spring of water, whose waters do not fail." (Isaiah 58:6-11 ESV).

***

The Israelites took a stone and made an idol to bow down to.

They took a piece of wood and said to it, "You are my god who created me."

They formed idols from gold and bronze and bowed down to them.

How does the One true and living God feel when man takes the things He creates and fashions an idol, a god for us to worship?

> "and I will cut off your carved images and your pillars from among you, and you shall bow down no more to the work of your hands; and I will root out your Asherah images from among you and destroy your cities. And in anger and wrath I will execute vengeance on the nations that did not obey." (Micah 5:13-15 ESV).

And have we learned this lesson today? Sadly not.

We still take the creation and say to it, "You created us."

Listen to what the wisest among us say today:

"You and I are made of stardust. We are the stuff of exploded stars. We are therefore, at least 1 way that the Universe knows itself. That, to me, is astonishing." Bill Nye.

"There is stardust in your veins. We are literally, ultimately children of the stars." Jocelyn Bell Burnell.

"The nitrogen in our DNA, the calcium in our teeth, the iron in our blood, the carbon in our apple pies were made in the interiors of collapsing stars. We are made of starstuff." Carl Sagan.

Even in our wisest moments, we still look to that which is created and say to it, "You made me."

***

He would still gather us together as a hen gathers her brood under her wings.

Are we willing to let Him?

> "O Jerusalem, Jerusalem, the city that kills the prophets and stones those who are sent to it! How often would I have gathered your children together as a hen gathers her brood under her wings, and you were not willing!" (Luke 13:34 ESV).

***

I've been scrolling through random Facebook posts and was blown away by how many inspirational quotes people leave on their walls.

Many are good. A few are funny.

If you'd like to see some of the most profound, instructional and inspirational quotes you'll ever read, might I suggest you start reading Matthew 5?

***

When we preach, would we rather hear 1000 "Amens!" or one "Well done, good and faithful servant?"

When we post, would we rather get 10,000 likes or one "Well done, good and faithful servant?"

When we work, would we rather receive vocational awards or one "Well done, good and faithful servant?"

When we serve, would we rather get 100 comments blessing us for our service or one "Well done, good and faithful servant?"

The danger is not in receiving "Amens!", likes, awards, or comments;

The danger lies in what we want more.

"Not to us, O LORD, not to us, but to your name give glory, for the sake of your steadfast love and your faithfulness!" (Psalm 115:1 ESV).

***

We love the goodness of the Lord, but we want to be blind to His severity.

The Lord is rich in love, showing his longsuffering to us, not willing that any should perish but that all should repent.

But God's longsuffering is not endless. The Day of the Lord will come.

In my daily Bible reading in Jeremiah, I read something that I don't think we like to acknowledge:

"You have rejected me, declares the LORD; you keep going backward, so I have stretched out my hand against you and destroyed you-- I am weary of relenting." (Jeremiah 15:6 ESV).

Is it true that we can continue to reject the Lord over and over, as He is extending His longsuffering to the point where God becomes weary of relenting?

God's longsuffering is for one purpose. It is to give us time to repent and turn to Him.

It is not so we can continue to live in our sins until it is convenient for us to repent.

It is not so we can feel safe in our sins and rejection of His call to us.

It is not so we can enjoy the pleasures of sin for a season.

His longsuffering is to bring us safety today.

The Lord, in his lovingkindness, is waiting, patient, and longsuffering for us this very day.

But one day, His longsuffering will come to an end.

One day, God will say. "Enough, no more."

One day, God will become "weary of relenting."

> "For he says, "In a favorable time I listened to you, and in a day of salvation I have helped you." Behold, now is the favorable time; behold, now is the day of salvation." (2 Corinthians 6:2 ESV).

***

Tough Talk From Jesus

In Luke 17, Jesus has some straight talk for His disciples that should cause us to think long and hard about things we may often overlook. And these words are coming from the One whose words will judge us on the last day. So let's spend a few moments listening to the Savior speak through the first two verses of Luke 17:

> "And he said to his disciples, "Temptations to sin are sure to come, but woe to the one through whom they come!" (Luke 17:1 ESV).

Jesus tells us that temptations will come. Unfortunately for us, this is a part of life. Because God has given us free will, we must deal with the consequences of having free will. One consequence is the pull to do what I want rather than having the discipline to do what God wants me to do. James says that these temptations come when we are drawn away and enticed by our own desires (James 1:14).

But Jesus also has something to say for the one through whom temptations come. While each of us will stand in judgment for our own sins and actions, if we are the cause of temptations to our brothers, understand that Jesus will look harshly upon that. Listen to His language: "woe to the one through whom they come!" Jesus pronounces a woe upon us if we are the one who brings the temptation to our brothers.

We should have a love for each other to help our brothers and sisters endure hardships and trials, but when we are the ones who lay temptations before each other, Jesus looks at it about as harshly as He looks at anything. To put a fine point on it, look at what King Jesus says about this one:

> "It would be better for him if a millstone were hung around his neck and he were cast into the sea than that he should cause one of these little ones to sin." (Luke 17:2 ESV).

Too often, we might be tempted to think of the great separation of the sheep and the goats based solely on our own struggles with temptations and sins. But I think there might be a few goats on the left, not because of their struggles with temptations, but because of the temptation to sin they lay before their brothers and sisters. This harsh language Jesus has about these people makes me wonder how much grace and mercy He will extend to them.

The lesson for me is simple. I have enough trouble with my own temptations. I need to ensure that I am helping my brothers and sisters with their burdens. At the least, I absolutely need to stay away from being the cause of their temptation.

Do I tempt them by encouraging them to commit sexual sins?

Do I tempt them by encouraging them to drink or do drugs?

Do I tempt them by encouraging them to forsake the assembly and choose to be somewhere else?

Do I tempt them by encouraging them to lie?

Do I tempt them by encouraging them to engage in course jesting?

Do I encourage my brothers and sisters to do good, or do I encourage them to sin? Am I the one through whom temptations come? If so, do we understand just how much King Jesus detests this? "It would be better for him if a millstone were hung around his neck and he were cast into the sea than that he should cause one of these little ones to sin."

Let us be very careful before we bring temptations to our brothers and sisters. As gracious as our Savior is to us as we struggle to maintain our walk with Him, we do not want on the receiving end of His wrath. He seems to show little patience with the ones who bring temptations to others.

***

When Paul says that love believes all things in 1 Corinthians 13:7, he's not talking about believing the lies and rumors people spread about others. He's talking about believing the best in people and giving them the benefit of the doubt.

When given a choice between making harsh assumptions and assuming good about others and their motives, always believe the best.

***

The story of Abraham may be more amazing than we have given it credit for. I believe that when we think of this great man of faith, who "believed the LORD, and he counted it to him as righteousness" (Genesis 15:6), we start his life in our minds at age 75 when God called him (Genesis 12:4).

But Abraham had a history. The Bible said that he was from Ur of the Chaldeans (Genesis 11:27-28). For 75 years before being called, Abram was a Chaldean. This is the same group of people who founded the Babylonian empire; not the new, or Neo-Babylonians of Nebuchanezzar, but the old Babylonian Empire of Hammurabi.

Before Abram was called by God, Joshua tells us,

> "And Joshua said to all the people, "Thus says the LORD, the God of Israel, 'Long ago, your fathers lived beyond the Euphrates, Terah, the father of Abraham and of Nahor; and they served other gods.
>
> Then I took your father Abraham from beyond the River and led him through all the land of Canaan, and made his offspring many. I gave him Isaac." (Joshua 24:2-3 ESV).

Before God's call, it seems Abram worshiped the false gods of the Chaldeans. Yet, the one true God separated him and took this Chaldean and made him and his offspring a special people. Abraham's seed became an ark through which the Messiah would enter the world to bless all nations.

If God could take a pagan idol worshipper out of an evil land and create a nation of chosen people for Himself who would bring the Savior of the world, then I suppose that nothing in my life is so messed up that God can't make right if I believe Him.

> "And he believed the LORD, and he counted it to him as righteousness." (Genesis 15:6 ESV).

Do we believe the Lord?

***

As I move through the book of Jeremiah in my daily Bible reading, it's hard not to focus on the things that Israel did to provoke the Lord to anger so much that moved Him to bring judgment upon His people. Time after time, God, in His longsuffering, had delayed judgment when good Kings repented and obeyed.

But the sins of the people were great and in the days of King Zedekiah, there was no repentance from God and the people found no remedy. Perhaps the people were banking on God continuing to show His patience. But God had said to the people, "No more."

What was it that caused God to get to this point? Jeremiah 32 gives us a taste of the sins of the people. When I read them, it sent chills through me. Many of these sins are the same ones that we, as a nation today, commit. While I am no prophet and I will not presume to speak for the Lord as to His intentions with our nation today, I do know that the things that angered God then anger God today.

Listen to these words and ask yourself if we are much better than the Israelites to whom God brought judgment in the days of Jeremiah:

> "The Chaldeans who are fighting against this city shall come and set this city on fire and burn it, with the houses on whose roofs offerings have been made to Baal and drink offerings have been poured out to other gods, to provoke me to anger.
>
> For the children of Israel and the children of Judah have done nothing but evil in my sight from their youth. The children of Israel have done nothing but provoke me to anger by the work of their hands, declares the LORD." (Jeremiah 32:29-30 ESV).

Can we call ourselves a Christian nation anymore when we replace God with our own creations that we bow before? We use science and evolution to deny the Creator when pure science itself attests to the Creator. We commit abominations and perversions and force them upon our people and our children. We call good evil and we call evil good. We persecute the ones who stand for the ways of the Lord, calling them bigoted and prejudiced while lifting up the immoral and perverse men and women and celebrating their perversion.

Jeremiah continues:

> "They have turned to me their back and not their face. And though I have taught them persistently, they have not listened to receive instruction.

They set up their abominations in the house that is called by my name, to defile it.

They built the high places of Baal in the Valley of the Son of Hinnom, to offer up their sons and daughters to Molech, though I did not command them, nor did it enter into my mind, that they should do this abomination, to cause Judah to sin." (Jeremiah 32:33-35 ESV).

I cannot imagine what the Lord thinks of a people who abort millions of babies and revel in it. It's almost as if a nation of people has become drunk on the blood of the innocent, sending themselves into a frenzy over their murderous evil desires. Their bloodlust for murder will not be restrained.

How long do we think that the holy and sovereign God, who calls Himself the Father of the orphans and the protector of the widows will stand by and allow this to continue?

I don't know. I won't presume to speak for the Almighty. But I do know His character. I know His character of justice and mercy; His propensity to withhold His hand and His propensity to protect the innocent.

We live in an evil land but we have the blessing of having men and women with the character of salt sprinkled throughout this evil land. That is our redeeming grace. But when we see this land continue to descend into unspeakable evil, it should be a warning and a sign for us to draw closer to the Lord. When and if His cup of wrath is poured out against this nation in our lifetime, we need to be like the good people in the days of Jeremiah whom the Lord saw that put their trust in Him.

***

The judgment had been executed on Judah. They lost their land and were taken captive into the land of Babylon. God told the people not to expect deliverance anytime soon. His message to them: build houses and have a family in Babylon, for they would be there for a while.

But there was a remnant left in Judah. Their lives had been upended. They had lived through the horror of war and invasion. They had seen the temple and the city of Jerusalem burned with fire. But Jeremiah had stayed with them. What did this remnant do when their lives had been shattered?

They turned to Jeremiah, knowing that he spoke as a prophet of God:

"Then they said to Jeremiah, "May the LORD be a true and faithful witness against us if we do not act according to all the word with which the LORD your God sends you to us.

Whether it is good or bad, we will obey the voice of the LORD our

God to whom we are sending you, that it may be well with us when we obey the voice of the LORD our God." (Jeremiah 42:5-6 ESV).

What do we do when our world is shattered?
Where do we turn when there is nowhere else to turn?
Where do we turn when we are afraid, lost, and in need?
Some turn to drugs and alcohol to hide the shattered vestiges of their lives. Some turn to false gods and beliefs rather than seeking the Lord. But the remnant surrendered to the Lord. They told Jeremiah they would obey the Lord, "whether good or bad;" that is, no matter what God wanted them to do, they would do it, even if it was hard.

When we get to the point where we will submit to the Lord, "whether good or bad," then we are where the Lord needs us to be. This is total submission to Him.

No conditions; no half-hearted obedience; no obedience on our terms.

When our world is shattered, where do we turn? Is it to the Lord? Is it wholly, with all of our hearts and in total submission to Him?

The book of Jeremiah goes on to tell us that the people would live among others who did not want to listen to the Lord, but this remnant made a choice. Even when their fellow Jews rebelled, they said they would remain true.

Let us always have a heart to obey God, "whether good or bad" and let us do so even when our own people may be urging us to not follow the Lord.

***

There is a war going on around us, and many do not know they are on the losing side.

Many people battle on Satan's side because, as Jesus says,

> "And this is the judgment: the light has come into the world, and people loved the darkness rather than the light because their works were evil.
> For everyone who does wicked things hates the light and does not come to the light, lest his works should be exposed." (John 3:19-20 ESV).

God is mocked, blasphemed, and ridiculed by people around us living in our nation. Just like the people who came before them, they are convinced they will be the ones who kill God once and for all.

And so they battle on the dark side because they hate the light. And the attacks against God and our faith are growing more and more brazen.

They don't know that no matter what they do or how hard they fight, they can never win the war against God.

People who kill, steal, lie and mock the values of righteous living do not understand that when God brings an end to the war, they will bow their knees to God and confess Jesus as Lord.

Do not let the evil you see cause you to forget the victory that is King Jesus' when He wins the war.

Stay on the side of the light, and He will vindicate you when those around you persecute you.

> "for it is written, "As I live, says the Lord, every knee shall bow to me, and every tongue shall confess to God." So then each of us will give an account of himself to God." (Romans 14:11-12 ESV).

***

When Jesus walked on the water, we look at Peter's response and miss what I think is the most amazing part of the story.

We either praise Peter as being the one with enough faith to step out of the boat,

Or we condemn Peter for having little faith when he took his eyes off Jesus and focused on the waves.

Both are true, but miss the most amazing thing in my opinion.

Jesus was walking amid the same waves as Peter, but He was not afraid.

Jesus did not fear the waves, the wind, or the darkness.

When we are in the midst of the storm and look to Jesus, we are looking to the one Who is not afraid of what makes us afraid.

We put our trust in Him because He swallows up fear for us and He becomes our courage.

We gain confidence because our King is not afraid.

***

My God Knows Me

We live in a world where we are a number. We have a social security number and a driver's license number. When we buy things, a company assigns us a customer number. Any individuality we have is attached to the number. If a company or the government wants to know anything about us, they look at the details attached to our number.

That means that it's possible for us to slip through the cracks. If nothing about us is outside the norms, then we really are just a number. We often hear talk of "going off the grid." What we mean is removing ourselves from any way an entity can track us. We won't use credit card numbers, bank account numbers, or any other number that allows someone or something to know who we are or where we are.

Are we sometimes tempted to think that God feels the same way about us? Do we feel that we are just a number to God? With billions of souls on the earth, what are the chances that God really knows me? When I add my prayers to the tens of millions that are happening at any given time, what are the chances that God hears me with undivided attention?

Sometimes we play lip service to God's ability to know us, but in the back of our minds, we ascribe our limitations to Him. Is it possible that sometimes we feel like we are just a number to God and if we lay low, we can fly under His radar?

That's not the God I read about in the Bible. The one whose ways are not our ways, but higher than our ways. Listen to what the Bible says about God knowing us:

> "Are not five sparrows sold for two pennies? And not one of them is forgotten before God. Why, even the hairs of your head are all numbered. Fear not; you are of more value than many sparrows." (Luke 12:6-7 ESV).

Jesus, who is God the creator, tells us that He knows every sparrow He has created, and He even knows every single strand of hair on every person He has ever created. I have no clue how many billions of souls God has created since Adam and Eve, but His infinite mind knows every hair stand that He created on each of them.

When we pray to God, He knows who I am. He knows me. Not because I am famous or because I garner special attention. He knows me because He made me. He knows my name. We are not a number, not one of billions. We are one who He knows. We never slip through the cracks or fall off the grid with God.

> "But if anyone loves God, he is known by God." (1 Corinthians 8:3 ESV).

Someone estimated that there have been between 75 billion and 100 billion souls that God created since Adam and Eve. If so, He intimately knew every one of them. He knew every strand of hair on every person. He can do that because He is not a man. He is God. Another person estimated that there are 200 billion trillion stars in the universe and,

> "He determines the number of the stars; he gives to all of them their names." (Psalm 147:4 ESV).

We struggle to find names for our children, don't we? Yet God knows every one of the stars He made, and He has given each of them names, all 200,000,000,000,000,000,000,000+ of them.

So, when we pray to God, we need to understand that when we do, God is listening to us. He's not distracted by everything else going on with Him. He hears my prayers. He knows my name. My God knows me.

And the same is true when we want to hide from Him. Just as Adam and Eve learned, there is no place to hide from His presence. Just as we are more than a number to God, neither can we make ourselves anonymous to Him. We cannot fall off the spiritual grid with God. Listen to how David put it:

> "Where shall I go from your Spirit? Or where shall I flee from your presence? If I ascend to heaven, you are there! If I make my bed in Sheol, you are there! If I take the wings of the morning and dwell in the uttermost parts of the sea, even there your hand shall lead me, and your right hand shall hold me. If I say, "Surely the darkness shall cover me, and the light about me be night," even the darkness is not dark to you; the night is bright as the day, for darkness is as light with you." (Psalm 139:7-12 ESV).

Whether we like it or not, my God knows me. To those who love Him, we should take great comfort in this. To those who love darkness, it should be terrifying to us. One day we shall see Him face to face. When He looks into the books that will lay open before Him, it will not be to look up who we are. He knows that. It will be the record He shares with us. The books will be our evidence that He knew us all long. We will see the things in ourselves that He sees in us through the books in heaven that are written.

The books are evidence that He truly sees us and knows us. That we don't fall through the cracks or off the grid. We cannot slip unnoticed into heaven or be sentenced unjustly to eternal punishment. When we see Jesus face to face, we will be looking into the eyes of the one Who knows everything about us, including every strand of hair He made on our body.

He will know our thoughts, our actions, and our words. He will not confuse us with someone else. He will know us then because He knows us now. This is the God we serve. We need to always remember that our God is a God who knows me. He always has and He always will.

And we should take tremendous comfort and strength in this in this truth.

***

In the spirit of the political season, I thought I'd perform my own poll this morning:

Q: What do you fear most for you and your family today?
A- Inflation
B- Crime
C- Immigration
D- Foreign Affairs
E- Climate Change
F- Healthcare
G- God

"The end of the matter; all has been heard. Fear God and keep his commandments, for this is the whole duty of man." (Ecclesiastes 12:13 ESV).

***

One day,
God will give me a home I did not build
Feed me food I did not grow
and clothe me with clothes I did not make.
One day, God will take me from poverty and make me rich beyond my imagination.
One day, I will look back to this life and wonder why I ever entertained the idea of sinning against my God.

"Brothers, I do not consider that I have made it my own. But one thing I do: forgetting what lies behind and straining forward to what lies ahead,

I press on toward the goal for the prize of the upward call of God in Christ Jesus." (Philippians 3:13-14 ESV).

***

As I continue in my daily Bible reading, I am in the book of Ezekiel. Something I read today helped me understand a phrase that Jesus said a lot:

> "Indeed, in their case the prophecy of Isaiah is fulfilled that says: "You will indeed hear but never understand, and you will indeed see but never perceive."
> For this people's heart has grown dull, and with their ears they can barely hear, and their eyes they have closed, lest they should see with their eyes and hear with their ears and understand with their heart and turn, and I would heal them.'
> But blessed are your eyes, for they see, and your ears, for they hear." (Matthew 13:14-16 ESV).

Having ears but do not hear and eyes but do not see.

Some believe that God will prevent people from hearing and seeing despite free will. But listen to what Ezekiel says. It helps to set it in context:

> "Son of man, you dwell in the midst of a rebellious house, who have eyes to see, but see not, who have ears to hear, but hear not, for they are a rebellious house." (Ezekiel 12:2 ESV).

When we do not hear though we have ears and do not see though we have eyes, it is because we are rebellious people. If we have a heart set on rebellion against God, we will not hear or receive the Word of God. Though we have eyes, if our heart is set on rebellion, we will not see the message.

Jesus preached to people with eyes and ears, knowing they would not hear or see; but not because they couldn't or because God prevented them. It was because they had no intention of seeing or hearing what Jesus was teaching.

If we are set in our rebellion, we will not see or hear the message of the Gospel. It will sound foolish, and we will scoff at the message. To see with our eyes and hear with our ears, we must have a heart ready to submit to God.

May we never be one who God allows to believe a lie or one whose heart and conscience turn to stone. May we be people who see and hear because we have tender hearts ready to submit to Him and His message.

***

Snapchat is an interesting platform. You can post something on it, and it is automatically deleted after a certain time.

While there may be harmless ways of using this tool, don't let it lull you into a false sense of safety from God.

Be careful what you choose to share. Anonymity only exists among men. Even a deleted Snapchat may come back to haunt you one day when it really matters:

> "For God will bring every deed into judgment, with every secret thing, whether good or evil." (Ecclesiastes 12:14 ESV).

***

While I am catching up on the news this morning,
Getting Ryder ready for school,
Planning what I will do today,
And getting ready for a trip to Canton with my parents tomorrow,
Angels surround the throne of God, singing praises to Him,
While the Father is poised in His time to whisper to His Son,
"It's time. Go get your bride."

> "But concerning that day and hour no one knows, not even the angels of heaven, nor the Son, but the Father only." (Matthew 24:36 ESV).

***

If you're in the Dallas, TX area, you probably just witnessed one of the biggest downpours we've seen in a while.

The clouds are thick, low, and dark.

Take a look outside.

How amazing would it be to see those clouds part today to reveal the return of the Lord?

> "And when he had said these things, as they were looking on, he was lifted up, and a cloud took him out of their sight.
>
> And while they were gazing into heaven as he went, behold, two men stood by them in white robes,
>
> and said, "Men of Galilee, why do you stand looking into heaven? This Jesus, who was taken up from you into heaven, will come in the same way as you saw him go into heaven." (Acts 1:9-11 ESV).

***

We rely on God for everything.

He wouldn't have to lift His hand against us for us to learn how powerful His presence is in our lives;

All He would have to do is stop showing kindness to us for us to see how much we do truly rely on Him daily.

"For the Gentiles seek after all these things, and your heavenly Father knows that you need them all.

But seek first the kingdom of God and his righteousness, and all these things will be added to you." (Matthew 6:32-33 ESV).

***

I am still in Ezekiel and I am so ready to move past the prophets. Not because I don't see value in them, but because it reminds me that God expects me to walk with Him to avoid negative consequences.

Even though we see His grace repeatedly offered, His people repeatedly walked away from it.

God, at times, begged His people to return to Him, but they stiffened their necks in pride against Him.

Things haven't changed much today.

God offers His grace and begs us to walk with Him.

But we often stiffen our necks to Him.

The prophets show the judgment of God. I wonder how many of us will be shocked, surprised, and in disbelief when His judgment comes.

The prophets are a shot of reality that we need, but it's not fun to read through the messages. We like to focus on promises, grace, and forgiveness.

Sometimes, only hearing what we want to hear will cause us to close our ears and stiffen our necks to what we don't want to hear.

So I will continue through the prophets until done. The redeeming message I long for is their promise that something better is coming.

Something better is here now.

***

I just read about God breathing life into the dry bones in Ezekiel. What was God trying to teach Ezekiel? Simply, He has the power, the desire, and the inclination to take us when we are dead and without hope and breathe into us life and vitality.

Sin kills us and separates us from God. We all have been or are dead before God. Without God breathing life into our dead bones, we are without hope.

But Ezekiel shows us that God gives hope. We can never be so dead that God cannot restore life to us.

What is stopping me from calling on the name of the Lord today and having His Spirit breathe life into me, washing away my sins?

***

This is still God's world.
We can jockey for a piece of it
We can plan, scheme, buy and sell
But that doesn't change the fact that we are all playing with what is, and always will be God's possessions.
God can give or take away
God can lift up or bring down
God doesn't need to consult with you or me when it comes to what He does with His possessions.
He doesn't seem to be as concerned about who gets what
As He is about what we do with His stuff.
Naked we came into the world, and naked we will return.
Let's ensure we have the proper perspective about His stuff in His world.

"and the dust returns to the earth as it was, and the spirit returns to God who gave it." (Ecclesiastes 12:7 ESV).

***

Excruciating Pain

I wonder if we can understand the pain that Jesus went through when He suffered on the cross. When Jesus came to earth as the Messiah, He was the one who chose to enter the world during a time when Rome had perfected the awful, torturous execution method of the cross. He chose to come to earth and die knowing the pain He'd have to endure.

At the Mount of Olives, He spent time in prayer with such anxiety over the torture He would be enduring in a few hours that the text says,

> "And being in agony he prayed more earnestly; and his sweat became like great drops of blood falling down to the ground." (Luke 22:44 ESV).

We can read historical records that describe the way Rome used the cross as a means to show unspeakable cruelty to their fellow man. The cross was not a humane means of execution; it was designed to extract every bit of torture possible.

The pain that the cross inflicted was so bad, we had to invent a word to describe it: "Excruciating." It was of Latin origin based on "crux", "cruc- a cross" Excruciating was pain "of the cross." This is what Jesus endured as He willingly laid down His life to become the sacrifice for us.

And this was foretold from the beginning. When Satan tempted man to sin, God spoke to this excruciating sacrifice He would one day make to bring back together what sin had separated. Speaking to Satan, God said,

> "I will put enmity between you and the woman, and between your offspring and her offspring; he shall bruise your head, and you shall bruise his heel." (Genesis 3:15 ESV).

It was this bruising of Jesus' heel that was found on the cross. But in this pronouncement, we see God's wrath unleashed upon Satan for the role he played in tempting Adam and Eve to sin. Where the excruciating pain of the cross which led to death was described as a bruised heel, God told Satan that what would happen to him would be far worse than what Jesus would endure on the cross. Jesus would bruise Satan's head which was a more devastating injury.

What should that tell us? To me, it serves as a warning that God isn't playing around with sin. As bad, as painful, and as excruciating as the pain that Jesus had to endure on the cross, it would be nothing compared to the punishment that awaited Satan. Jesus would crush him.

This fatal injury began when Jesus conquered death and will be brought to completion at Judgement when Satan and his angels are sentenced to eternity in the lake of fire.

> "and the devil who had deceived them was thrown into the lake of fire and sulfur where the beast and the false prophet were, and they will be tormented day and night forever and ever." (Revelation 20:10 ESV).

If man had to invent a word to describe the painful death that the cross created, can we even begin to imagine how horrific the torment from the lake of fire will be? If the bruised heel Jesus endured was excruciating, then what must the pain that represents a bruised head be like? This is reserved for the devil and His angels.

But our Lord tells us something that we should all should heed:

> "Then he will say to those on his left, 'Depart from me, you cursed, into the eternal fire prepared for the devil and his angels." (Matthew 25:41 ESV).

Those who are created in the image of God and refuse to submit to their Creator, rebel and go their own way, and let sin reign over them, will share the same judgment reserved for the devil and his angels. But God, in His rich love and grace, is pleading with us to choose the life which is found only in His Son. He is not willing that any should perish, but that all should come to repentance.

Jesus experienced excruciating pain so we can avoid a far worse punishment. This is how deep His love is for us. He was willing to endure the cross so we wouldn't have to endure eternal death. And this is the reason why we should give everything to Him. He has offered us more than we could ever repay.

***

The words I long to hear the most are not,
"I love you"
Or
"You'll never have to worry again"
Or
"You've accomplished all your goals"
The words I long to hear most are,
"Well done, good and faithful servant"

***

I am in Daniel in my Daily Bible reading. It's amazing how God taught Nebuchadnezzar what true sovereignty was. But the lesson God taught centered on the King's goodness, not his greatness. I wonder if we often confuse goodness and greatness today.

Notice, in chapter 4, God sends the king a dream that shows that God was about to raise His hand against Nebuchadnezzar. This frightens Daniel, who seemed to have developed a close relationship with the king by this time. Notice the advice that Daniel gives the king:

> "Therefore, O king, let my counsel be acceptable to you: break off your sins by practicing righteousness, and your iniquities by showing mercy to the oppressed, that there may perhaps be a lengthening of your prosperity." (Daniel 4:27 ESV).

He did not council that the king should make great proclamations about the true God or build a beautiful temple for Him. He simply said to show mercy to the oppressed and practice righteousness.

Then, in the next chapter, Nebuchadnezzar is dead and one of his descendants is on the throne. This king sees a hand writing on the wall and calls in the aged Daniel to interpret the writing. Listen to what Daniel says as he recounts the lessons of king Nebuchadnezzar:

> "But when his heart was lifted up and his spirit was hardened so that he dealt proudly, he was brought down from his kingly throne, and his glory was taken from him." (Daniel 5:20 ESV).

Referring back to the same account, Daniel tells the king about how God dealt with Nebuchadnezzar when his heart was lifted in pride. Together, we see that God taught Nebuchadnezzar He wanted the king to show humility and serve others who were in need.

This is a hard lesson for rulers to learn but it is also a hard lesson for us to learn today, especially those of us who live in a land where we value the individual and we are brought up learning the social values of looking out for number one. But Jesus gives us fair warning that He will expect the same from us, and one day, these will be the expectations we will be judged by.

Listen to what Jesus says is coming for each of us. As we read these words, we need to ask ourselves if we are living in self-center pride or if are we showing righteousness by humbling ourselves in selfless service to others.

> "Then he will say to those on his left, 'Depart from me, you cursed, into the eternal fire prepared for the devil and his angels.
> For I was hungry and you gave me no food, I was thirsty and you gave me no drink,
> I was a stranger and you did not welcome me, naked and you did not clothe me, sick and in prison and you did not visit me.'
> Then they also will answer, saying, 'Lord, when did we see you hungry or thirsty or a stranger or naked or sick or in prison, and did not minister

to you?'

Then he will answer them, saying, 'Truly, I say to you, as you did not do it to one of the least of these, you did not do it to me.'

And these will go away into eternal punishment, but the righteous into eternal life." (Matthew 25:41-46 ESV).

***

I am convinced that on the Day of Judgment, every man who was ever created will bow their knee and confess with their mouth of their own free will Jesus as Lord.

I do not think God will force anyone to do anything against their will, just as He does not force us to sin or act righteously today.

I am not sure we are prepared for the awesome experience of standing before the One true God.

Being in His presence will be overpowering as we witness His unlimited glory, power, and majesty compared to our frail, weak and limited existence.

Even the most rebellious blasphemer on earth today will be in awe when standing in the presence of God the Creator.

In His presence, there will be no fight, no argument, no accusation against the holy and mighty I AM.

On the Day of Judgement, before His Throne, we will all finally understand who we are and who He is.

Sadly, for many of us, the free-will kneeling and confession will be too late.

Today is the day to humble ourselves in the presence of God Almighty and prepare to meet Him on His terms when Judgment Day comes.

We want to kneel and bow at His right hand, not at His left hand on that Day.

> "for it is written, "As I live, says the Lord, every knee shall bow to me, and every tongue shall confess to God." So then each of us will give an account of himself to God." (Romans 14:11-12 ESV).

***

Today, I am in the book of Hosea in my daily Bible reading. This is a book where God tries His best to get the people to understand that they are being unfaithful to Him. But here's the thing… outwardly, they keep some form of worship of God, yet they mix it with idol worship and "villainy" as Hosea puts it.

God tells them that He doesn't want their outward service, He wants their heart.

> "For I desire steadfast love and not sacrifice, the knowledge of God rather than burnt offerings." (Hosea 6:6 ESV).

Perhaps, we do the same thing the people of Israel did in the days of Hosea. Perhaps we have enough God in our lives to make us feel comfortable and ease our conscience. Yet, we "move the landmarks" (5:10), we look for ways to take from others and commit villainy (6:9), "A merchant, in whose hands are false balances" (12:7), (Think cheat on our taxes or misrepresent the truth).

> "there is swearing, lying, murder, stealing, and committing adultery; they break all bounds, and bloodshed follows bloodshed." (Hosea 4:2 ESV).

And after we do these things, we come together on Sunday to worship and pray to the Lord.

This is what Israel did and it pained God as one who was a husband with a cheating wife.

God wants our worship, but He wants it from a pure heart. If we intend to play the harlot with God, then it's best to stay home. He finds no joy in our sacrifice and worship unless it comes from a faithful heart.

I pray we never grow so comfortable with our whoredom against God that we get to the point where we will never return to Him.

> "Their deeds do not permit them to return to their God. For the spirit of whoredom is within them, and they know not the LORD." (Hosea 5:4 ESV).

But our Lord is rich in mercy and offers abundant grace, seeking a relationship with His children. Therefore, He calls us to come out of our whoredom and again become one with Him.

> "Return, O Israel, to the LORD your God, for you have stumbled because of your iniquity." (Hosea 14:1 ESV).

***

As we make plans to worship God with our brothers and sisters today, think about the words of the aged apostle John. It has to do with owning our sins so we can have them forgiven.

It is one thing to say, "Yeah, I sin." But it is another thing to be able to identify what our sin is to God.

When we name our sin, we take ownership of it. We can't hide behind generalities. We can't group ourselves with other sinners. We look at God and say, "This is my sin against you. I am guilty of this."

I encourage all of us this morning to search our hearts for sins and call them out before God. Ask the one Who is able to forgive those sins to wipe their guilt from us.

Naming our specific sin takes humility. It takes accountability. It takes faith because we recognize that we need something from God.

But this kind of confession makes builds a character of being open and honest before God. It creates a character of dependency on God.

So let us all look into our own hearts, identify our own sins, own them, confess them, and ask our God to forgive them.

Then let us worship our God together with a pure and clean heart.

"If we say we have no sin, we deceive ourselves, and the truth is not in us.

If we confess our sins, he is faithful and just to forgive us our sins and to cleanse us from all unrighteousness.

If we say we have not sinned, we make him a liar, and his word is not in us." (1 John 1:8-10 ESV).

***

I am in the minor prophets in my daily Bible reading. A verse in Amos struck me this morning. God is naming all the nations, including Judah and Israel, and saying because of their iniquities, He will bring judgment that will not be revoked.

Amos mentions the sins of nations that bring God's judgment upon them. Most have to do with the way that nations deal with people by mistreating them or taking advantage of those who are weak. But listen to the specific charge God brings to Israel:

"But you made the Nazirites drink wine, and commanded the prophets, saying, 'You shall not prophesy.'" (Amos 2:12 ESV).

Two of the charges that God brings against Israel are forcing the people of God to violate their commitment to the Lord and commanding that they no longer speak the things of the Lord.

While we do not have Nazarites or prophets today, we do have people who are keeping vows to the Lord when they called upon His name and we have preachers and teachers who speak His message to a lost world.

Our nation is growing increasingly hostile to God and His people. We are living in a society that tries to force the people of God to violate their vows in the name of diversity. We live in a society that is trying to censor the message of repentance from sin that we preach from the Word of God.

Could we be within the generation who sees the weight of law fall upon us for keeping our vows to the Lord or for speaking the message of sin and repentance?

We may have to endure persecution unlike any we have seen in our lifetime, but the message of the prophets is that God is always in control. His eye sees and in the end, He will act against those who lift their hand against Him and His people.

These are the times when we act in faith though we live among people who try to silence God and His people. Let us do good and rely on God to sort out injustices in His time. Let us not trade our crown for a mess of pottage when and if we face the same type of persecution we read in Amos.

***

Choosing Righteousness

In Hebrews 11:24, the writer tells us that Moses "refused to be called the son of Pharaoh's daughter." There came a point when Moses could choose to live as a prince or choose to suffer mistreatment with the people of God. This choice led him to become the leader of a people chosen by God rather than die in the depth of the Red Sea with the armies of Egypt.

Choosing righteousness is a choice and Satan will not make it easy. The devil will always present a choice that appeals to our vanity, our lusts, and our carnal desires. The choice will be like a hit of narcotics to us, appealing to what makes us feel good at the moment.

But choosing righteousness means that we will make decisions based on what we know God wants from us and not based on what feels good to us at the moment. Righteous choices will often deny self now to do what God wants us to do, even though we don't get to enjoy the pleasures of sin for a season.

Our righteous choices are not often the big life decisions that shape our destiny here on earth. Often, they are the small things we choose that may never affect the day-to-day living we experience, yet can affect our eternal destiny.

Here are two choices that I put before us as we consider choosing righteousness. Think about what we want versus what God wants. Consider the effect that these choices will have on our minds, our hearts, and our ability to grow into the image of Christ that God is committed to transforming us into.

What do we choose to watch on TV? This seems so innocuous, doesn't it? How much skin is too much? How many curse words cross the line before we say enough? How much coarse jesting (dirty jokes) do we need to hear before we say it crosses the line and we turn off the TV? How much violence, hatred, evil plotting, sin, or blasphemy do we allow into our minds before we watch something else?

What we allow into our hearts through television is a choice. We invite it into our hearts. This choice hinges on two considerations. First, are we turning a blind eye to evil for our own pleasure and entertainment? Second, are we passing by opportunities for the wholesome entertainment readily available to us? It is a choice. Do we think on good things or do we think on evil things? If Jesus were sitting on the couch next to us, would that influence the choice of what we would watch?

Where do we spend our time? We all have the same 24 hours a day to spend that everyone else has to spend. Kings and peasants alike are given an equal allotment. Do we cram in hours of work beyond what we need and trade time with family and spiritual growth for more cash? Do we trade time at worship with God's people for entertainment or sleep? Do we choose to visit places that will tempt us to sin rather than strengthen us to be more like the men and women God wants us to be? Do we choose to spend time with people who do not value God rather than brothers and sisters who are trying to get to heaven? Where we choose to spend our time is a choice we make. Do we choose righteousness?

What we choose to enter our minds as we entertain ourselves and where we choose to spend time are things that may have little impact on our lives at the moment, but over time, these choices will affect who we are and the kind of people we will become. As we think in our hearts, so are the people we become.

"Do not be conformed to this world, but be transformed by the renewal of your mind, that by testing you may discern what is the will of God, what is good and acceptable and perfect." (Romans 12:2 ESV).

***

Before you stress too much, remember...
It doesn't matter how many missiles fall into the wrong place,
or who does or does not get elected to office,
or who does or does not run for president,
or who does or does not take over major companies...
Regardless of what happens in our world,
God has always been sovereign,
God is sovereign,
and God will always be sovereign.
If you belong to Him, then nothing else is really that stressful...

***

I am wrapping up the minor prophets in the Old Testament before I move into the New Testament on Friday. Much of the messages they speak are about impending judgment. The "day of the Lord" is near.

Listen to the words of Zephaniah:

> "Be silent before the Lord GOD! For the day of the LORD is near; the LORD has prepared a sacrifice and consecrated his guests." (Zephaniah 1:7 ESV).

The prophet goes on in the next few verses to say whom the Lord will punish. But when he gets to verse 12, he says something interesting:

> "At that time I will search Jerusalem with lamps, and I will punish the men who are complacent, those who say in their hearts, 'The LORD will not do good, nor will he do ill.'" (Zephaniah 1:12 ESV).

It seemed that the warning of the coming of the Day of the Lord was falling on deaf ears. People were complacent and not moved to repentance like the people of Nineveh were at the preaching of Jonah.

In fact, their disposition toward the message of impending judgment was that God was not in the picture at all. He wouldn't do good or ill toward the people. He was impotent or inactive.

Jesus promises that He will return again one day to bring judgment to the people of the earth. Today, we also scoff and say,

> "Where is the promise of his coming? For ever since the fathers fell

asleep, all things are continuing as they were from the beginning of creation." (2 Peter 3:4b ESV).

This is the same as saying, "The LORD will not do good, nor will he do ill."

When the promised judgment spoken by the prophets came, people were not prepared. The question for us is,

Will we repeat the actions of the people of God who did not repent of the message from the prophets and heed their warnings?

Or will join in with scoffers who yawn at the call to repentance and expect the sun to again rise and set as it has always done before?

One day, the sun will rise but never set. Will we be ready?

That day could very well be today.

***

What does it mean to live in an absolute sovereign kingdom?

1. We have no input when it comes to the law.
2. The king is our ruler until death. We don't get to vote him out.
3. We never get to put the king on trial or demand he makes a defense for his actions.
4. The king chooses the punishment and when to extend his grace.
5. The king provides all sustenance, protection, and allocation of possession. All blessings flow from the king.

Perhaps our first response is to argue against living under the kingship of Jesus because there are some aspects of sovereignty we don't want to give up.

But until we are willing to live under His sovereign kingship, we will not receive the benefits of His kingship.

Sovereignty is often hard to submit to. Perhaps it is even harder to release to another.

> "But his citizens hated him and sent a delegation after him, saying, 'We do not want this man to reign over us.'" (Luke 19:14 ESV).

***

Let's be careful when we feel pressure to follow the majority...

"The Lord saw that the wickedness of man was great in the earth, and that every intention of the thoughts of his heart was only evil continually.

And the Lord regretted that he had made man on the earth, and it grieved him to his heart.

So the Lord said, "I will blot out man whom I have created from the face of the land, man and animals and creeping things and birds of the heavens, for I am sorry that I have made them."

> But Noah found favor in the eyes of the Lord." (Genesis 6:5-8 ESV).

***

I started the New Testament in my Daily Bible Reading this morning. In the book of Matthew, we read about the birth of Jesus. On this joyous occasion, we see the sinister plot by Herod take root. Rather than join in the joyful occasion, celebrating the coming of the promised Messiah and King, Herod saw the child as a threat to his legacy.

When the wise men from the East came to Herod, they asked him where the King of the Jews who was born was. The next verse is troubling:

> "When Herod the king heard this, he was troubled, and all Jerusalem with him;" (Matthew 2:3 ESV).

I guess it isn't troubling that King Herod was troubled. Perhaps we understand why. Jesus represented to him a threat to his kingship. But what was troubling was that all Jerusalem with him was troubled.

Yesterday, I wrote that we need to be careful when the majority pulls us to their way of thinking if that way is evil. Matthew 2:3 reminds us that we also need to be careful that we don't let those in power and influence shape our thoughts.

All of Jerusalem should have been glad when they heard about the promised birth of the Messiah, the coming King of Israel. Instead, they were troubled because their current king was troubled.

In the end, their king would die and this infant would inherit a Kingdom and having conquered death, rule the Kingdom forever.

Let us be careful about which voice of authority we listen to and not allow those with influence to cause our hearts to trouble with theirs when God's purposes get in their way.

***

Imagine that war came to our soil.
Everyone is forced to choose one side or the other.
Remaining neutral is not an option.
We must choose to fight for our homeland or fight for the invading army.
This war will be a war until there is one victor and one vanquished.
It is a fight to the death.
Before you make the choice, here is one piece of information you might want to consider.
The invading force has the power to make it invincible. There is no way our homeland can win against it.
No hope whatsoever.
Which side do we choose?
The Kingdom of heaven is fighting the power of the god of this world.
We must choose a side.
Remaining neutral is not an option.
If we fight for the god of this world, it will be a popular choice, but it will lead to our death.
If we fight for the King of kings, the Lord of lords, then we will be assured victory, but those of the homeland will accuse us of being a traitor and will hate us.
What side will we choose today?
Will we choose life or death; will we choose the kingdom of heaven or the kingdom of Satan?
Will we choose victory or defeat?
The war's end is a foregone conclusion.
Which choice will we make?

"You will be delivered up even by parents and brothers and relatives and friends, and some of you they will put to death. You will be hated by all for my name's sake. But not a hair of your head will perish. By your endurance you will gain your lives." (Luke 21:16-19 ESV).

***

Well, Jesus didn't come yesterday, on His, the Lord's day.
Perhaps the Father is about to give Him the word this morning to come.
With our thoughts in full planning mode for Thanksgiving, perhaps we are planning for the thing that may not occur.
If so, have we planned for the event that really matters for our eternity?

"For as in those days before the flood they were eating and drinking, marrying and giving in marriage, until the day when Noah entered the ark, and they were unaware until the flood came and swept them all away, so will be the coming of the Son of Man." (Matthew 24:38-39 ESV).

***

Jesus, Matthew 25, and Grace vs Works

There are a lot of people who teach that we are saved by grace and there is nothing we do for our salvation. Even though Jesus said to baptize people in the name of the Father, the Son, and the Holy Spirit (Matthew 28:19), many say that we don't have to listen to that instruction since it constitutes a work.

Perhaps they also think that Jesus misses the point of grace vs works when He spoke in Matthew 25. Here is what I mean…

When we read about the 10 virgins, the five unwise ones didn't prepare their lamps. When the bridegroom came, they were at the marketplace buying oil and missed his arrival. When the 5 virgins returned, the door was shut:

"Afterward the other virgins came also, saying, 'Lord, lord, open to us.' But he answered, 'Truly, I say to you, I do not know you.'" (Matthew 25:11-12 ESV).

Perhaps some people need to remind Jesus that preparing for His return is a work of men, therefore, these foolish virgins will still be saved by His grace.

Perhaps some also think that Jesus misses the point of grace vs works in the next section when He talks about the men who were given talents. The men who were given 2 and 5 talents respectively worked, which many today believe is not necessary for salvation, but the one who was given 1 talent just buried his talent and returned what the Lord gave Him.

When the Lord returned, the man with one talent, who didn't work for the Lord, returned the talent back to the Lord. This is what the Lord said to him:

"Then you ought to have invested my money with the bankers, and at my coming I should have received what was my own with interest. So take the talent from him and give it to him who has the ten talents.

For to everyone who has will more be given, and he will have an abundance. But from the one who has not, even what he has will be taken away. And cast the worthless servant into the outer darkness. In that place there will be weeping and gnashing of teeth.'" (Matthew 25:27-30 ESV).

Perhaps some people think they need to remind Jesus that working to grow our talents is a work of men, therefore the man who buried his talent will still be saved by grace instead of being cast into the outer darkness.

And then, when Jesus is sitting on the judgment throne, there will be many people who do not feed the hungry, clothe the naked, and visit the sick and those in prison and not minister to them:

> "Then he will answer them, saying, 'Truly, I say to you, as you did not do it to one of the least of these, you did not do it to me.' And these will go away into eternal punishment, but the righteous into eternal life." (Matthew 25:45-46 ESV).

Perhaps some people today think that Jesus was mistaken because it sounds like people weren't saved because they didn't work.

I know many people today believe that we do not have to obey God and His grace will still cover our sins, but this goes against the very purposes of Jesus' message in Matthew 25. Certainly, our obedience will not merit salvation, but it seems that Jesus will give His grace on Judgment Day to those who obey Him.

No matter how much we insist that this constitutes earning our salvation, it does not. It simply means that we must obey the Master if we hope to receive His grace.

***

I'm in Matthew in my daily Bible reading. In chapter 15, we read an interesting story about Jesus. A Caananite woman comes to Him, pleading for Him to heal her daughter from demon possession.

At first, Jesus ignores her, but she persists. Wouldn't you if you were in her shoes? Undoubtedly.

The disciples urged Jesus to send her away. Notice Jesus' response to the woman:

> "He answered, "I was sent only to the lost sheep of the house of Israel." (Matthew 15:24 ESV).

Understand, this statement was true. Though Jesus did interact, heal, and forgive Gentiles, His mission was very specific and aimed at the Jews. He would not allow the floodgates to open to the rest of the world at this time.

That would come later with the baptism of Cornelius.

Now, Jesus goes on to heal this woman's daughter because of her great faith. But there is a lesson of sovereignty for us in this story.

Thorough Jesus only came for the lost sheep of the house of Israel, it was His prerogative to do what He wished.

No one had the right to criticize His choice.

No one had the right to forbid Him from healing this woman's daughter.

No one had the right to demand a defense for His decision to heal the woman's daughter.

The Scriptures are ripe with lessons of God's sovereignty. I fear that we feel much too comfortable questioning Jesus, demanding Him to defend His words, and forbidding Him from teaching what He teaches.

The way He dealt with compassion toward this Caananite woman in spite of His specific mission should cause us all to drop to our knees in humble submission to His absolute sovereignty.

The lesson: Jesus can do whatever He wants; we must seek His will and conform to it, not fight against it.

***

Today, Thanksgiving, I finished the book of Matthew in my daily Bible reading.

I couldn't have had a better reading for this day of Thanks.

In a few hours, I will be surrounded by family, feasting on a rich man's feast, for most of us have been abundantly blessed by God beyond what we deserve.

I have so many things to be thankful for, but having read about the crucifixion and resurrection of my Lord and King, I will keep the most precious thankfulness front and center in my heart today.

Happy Thanksgiving, friends. Today is truly a good day to remember all that the Lord has made us thankful for.

***

If we see Jesus today, how will we answer this charge before the Judge?

Did you love Me with all your heart, soul, and mind?

Did you love your neighbor as yourself?

"And he said to him, "You shall love the Lord your God with all your heart and with all your soul and with all your mind.
This is the great and first commandment.
And a second is like it: You shall love your neighbor as yourself.
On these two commandments depend all the Law and the Prophets." (Matthew 22:37-40 ESV).

***

In Matthew, Jesus tells a couple of parables that speak to good and evil people being allowed to exist in His kingdom together until the end, when He will send His angels as reapers to separate the good from the bad.

"Let both grow together until the harvest, and at harvest time I will tell the reapers, "Gather the weeds first and bind them in bundles to be burned, but gather the wheat into my barn."" (Matthew 13:30 ESV).

And...

"Again, the kingdom of heaven is like a net that was thrown into the sea and gathered fish of every kind. When it was full, men drew it ashore and sat down and sorted the good into containers but threw away the bad." (Matthew 13:47-48 ESV).

In both parables, I am sure that the weeds thought they were wheat, and the bad fish thought they were good fish.

So, how can we be sure we are wheat and good fish? The parables Jesus teaches talk about good and honest hearts. We must look into the words He brought to us and consider our disposition toward them.

If we hunger and thirst after His words, then our heart is good. If we shut off His words from transforming us, then we are weeds and bad fish.

If we love our neighbors and seek their welfare, then our heart is good. If we ignore those in need or make excuses why we do not need to help when we have the means to help, then we are weeds and bad fish.

If we are quicker to find the good in people than we are in finding the bad in people, then our heart is good. If we tear down and sow discord instead of edifying, then we are weeds and bad fish.

Being wheat and weeds, good fish or bad fish isn't about knowing the Scriptures well or simply attending the right church. A lot of weeds and bad fish will know the Scriptures and attend the right church in the Kingdom.

The King will allow the weeds and bad fish to coexist with the wheat and good fish until His reapers come.

We must always examine our hearts and produce the fruits of a good heart. What a terrifying day it will be if, on that day, reapers remove us after we spend a lifetime in the right church and living among the right people because our hearts are bad.

***

Excerpt: The Potter and the Clay

This Sunday, I will be teaching a class on The Sovereignty of God at Campbell Road Chruch of Christ in Garland, TX. Here is an excerpt from my book, The Sovereignty of God regarding the Potter and the Clay:

The Potter and the Clay: Over Nations

To illustrate His sovereignty as Creator, God spoke to the prophets and used the illustration of a potter and clay. He did this with both Isaiah and Jeremiah. Let's look at what He said to Jeremiah because He walks us through the illustration using a real-life potter and not just imagery.

> "The word that came to Jeremiah from the LORD: "Arise, and go down to the potter's house, and there I will let you hear my words." So I went down to the potter's house, and there he was working at his wheel." (Jeremiah 18:1-3 ESV).

Jeremiah gets a visual lesson of God's sovereignty. He is instructed to go to the potter's house and watch him create a vessel on his wheel. In this object lesson, Jeremiah observes that the clay vessel has some defect. So, what happens when the potter sees something he does not like with the clay vessel he is creating?

> "And the vessel he was making of clay was spoiled in the potter's hand, and he reworked it into another vessel, as it seemed good to the potter to do." (Jeremiah 18:4 ESV).

The potter had some choices to make, didn't he? He could have destroyed the clay vessel and given up on his creation, or he could have left the defect or spoil in the vessel. But in this case, the potter chose to refashion the clay into the vessel he wanted it to be. This potter was sovereign over the lump of clay. Then God speaks to this object lesson:

> "Then the word of the LORD came to me: "O house of Israel, can I not do with you as this potter has done? declares the LORD. Behold, like the clay in the potter's hand, so are you in my hand, O house of Israel." (Jeremiah 18:5-6 ESV).

God is saying to Israel that He is the Potter and Israel is the clay. As their creator, He can do with Israel whatever He chooses to do with them. He can mold or fashion them into anything He wants them to be. The potter didn't have to consult with the clay to see if it was all right for him to fashion it into something else, did he? Neither does God have to consult and agree with Israel on what He will make of it.

> "If at any time I declare concerning a nation or a kingdom, that I will pluck up and break down and destroy it, and if that nation, concerning which I have spoken, turns from its evil, I will relent of the disaster that I intended to do to it." (Jeremiah 18:7-8 ESV).

God even extends His sovereignty over Israel to all nations. We will look at this in more detail later in the book, but His point here is that just as He is sovereign over Israel, so is He sovereign as the potter over all nations. He has the power to break up and destroy anytime He chooses.

Put another peg in this verse that we will discuss later. As part of His sovereignty, God is free to devote a nation to destruction, and if that nation repents, God in His sovereignty can choose to relent and spare the nation from the harm He "intended to do to it." There is so much about free will and the sovereignty of God that many can't wrap their minds around. And with good reason. God's sovereignty is so far above our finite ability to comprehend that we may never have all the answers. Spoiler Alert- I will not be able to explain all there is about God's sovereignty in this book. But I will encourage us to be slow to build elaborate belief systems based on things we think might be true. More on this later. But God not only discusses His sovereignty over nations to break and destroy them, but He also tells Jeremiah that He has the sovereignty to build and plant:

> "And if at any time I declare concerning a nation or a kingdom that I will build and plant it, and if it does evil in my sight, not listening to my voice, then I will relent of the good that I had intended to do to it." (Jeremiah 18:9-10 ESV).

As the potter over nations, God can also choose to build up and plant any nation. We say nations rise and fall at God's will, which is true. God establishes the governments (Romans 13:1). Just as repentance can change the decree of God against the ones He intends to destroy, so can evil from the nations cause God to relent from the good He had "intended to do to it."

And so, the message of the potter and the clay to Jeremiah is that God is building/planting a nation to be His instrument of wrath against Israel, which he intends to break down and destroy:

> "Now, therefore, say to the men of Judah and the inhabitants of Jerusalem: 'Thus says the LORD, Behold, I am shaping disaster against you and devising a plan against you. Return, every one from his evil way, and amend your ways and your deeds.'" (Jeremiah 18:11 ESV).

God's illustration here is that He is sovereign over even the nations. He can do what He intends to do to them because He is powerful enough to do it, He has the will to do it, and He can ensure that it turns out exactly as He intends. Things never get out of God's control. He never has a miscalculation where He unleashes a monster that does more damage than He intends or inadvertently judges a nation more harshly than He intends. God is in perfect control over everything that He intends, and as we will see later, He will accomplish all of His purposes:

> "remember the former things of old; for I am God, and there is no other; I am God, and there is none like me, declaring the end from the beginning and from ancient times things not yet done, saying, 'My counsel shall stand, and I will accomplish all my purpose,'" (Isaiah 46:9-10 ESV).

***

In the book of Matthew, it's interesting how Jesus and the religious leaders asked each other questions. The religious leaders did it to trap Jesus because they had preconceived ideas they wanted to defend. Jesus was a challenge to their belief, and they refused to submit to the truth. Instead, they sought to discredit Him by setting traps for Him.

> "And when he entered the temple, the chief priests and the elders of the people came up to him as he was teaching, and said, "By what authority are you doing these things, and who gave you this authority?"

(Matthew 21:23 ESV).

"And they sent their disciples to him, along with the Herodians, saying, "Teacher, we know that you are true and teach the way of God truthfully, and you do not care about anyone's opinion, for you are not swayed by appearances. Tell us, then, what you think. Is it lawful to pay taxes to Caesar, or not?" (Matthew 22:16-17 ESV).

"In the resurrection, therefore, of the seven, whose wife will she be? For they all had her." (Matthew 22:28 ESV).

In all of these instances, the religious leaders were not seeking knowledge; they were seeking to trick Jesus and prove He was a fraud. They didn't have a good and honest heart, seeking truth. They were only concerned about defending their carefully crafted beliefs.

There is a lesson for us. Do we seek the truth, or do we seek to defend our carefully crafted beliefs? If our hearts refuse to consider truth, then we run the risk of standing condemned because we defend our beliefs rather than let His words fashion what our beliefs should be.

Truth is never concerned about an honest examination, but our own crafted beliefs will seek to silence examination.

Tomorrow, we will discuss the purpose of the questions that Jesus poses to the religious leaders in the book of Matthew.

***

I just saw a couple of old people on TV. Wrinkles, slow moving, and gray hair were the tell-tale signs.

Then I found out that they were my age.

Ecclesiastes 12 came to mind.

The good thing about growing old and seeing signs of aging in your body is that it gives you a greater appreciation for the promised new body that awaits us in heaven.

***

I just saw this on a T-shirt and I love it:

"The devil saw me with my head down and thought he had won...

Until I said 'Amen.'"

***

Yesterday, we looked at some of the questions that the religious leaders asked Jesus in the book of Matthew. These questions were not asked to seek truth, but to trap Jesus because they wanted to defend their carefully crafted beliefs, and Jesus posed a threat to those beliefs.

Today, let's look at some of the questions that Jesus asked the religious leaders. What can we learn from the questions He posed to them?

When Jesus was asked if we should pay taxes, Jesus responded by asking for a coin.

> "And Jesus said to them, "Whose likeness and inscription is this?" (Matthew 22:20 ESV).

When the religious leaders asked Him by what authority he was doing things,

> "Jesus answered them, "I also will ask you one question, and if you tell me the answer, then I also will tell you by what authority I do these things.
> The baptism of John, from where did it come? From heaven or from man?" (Matthew 21:24-25b ESV).

And Jesus asked about their perception of who the Messiah was:

> "Now while the Pharisees were gathered together, Jesus asked them a question, saying, "What do you think about the Christ? Whose son is he?" They said to him, "The son of David." (Matthew 22:41-42 ESV).

Jesus went on to quote Scripture that talks about the Messiah and finished with:

> "If then David calls him Lord, how is he his son?" (Matthew 22:45 ESV).

Unlike the religious leaders, Jesus was not asking these questions to trap people, nor was he asking questions to avoid answering the hard questions. Jesus was asking questions to get to the heart of the religious leader.

His questions were designed to force them to address their heart. On paying taxes, Jesus saw through their attempt to trap Him rather than seek an answer to a genuine question, and He asked them a question that demonstrated they could obey God while obeying the powers God had instituted (Romans 13:1).

When asked by what authority He was doing things, Jesus responded with a question that demonstrated they were not really interested in the answer He would give. The religious leaders would have pounced on whatever answer He gave, so Jesus turned the question on them and put them in the position they sought to put Him in.

And when Jesus asked whose son David was and what it meant that David called Him Lord, Jesus was forcing the religious leaders to make a decision about who the Messiah was. They expected the Messiah to be a physical leader who would deliver Israel from Rome and from all enemies, yet in their minds, the Messiah would live neatly within the social structure they built for Him.

By asking these questions, Jesus challenged the carefully crafted beliefs and made them come face-to-face with their beliefs, and forced them to choose what to defend. Jesus didn't ask these questions to trap people but to shine the light of truth into their hearts and to expose what they believed.

Jesus asks us questions throughout His word which are designed to shed light into our hearts. What do we do with His questions? Do we seek to ignore or explain away the questions we face or do we let them fashion the truth we hold fast to?

Jesus asks us:

Who am I?

Do you love Me? Do you love your neighbor?

Will you choose me or your fleshly appetites?

Am I worth sacrificing for, or will you choose your desires over serving me?

These questions go to our hearts, and Jesus forces us to answer. There is no middle ground, no mediocre path, and no room for compromise.

Jesus asks us questions that will draw a sharp distinction between what we will give to Him versus how we will live to ourselves.

These questions will shine light into our hearts. We can ignore these questions and refuse to answer, but this in and of itself is an answer that exposes our hearts.

Jesus asked the religious leaders some tough questions that required tough answers that they were not willing to give. Because of this, their place at His table was given to someone else.

That place at his table is reserved for you and me, provided we have a good and honest heart that listens to the questions He asks and seeks to bring our answers into subjection to the Messiah's will.

***

Something to think about... On the Day of Judgment:
There will be no protests.
There will be no bribes.
There will be no bail, cashless or otherwise.
There will be no defense lawyers to speak on our behalf.
There will be no preponderance of the evidence.
There will be no false convictions.
There will be no appeals.
Judgment will be swift, perfect, just and merciful from an infallible Judge.
Judgment will be final.
Don't confuse human judgment and justice with Divine judgment and justice.

***

While we watch TV,
Eat dinner with family and friends,
Plan for the Christmas holiday,
Prepare for the weekend,
And get ready for the New Year 2023,
Angels are singing around the throne,
While our King and High Priest is awaiting word from the Father to return for His people.
As we make plans, let's not forget to prepare for the most important plans of all.

"You also must be ready, for the Son of Man is coming at an hour you do not expect." (Luke 12:40 ESV).

***

As I am reading the book of Mark, I see over and over how the Scribes and Pharisees have a problem they cannot get past; a problem that will ultimately damn them because it causes them to reject Jesus:

"And when Jesus saw their faith, he said to the paralytic, "Son, your sins are forgiven."

> Now some of the scribes were sitting there, questioning in their hearts, "Why does this man speak like that? He is blaspheming! Who can forgive sins but God alone?" (Mark 2:5-7 ESV).

From one standpoint, we understand this. Anyone who claims that which belongs to God alone should be condemned as a blasphemer. But in light of the promised prophesies that pointed to Jesus, they should have been open to testing His claims in light of prophecies.

But they would not. They didn't give Jesus a chance to show that He was the promised Messiah. Instead, they rejected Him outright. Why did they do this?

They did this because they held Jesus to their standards. If Jesus were held to the standards of man, then they would be correct. But God can do what man cannot do. God can forgive sins; man cannot.

Once they held Jesus to their own standards, then nothing would allow His acceptance within their hearts.

This is a danger that we must all be careful of. God is not held to our standards. We must fight against holding him to our expectations. Instead, we must study to understand the expectations that the Scriptures give us about Him.

If we hold Him to the standard that He must forgive the way we expect Him to forgive, then we are guilty of the same closeminded sinfulness of the Scribes and Pharisees.

If we hold Him to the standard to teach what we think He should teach, then we are guilty of the same closeminded sinfulness of the Scribes and Pharisees.

If we hold Him to the standard to rule the way we expect Him to rule, then we are guilty of the same closeminded sinfulness of the Scribes and Pharisees.

If we bring our standards to Jesus without having a heart open to see Him for who He is, then we will only be happy by making Jesus into our image of Him.

We must have a heart that seeks to know Him and a heart ready to accept Him for who He is. These are the ones who will be invited to dine at His table with Him.

***

Questions I ask myself:
Am I a peacemaker or a troublemaker?
Am I encouraging or unsupportive?

Do I assume the best in others or do I assume the worst?
Am I a giver or a taker?
Do I demand or do I serve?
Do I spread hurtful things or do I protect others' reputation?
Do I give grace or exact revenge?
I have a lot of work to be more like my Savior.

"For those whom he foreknew he also predestined to be conformed to the image of his Son, in order that he might be the firstborn among many brothers." (Romans 8:29 ESV).

***

This is what you live for as a father...
My six-year-old and I went to a Bible study at the preacher's house tonight. Ryder went upstairs to play with the other kids during the study.

When we got home, he mentioned that he told some other kids about Jesus.

I pray Emily and I can continue to cultivate this heart in him as he gets older.

***

There is a very interesting thing that Jesus says in the book of Mark. As He is eating with tax collectors and sinners, the disciples of John and the Pharisees ask Him this question:

"Now John's disciples and the Pharisees were fasting. And people came and said to him, "Why do John's disciples and the disciples of the Pharisees fast, but your disciples do not fast?" (Mark 2:18 ESV).

The disciples of John and the Pharisees are guilty of what we are often guilty of doing. We have a preconceived idea of what Jesus should be like and when He doesn't fit our idea of Him, we question Him.

Here is how Jesus explains it:

"And Jesus said to them, "Can the wedding guests fast while the bridegroom is with them? As long as they have the bridegroom with them, they cannot fast.

The days will come when the bridegroom is taken away from them, and then they will fast in that day.

No one sews a piece of unshrunk cloth on an old garment. If he does, the patch tears away from it, the new from the old, and a worse tear is made.

And no one puts new wine into old wineskins. If he does, the wine will burst the skins--and the wine is destroyed, and so are the skins. But new wine is for fresh wineskins." (Mark 2:19-22 ESV) .

Jesus came to bring "different". He came to fulfill the law, not to perpetuate the law. If Jesus merely conformed to the old ways of doing things, then He could not fulfill what He came to do.

Jesus would be different and teach differently. If He tried to conform, then it would be like putting a new patch on old wineskins.

For the Jews, it meant that Jesus didn't come to simply be like all the other Rabbis. For us, it means that Jesus will not conform to our expectations. We must conform to His. When His expectations and our expectations clash, it's like putting a new cloth on old wineskins. Something is going to tear.

The only way our life will find harmony is to see Jesus for Who He is and to conform our lives to His. Approaching Him any other way will simply not work.

***

We are interesting creatures.

We can see a moment of good in an evil person and forever see them as good afterward.

And we can see a moment of weakness in a righteous person and forever see them as evil afterward.

There is truth that we only get one chance to make a first impression,

But it's important to be willing to let our first impressions of people change if it's warranted.

How willing we are to change our first impressions of someone goes to our character and to the people God wants us to be.

***

Ask And It Will Be Given To You

When Jesus spoke to the multitude, He said some pretty amazing things.

One thing He said should bring us tremendous joy and comfort. In Matthew and Luke, we read Him say this:

> "Ask, and it will be given to you; seek, and you will find; knock, and it will be opened to you. For everyone who asks receives, and the one who seeks finds, and to the one who knocks it will be opened." (Matthew 7:7-8 ESV).

And

> "And I tell you, ask, and it will be given to you; seek, and you will find; knock, and it will be opened to you. For everyone who asks receives, and the one who seeks finds, and to the one who knocks it will be opened." (Luke 11:9-10 ESV).

Isn't that amazing? The Creator invites us to ask and says we shall receive; seek, and we shall find. Unfortunately, when we read these passages, we tend to focus on a couple of thoughts that cause us to lose the power and wonderful gift that Jesus is offering.

Sometimes, we read into this invitation to ask something that Jesus is not speaking about. This is a pity because it dredges up disappointment that shouldn't be there and causes us to miss the powerful invitation to ask and receive. What do I mean?

Many read these passages and think, "God is telling me to ask for anything I want, and He will give it to me." If we ask for money, God will make us rich. If we ask for a car, God will give is a Lamborghini. If we ask for a job, God will make us CEO. Some people read this like God is a genie in a bottle, ready to grant our every wish of Him.

But these passages never come close to indicating that God will answer every wish we have of Him. In fact, Jesus is promising us something even more wonderful. We will look at that in a moment.

But some also focus so much on the thought that God will not grant us all we ask and miss the powerful thing the Creator is offering to His children in this invitation to ask and receive. This is as equally sad as the one who thinks that God will grant every whim we offer up to Him.

So, what is it that Jesus is inviting us to ask for? He goes on to explain in the next few verses in each account. First, in Matthew, Jesus goes on to say this:

> "Or which one of you, if his son asks him for bread, will give him a stone? Or if he asks for a fish, will give him a serpent? If you then, who are evil, know how to give good gifts to your children, how much more will your Father who is in heaven give good things to those who ask him!"

(Matthew 7:9-11 ESV).

And in Luke, Jesus goes on to say this:

"What father among you, if his son asks for a fish, will instead of a fish give him a serpent; or if he asks for an egg, will give him a scorpion? If you then, who are evil, know how to give good gifts to your children, how much more will the heavenly Father give the Holy Spirit to those who ask him!" (Luke 11:11-13 ESV).

In both cases, we are invited to ask God to take care of our needs, and He will abundantly do so because He is a good Father. He doesn't promise to give us everything we ask for; He promises something better: He promises to give us everything we need. That requires an act of faith from us, knowing that we will not go without the necessities of life.

As parents, if our adult children tell us that they are hungry, wouldn't we take them to the grocery store and provide for them abundantly, according to our ability? But if they called us and asked us for a Lamborghini, would it mean that we didn't love them if we said, "No?"

Jesus says it like this: "If you then, who are evil, know how to give good gifts to your children, how much more will the heavenly Father give the Holy Spirit to those who ask him!" God is both able and willing to take care of all of His children's needs. That is the point that Jesus is making to us. If we lack anything we need, He invites us to ask the Father, and He will give us what we ask for. He will provide for the needs we have.

If we want to read into this wonderful promise something which isn't there, we will be disappointed and miss the unbelievable gift that Jesus offers when He invites us to ask and receive from the Father. If we focus too much on how God will not give us everything we ask for, we may end up neutering the powerful promise we have from Jesus and walk away, dismissing the gift of asking and receiving altogether.

Jesus says to ask, and we will receive. What a wonderful blessing from the Father who loves us more than any earthly father loves his earthly children. This invitation to ask and receive should be one of the most precious gifts we cherish from our heavenly Father. It means that He loves us, listens to us, and will personally make sure each one of us has everything we need in life.

Don't neuter this promise, and don't read into it something that Jesus doesn't say. Rather, let us all drop to our knees and thank the Father for giving us this invitation to ask and receive, knowing He will honor our petitions to Him just as Jesus said He would.

***

In Mark, Jesus told the disciples:

"The Son of Man is going to be delivered into the hands of men, and they will kill him. And when he is killed, after three days he will rise." (Mark 9:31b ESV).

This statement tells me a lot about Jesus:
It tells me that His death was not a defeat but a victory.
It tells me that Jesus always put the Father's will first.
It tells me that Jesus is not afraid to tell His disciples the hard truths.
As His disciples:
We can be secure, knowing that victory is in Jesus.
To be like Him, we will put the Father's will first in our lives.
We should not sugarcoat the truth nor shy away from it.

***

What does it mean to walk with Jesus?
It means that my heart is set on living the way He wants me to live.
It means that I will seek a stewardship that serves and honors Him, not when it's convenient, but all the time.
It means that when I stumble, I reach my hand to Him for support and to be lifted up so I can continue my walk with Him.
Walking with Jesus, My King, doesn't mean I will be perfect,
But it means that in spite of being imperfect, I will not give up my desire to live as His servant,
Knowing that His grace will supply what I need when I fall.
Walking with Jesus is my choice to make.
Continuing the journey with Him is possible through His grace.

"Therefore, as you received Christ Jesus the Lord, so walk in him," (Colossians 2:6 ESV).

***

This is one of the verses that overwhelms me when I think about it. God visits His creation and spends 33 years living among us, knowing how His 33 years would come to an end:

> "And the Word became flesh and dwelt among us, and we have seen his glory, glory as of the only Son from the Father, full of grace and truth." (John 1:14 ESV).

How can we ever doubt the depth of our Savior and God's love for us?

***

This is interesting. Annas was the High Priest of Israel from 6 AD to 15 AD before being deposed. Annas had 5 sons that he was able to maneuver into the office of High Priest over the years.

He also was able to maneuver his son–in–law into the office from 18 AD to 36 AD. His son-in-law's name was Caiaphas. Sound familiar?

This is why Jesus was brought before Annas and Caiaphas during His trials. Though Caiaphas was the High Priest recognized by Rome, Annas was the patriarch who still wielded influence.

Luke tells us that when Jesus was 12, He stayed behind in Jerusalem to speak to the officials in the Temple.

> "After three days they found him in the temple, sitting among the teachers, listening to them and asking them questions. And all who heard him were amazed at his understanding and his answers." (Luke 2:46-47 ESV).

When you look at the timeline, Annas would have been in his 1st to 3rd year as High Priest when Jesus was sitting among the teachers in the temple.

Could it be that the family who would be responsible for executing the Messiah was first astonished at His understanding and answers when He was 12 years old?

When Jesus was 12 years old, Annas most likely met Him and had the opportunity to hear teachings from the young promised Messiah.

Yet political power would become more important to this young, new High Priest than his spiritual role as a shepherd to God's people. And when He was face to face with Israel's King and God, Annas chose to pursue earthly power and wealth.

> "For what does it profit a man to gain the whole world and forfeit his soul? For what can a man give in return for his soul?" (Mark 8:36-37 ESV).

***

Who knows what the future holds? Perhaps followers of Jesus will see persecution in our homeland like never before.

Perhaps society will turn on those who follow Jesus. Perhaps they will force Christians to deny Jesus or pay a terrible cost.

Perhaps those we love- family and friends- will turn on us and try to silence us.

Or perhaps God will still allow relative peace and safety as we follow His Son.

What is going to happen will happen. We have no control over that.

But we do have control over the relationship we have with our King.

Whether peace or persecution, if we lean on the Lord, then nothing can rob us of our hope.

I pray for peace, but I pray more for our faithfulness as our society starts to move further away from God.

"Blessed are those who are persecuted for righteousness' sake, for theirs is the kingdom of heaven.

"Blessed are you when others revile you and persecute you and utter all kinds of evil against you falsely on my account.

Rejoice and be glad, for your reward is great in heaven, for so they persecuted the prophets who were before you." (Matthew 5:10-12 ESV).

***

Why Sadducees Do Not Believe In A Resurrection

{Note: This is an excerpt from my book, "The Sovereignty of God." It looks at the error the Sadducees made when arriving at the conclusion that there is no resurrection. They used their reason to arrive at the wrong conclusion rather than using their reason to arrive at the correct conclusion. This serves as an example for us to be careful when we use reasoning to come to conclusions that we use to build our beliefs on. We must be careful we do not promote our reasoning to the level of "This saith the Lord."}

Excerpt:

In the days of Jesus, there were many sects, all believing something different. You had the Essenes, who lived a communal existence and many thought may have been the authors of the Dead Sea Scrolls. You also had the Zealots, who hated the Romans and believed God would conquer Rome through violence and might. Then you had the two more prominent sects who shared power in ruling the Jewish people through the Sanhedrin: the Pharisees and the Sadducees. The Pharisees were the more conservative of the two and followed the law and the oral traditions. In contrast, the Sadducees followed the law alone, limiting their appeal for authority to the first five books of the Old Testament. A significant distinction between them was in their view of the afterlife. Pharisees believed in an afterlife and angels, while the Sadducees didn't.

We see Jesus coming head-to-head with Sadducees on their view that there is no resurrection and no afterlife. The reasoning they used to arrive at this conclusion went something like this: The law taught what was referred to as the Levirate Marriage from Deuteronomy 25:5-10. If a man died without a son, his brother would take the widow as a wife and bear a son for his dead brother. The Sadducees reasoned that this inferred that there is no afterlife because if there was an afterlife and a resurrection, how would Levirate Marriages be handled when everyone met back up in the afterlife? This is how they would get Jesus to stumble and prove that there is no resurrection.

Remember, Jesus is God who created man in His image and instituted marriage in Genesis 1 at creation. The Sadducees had no idea the one they were about to test had firsthand knowledge of everything they were about to put to Him.

"The same day Sadducees came to him, who say that there is no resurrection, and they asked him a question, saying, "Teacher, Moses said, 'If a man dies having no children, his brother must marry the widow and raise up offspring for his brother.' Now there were seven brothers among us. The first married and died, and having no offspring left his wife to his brother. So too the second and third, down to the seventh. After them all, the woman died. In the resurrection, therefore, of the seven, whose wife will she be? For they all had her." (Matthew 22:23-28 ESV).

Understand, they had settled their authority that there is no resurrection, in part, by how they reasoned this situation through. Jesus tells the Sadducees that there is a resurrection and explains why. Remember, Jesus created man as an eternal being in His image. He was teaching the truth because He was the author of this truth. If you want to know how something works, there is no more qualified source than the creator of that something.

But look at the two charges Jesus lays at their feet which explains the error they made in how they arrived at their incorrect conclusion:

"But Jesus answered them, "You are wrong, because you know neither the Scriptures nor the power of God." (Matthew 22:29 ESV).

The first error was in not knowing the Scriptures:

"And as for the resurrection of the dead, have you not read what was said to you by God: 'I am the God of Abraham, and the God of Isaac, and the God of Jacob'? He is not God of the dead, but of the living." (Matthew 22:31-32 ESV).

The second error was not knowing the power of God:

"For in the resurrection they neither marry nor are given in marriage, but are like angels in heaven." (Matthew 22:30 ESV).

As we go through the rest of this study on the sovereignty of God, I will harken back to this lesson on the Sadducees' belief that there is no resurrection. Our challenge is not taking a passage, inferring from that passage, and then building a belief system that may not be true. If we make an inference about the sovereignty of God or about how our free will intersects and affects the sovereignty of God, and that inference is incorrect, then we may have a whole house of cards that come crashing down upon us.

And sometimes, we may have to admit that we can't figure out how everything works together because God has not told us. Sometimes we have to take what we read at face value and chalk it up to the power of God. Even though God has given us the ability to reason, there is no shame in saying, "I believe that God's purposes will always stand. I believe that God gave man free will. And I believe that God will not always get what He wants. And I still believe He is supremely sovereign." All of these statements are taught in Scripture, and nothing says we have to be able to fully understand things that may be too wonderful for us to understand.

To some, this may sound like a cop-out for an author. I get it. An author who has trouble backing up his point and says, "Well, you just have to have faith that my point is true," argues from a weak foundation. But sometimes, that foundation is the only correct foundation to stand on. There is no shame in saying that we don't understand how things work, but we believe it by faith.

***

The Lord is on His throne.
He is sovereign over all.
Choose to kneel before Him now,
Instead of kneeling as a conquered foe.
We either make a choice to kneel now,

or the choice will be made for us on Judgement Day.

***

The devil would have us look at the evil in the world, give up hope, and fall into despair with the direction away from God our society seems to be moving.

Jesus would have us lift up our eyes to see how ripe the fields are for harvest.

When despair starts to creep in, let's focus on the souls who are hungering for more than what this world can offer. Let's get out and feed them His Word that they are hungering for.

"Do you not say, 'There are yet four months, then comes the harvest'? Look, I tell you, lift up your eyes, and see that the fields are white for harvest." (John 4:35 ESV).

***

It's interesting that early Christians were often found guilty of being atheists because of their denials of other gods and their refusal to worship the emperors.

This shows how society will often define terms in a way to find fault in followers of Jesus while really being guilty of what they accuse us of being.

Case-in-point: We believe that Jesus is the only way to the Father and no one can come to the Father except through Him.

Our society accuses us of being exclusive and not being diverse.

But the truth is that we know that God opens the way to every man and woman to the Father, regardless of race, sex, economic level, or nationality.

True Christianity is diverse and inclusive because it is open to anyone who chooses Jesus.

But we will still be labeled as close-minded and exclusive.

I suppose that the early Christians could be considered atheists through the lens that society used the word, just like we might be considered exclusive and close-minded through the lens that our society uses the words.

But early Christians were also faithful believers in the one true God, just as we are part of a spiritual family that spans the globe, made up of men and women, rich and poor, and people from all races and nationalities.

We welcome all who bend the knee to King Jesus and submit to His rule, whomever you may be.

> "And Jesus came and said to them, "All authority in heaven and on earth has been given to me.
> Go therefore and make disciples of all nations, baptizing them in the name of the Father and of the Son and of the Holy Spirit,
> teaching them to observe all that I have commanded you. And behold, I am with you always, to the end of the age." (Matthew 28:18-20 ESV).

***

What an exciting thought that millions of people around the world are gathering to worship the Son of God and remember His death.

As we commune with Him, remember that His kingdom is gathering for this purpose all over the globe.

We do this today with a small number of people on earth, but the day is coming when we will gather around His throne with all His subjects and see Him with our eyes.

Faith will become sight.

***

Six days until Christmas.

We all have plans to meet with family, prepare feasts, and share gifts.

Some have plans with family to participate in annual festive events.

If King Jesus returned to earth before Christmas, would we be prepared, or is all of our preparation centered around a holiday which may or may not come?

Let us enjoy the holidays while always keeping our focus on being ready for our Lord's imminent return.

> "So then let us not sleep, as others do, but let us keep awake and be sober." (1 Thessalonians 5:6 ESV).

***

Is There A Little Naaman In Each Of Us?

When we read 2 Kings 5, we are introduced to a mighty general of the Syrian army, a man named Naaman. This man was mighty, as verse one says, "because by him the LORD had given victory to Syria." But there was a problem… he was a leper.

We know enough about this disease to know how devastating it could be to someone's life. It was painful and highly contagious. Most people were shunned and isolated. Yet, somehow, Naaman was a successful, highly honored man, despite suffering from this terrible condition.

The king of Syria thought enough of this mighty general to allow him to serve as commander of his army and even to send him to the enemy on the chance he might be healed.

> "And the king of Syria said, "Go now, and I will send a letter to the king of Israel." So he went, taking with him ten talents of silver, six thousand shekels of gold, and ten changes of clothing. And he brought the letter to the king of Israel, which read, "When this letter reaches you, know that I have sent to you Naaman my servant, that you may cure him of his leprosy." (2 Kings 5:5-6 ESV).

This was all because of an Israeli servant girl who told Naaman's wife about a prophet in Israel who could heal him. Well, Naaman found his way to this prophet and waited for a healing that could change the quality of his life instantly.

You know the story. Elisha sent his servant to tell Naaman to dip in the Jordan river seven times, and he'd be healed of his leprosy.

That's it. Nothing fancy or magnificent. Simply dip seven times in a dirty river far from home.

There would be no show, no waving of the hands, no ceremony fit for a mighty man of valor.

> "But Naaman was angry and went away, saying, "Behold, I thought that he would surely come out to me and stand and call upon the name of the LORD his God, and wave his hand over the place and cure the leper. Are not Abana and Pharpar, the rivers of Damascus, better than all the waters of Israel? Could I not wash in them and be clean?" So he turned and went away in a rage." (2 Kings 5:11-12 ESV).

Well, a couple of his servants calm him down with some simple advice:

> "But his servants came near and said to him, "My father, it is a great

word the prophet has spoken to you; will you not do it? Has he actually said to you, 'Wash, and be clean'?" (2 Kings 5:13 ESV).

And so this mighty man of valor humbles himself and dips seven times in a dirty river, just as God's prophet instructed him. The result? God cleansed Naaman of his leprosy and immediately transformed the quality of his life. Naaman goes on to do everything he can to show his undying gratitude for this act of grace from Israel's God.

But I wonder if there's a little bit of Naaman in each of us at times. Do we often look at what God asks of us and sometimes feel that what He's asking is beneath us?

Instead of a cup of cold water, do we seek to be given a banquet of food to share with those in need?

Instead of washing someone's feet, do we look for ways we can excuse ourselves from dirtying our hands in our service to others?

Instead of being immersed in baptism for the remission of sins, do we storm away in a rage because we think He should save us in a more theatrical manner?

Instead of repenting and asking our brother for forgiveness, do we wait for him to beg for our forgiveness? Or worse, do we cut him off with no chance in our hearts for reconciliation because he has wronged us?

I am ashamed when I find a little Naaman in my heart. The times when God tells me simply how I should conduct myself, and I huff and puff because what He's asking is not what I want to do. Sometimes I want to serve God my way so much that I am blind to see how He wants me to serve Him.

But no matter how much of a rage I fly into when God asks me to do something I don't want to do, the truth is the same truth that Naaman learned. Simply dipping seven times in a dirty river can change the quality of my life if that's what is asked of me.

When the Naaman inside of me starts to exert himself, I need to humble my heart and seek what the Lord would have me to do, and then trust that it can transform my life. God's ways are always best, and His instructions are always meant to transform my life if I give myself wholly to His will for me.

Is there a little Naaman in my life? Perhaps. But with God's grace and His help, hopefully, the Naaman in me that prevails is the one who finally submits in humility and dips seven times in a dirty river because that's what He has told me to do.

***

In my opinion, we are entering a Romans 14 time of the year. Whatever your disposition is toward the holidays, let's remember to abound in love and grace for one another.

This is a great opportunity to teach a world that thirsts for division how to love the way that Jesus loves.

> "By this all people will know that you are my disciples, if you have love for one another." (John 13:35 ESV).

***

What a joy to know that we may worship with people today who may not often think about God.

I pray that all of our hearts are touched with the good news of Jesus today.

***

He is coming back.

***

The Wonderful Lack Of Detail In The Parable Of The Good Samaritan

The parable of the Good Samaritan is one of the most beloved teachings of Jesus. In it, we learn the lesson of who our neighbor is. As we read it, the details that Jesus gives help us draw timeless lessons on how we should treat each other.

Sometimes, it's not the people we expect to be the compassionate ones who serve and sacrifice for others. Sometimes, it's the one we least expect, or worse, the ones our prejudices assume would not be good neighbors.

We are introduced to some interesting characters. At the story's beginning, we read about a man who was robbed and beaten nearly to death by robbers:

> "Jesus replied, "A man was going down from Jerusalem to Jericho,

and he fell among robbers, who stripped him and beat him and departed, leaving him half dead." (Luke 10:30 ESV).

Then, Jesus brings in the next two characters:

> "Now by chance a priest was going down that road, and when he saw him he passed by on the other side. So likewise a Levite, when he came to the place and saw him, passed by on the other side." (Luke 10:31-32 ESV).

And finally, we are introduced to the hero of the story, the one who Jesus teaches is the neighbor:

> "But a Samaritan, as he journeyed, came to where he was, and when he saw him, he had compassion.
> He went to him and bound up his wounds, pouring on oil and wine. Then he set him on his own animal and brought him to an inn and took care of him.
> And the next day he took out two denarii and gave them to the innkeeper, saying, 'Take care of him, and whatever more you spend, I will repay you when I come back.'" (Luke 10:33-35 ESV).

We draw some great conclusions from this parable, don't we? For instance, sometimes, the people who should be the ones who help are the ones who pass by, while the ones who we wouldn't give a second thought about end up being the ones who are the most compassionate toward others.

But the silence and lack of detail in the parable may speak as loud as what was said. For example, have we ever stopped and asked the question, "Why did the Priest and Levi pass by on the other side?" If you are like me, perhaps you think they didn't want to get their hands dirty helping a dying man, or perhaps they just didn't want to be bothered. This kind of person is easy to cast stones at and condemn. Certainly, we are not like these men.

But how would you feel if you found out that the Priest and Levi were on their way to a prominent synagogue where they were to meet an important VIP traveling to speak to them? What if hundreds of people were counting on them being there to make sure all the time and money spent planning for this great spiritual event didn't get wasted? Perhaps they sent others to follow up on the one who was robbed?

Or maybe the two were responding to a critical, time-sensitive crisis a member of the synagogue was having. Or we can think through a number of "legitimate" reasons that the Priest and Levi may have had to pass by on the other side. But casting them as uncaring and callous people makes it easier to see their evil while preventing us from seeing ourselves as the bad neighbor.

Neither was anything said about what was going on in the Samaritan's life. Did he have the spare time to help? Did he have an abundance of resources? Or did he have to use money meant for his family to help this man in terrible need? Did he miss an important appointment with a potential client to make the detour to the inn? Was the oil and wine he used on the man meant to be resources for his family? Jesus never gives us any details on his situation.

How often have we passed by on the other side rather than render help because we have "legitimate" reasons? Perhaps, we think, we need to focus our financial resources on our family or someone else. Or, perhaps we need to give our time and attention to someone more important to us at the moment. I'm sure if we think long enough, we will be able to come up with many ways to justify passing by on the other side when someone needs our help.

I don't know about you, but when I think about parables like these, I sometimes read into the silent details, things that make it easier for me to justify myself rather than see how the parable can transform me. I wonder how many other parables I have read into the silent details of things that justify me rather than things that help me become more of what Jesus wants me to be.

> "Which of these three, do you think, proved to be a neighbor to the man who fell among the robbers?" He said, "The one who showed him mercy." And Jesus said to him, "You go, and do likewise." (Luke 10:36-37 ESV).

***

Life points to one event: The judgment before Jesus
He is King and Lord
His words will be our judge
On that day, everything we do and say now will be our witness for or against us
Are we living our lives for His glory and service?
Or are we living our lives with little thought on how we should bring ourselves into submission to Him?

> "The one who rejects me and does not receive my words has a judge; the word that I have spoken will judge him on the last day." (John 12:48 ESV).

***

We are reaching the 2000 anniversary of the death of Jesus on the cross and His promised return.

Now is not the time to party while the Master is away (Matthew 24:48-51).

Now is not the time to stop preparing for His return (Matthew 25:1-13).

Now is not the time to stop working for the Master (Matthew 25:14-30).

Now is not the time to start thinking, "2000 years is a long time... Is He really coming back?"

> "knowing this first of all, that scoffers will come in the last days with scoffing, following their own sinful desires.
>
> They will say, "Where is the promise of his coming? For ever since the fathers fell asleep, all things are continuing as they were from the beginning of creation." (2 Peter 3:3-4 ESV).

Almost 2000 years have passed since Jesus was seated at His Father's right hand, clothed with power, glory, and honor.

The reason He has not returned in 2000 years is simple.

He is gracious.

He is loving.

He is merciful.

> "The Lord is not slow to fulfill his promise as some count slowness, but is patient toward you, not wishing that any should perish, but that all should reach repentance." (2 Peter 3:9 ESV).

But let us not be lulled into a false sense of security like the scoffers.

Let us not party while the Lord is away.

Let us not stop preparing for His imminent return.

Let us not stop laboring in His vineyard.

Because He IS coming back.

> "But the day of the Lord will come like a thief, and then the heavens will pass away with a roar, and the heavenly bodies will be burned up and dissolved, and the earth and the works that are done on it will be exposed." (2 Peter 3:10 ESV).

***

There has been a lot of talk about Big Tech and Government censorship lately.

When it comes to sounding the warnings and message of Jesus, they may mute, silence, or cancel us.

But they cannot mute, silence, or cancel the message.

If you are censored, or if I am censored,

The Lord has an army who will continue to sound out His words.

The good and honest hearts who seek Truth will always be able to find it.

***

Live today as though at any moment, the Father will whisper in the Lord's ear, "It's time... Go get your bride."

***

Happy New Year. 2023 is a gift to each of us from the patient and long-suffering Father. May 2023 draw each of us closer to Him.

***

We live in a society that is increasingly blurring the lines between right and wrong, absolutes and situations, standards and lawlessness. As we go through life, the Creator sets His will before us and calls us to Him.

We have a choice to make. Do we submit to Him and His will, or do we live unto ourselves? This fundamental decision we make will define who we are and what our destiny will be.

We were created to serve and dwell with the Creator forever. When we put that destiny in jeopardy through our own sins, our God became flesh, dwelt among us, and died for our sins so that He could redeem us and reconcile us back to the Father.

Jesus fixed what we broke. Yet the decision must be ours to reach out and accept what He has done for us. God will not impose His will upon us with force. He freely offers His grace.

But we will choose to love under His standard or live in lawlessness, seek out His absolute will for us or reject His will and apply situational ethics and justify ourselves with no thought of His word. We will choose to let Him define what is right and what is wrong, or we will change His definitions of right and wrong to justify how we want to live.

Our society is moving away from God and replacing His rule with its own. Let us all have a heart that submits to God, kneels before His Son, our King, and prepares for our rightful place at His feet for eternity.

If we cannot do that in this life, then we will be granted an eternity without Him to live with our lawlessness and with no gracious King to flow eternal blessings to us under His rule.

> "Woe to those who call evil good and good evil, who put darkness for light and light for darkness, who put bitter for sweet and sweet for bitter!
>
> Woe to those who are wise in their own eyes, and shrewd in their own sight!
>
> Woe to those who are heroes at drinking wine, and valiant men in mixing strong drink,
>
> who acquit the guilty for a bribe, and deprive the innocent of his right!" (Isaiah 5:20-23 ESV).

***

Banquets and Invitations

In Luke 14, Jesus speaks of banquets and invitations. In back-to-back illustrations, He speaks to us when we are the host and when we are the invitees. In each perspective, Jesus speaks to things He wants us to learn which are essential for us to internalize as His followers. These things make His kingdom different from the kingdoms of this world.

In verses 7-11, Jesus observes how, at a banquet, people jockey for the best seats and positions of honor. It must have been interesting to see Jesus watch the invitees make their grand entrances. I'm not sure that Jesus is really concerned about the seating arrangements as much as He is about the hearts of people who are swallowed up in pride so much that they feel they are better than others.

How disappointed the Master, who said we would be great by serving others, must have been to witness this shameful exhibition. This is why Jesus tells us not to seek the places of honor. By humbling ourselves, we will be exalted:

> "But when you are invited, go and sit in the lowest place, so that when

your host comes he may say to you, 'Friend, move up higher.' Then you will be honored in the presence of all who sit at table with you.

For everyone who exalts himself will be humbled, and he who humbles himself will be exalted." (Luke 14:10-11 ESV).

We should ask ourselves, "How do we react when we are in the presence of others who have a place of honor?" Do we subtly do things to ensure attention is on us, or are we content to let others take the seats of honor? If Jesus were with us in a social setting, what would He observe as we entered a banquet?

Then Jesus speaks to the man who invited Him to this banquet and tells him that he should not invite people who will simply return the favor by inviting him to their banquets. Instead:

"But when you give a feast, invite the poor, the crippled, the lame, the blind,
and you will be blessed, because they cannot repay you. For you will be repaid at the resurrection of the just." (Luke 14:13-14 ESV).

Jesus gives this admonition after watching people trying to outdo each other for the places of honor; but the poor, the crippled, the lame, and the blind would be humble and appreciative of the invitation. They wouldn't be the ones who sought the best seats or the ones who wanted to be seen by others. They wouldn't grab the places of honor.

So the attention shifts from the invitees to the host. Jesus wants the host to consider who he wants to invite to his banquet and why he wants these people to come to his party. Is he more concerned with putting together a "who's who" list for his banquet with the hopes that he will be on their lists when they throw a party, or is he more concerned with honoring the people who others dishonor? Followers of Jesus are cut from a different cloth from the rest of society.

And why should we take heed of Jesus' words? Because He has a banquet that we all want to be invited to. How thankful should we be that Jesus doesn't seek a "who's who" list for His banquet? Instead, He reaches out to sinners like you and me.

One person at the banquet is listening to all the things that Jesus is telling the host:

"When one of those who reclined at table with him heard these things, he said to him, "Blessed is everyone who will eat bread in the kingdom of God!" (Luke 14:15 ESV).

This opens the door for the last parable on banquets that Jesus teaches.

He talks about a man who threw a great banquet and invited all the usual "who's who" "A" listers. But the invitees all began to make excuses as to why they couldn't come.

Indeed, "Blessed is everyone who will eat bread in the kingdom of God!" The problem is that many of the people who the Lord will invite to His banquet don't want to be there. There is something more important to them, and so they make excuses. How did the host of the great banquet respond when the RSVPs came back, "Sorry, I can't make it to your banquet"?

> "So the servant came and reported these things to his master. Then the master of the house became angry and said to his servant, 'Go out quickly to the streets and lanes of the city, and bring in the poor and crippled and blind and lame.'" (Luke 14:21 ESV).

And so the man in the parable fills his banquet with the very people Jesus tells His host that he should invite to his banquets. And what is to be done with people who have more important things to do than to "eat bread in the kingdom of God?"

> "For I tell you, none of those men who were invited shall taste my banquet.'" (Luke 14:24 ESV).

Jesus gives all of these lessons simply by watching how the host and the invitees of the banquet He was at acted toward each other. How carefully should we guard our hearts against pride when we are in the position of hosting or being hosted? Who is it that we are trying to impress? What are we seeking from others when we serve?

This is what makes the servants of Jesus different from the people in the world. We serve in the same way Jesus serves.

***

What is it to know that God is sovereign in my life?

It's opening a pantry full of food, realizing that God has given it to me by His grace and that if He chooses, He can take it all away today before I eat another bite.

Knowing God is sovereign in my life means respecting His awesome power to give and take away, regardless of how unlikely it may seem to me.

Knowing God is sovereign in my life means that He can make the decisions to give and take away for His glory and good pleasure without having to explain Himself to me.

I must always trust my sovereign God, not only when I witness His goodness but knowing that His goodness is still there, even when I can't see or understand it.

Faith is that step I take when I cannot see with my eyes, but I know in my heart that God always maintains His sovereignty in all things.

> "But Elisha said, "Hear the word of the LORD: thus says the LORD, Tomorrow about this time a seah of fine flour shall be sold for a shekel, and two seahs of barley for a shekel, at the gate of Samaria."
>
> Then the captain on whose hand the king leaned said to the man of God, "If the LORD himself should make windows in heaven, could this thing be?" But he said, "You shall see it with your own eyes, but you shall not eat of it." (2 Kings 7:1-2 ESV).

***

What do we do with this verse?

Do we bow at the feet of Jesus and submit to Him as Lord, Creator, and the sovereign I AM?

If this verse means what it says, then fear and awe should fall upon us when we face the decision of what we do with Jesus.

The greatest decision we make will be what we do with this verse:

> "Jesus said to them, "Truly, truly, I say to you, before Abraham was, I am." (John 8:58 ESV).

***

John tells us that God preserved an inspired account of what happened to Jesus so that when we read, we would believe.

Reading the Word of God is how we build our faith. God doesn't zap faith into us.

Faith doesn't come supernaturally or irresistibly from God.

All who read can believe and have faith. No one is prevented, and no one is compelled.

But to have the faith that leads to salvation, we must spend time in the Word.

We do that by reading, or we do that by hearing.

We gain faith by bringing the Word into our hearts. It is our choice, and we must open the door of our hearts to receive it.

But if we neglect to hear or read, then the very things God provided for our faith cannot work in us.

When was the last time we were in the Word of God, whether reading or hearing?

If it's been a while, Satan can easily gather away the seeds that fall before they can take root.

Read, hear, and have faith.

> "Now Jesus did many other signs in the presence of the disciples, which are not written in this book;
>
> but these are written so that you may believe that Jesus is the Christ, the Son of God, and that by believing you may have life in his name." (John 20:30-31 ESV).

***

I am in the book of John in my daily Bible reading. John shows that Jesus is divine, coming down from heaven, having existed from the beginning with God.

John calls Him the Creator and says He is the only way to the Father.

John shows us men who worshiped Him while He never chastised them for doing so.

But John also shows us that Jesus obeys God the Father and is in submission to Him.

John shows us that Jesus serves men.

John shows us that Jesus seeks to do things that glorify the Father.

John shows us that Jesus extends mercy to those who, by their guilt, deserve condemnation.

John shows that Jesus forgives and extends grace to others.

What should this mean to me?

If Jesus, who is worthy of praise, worship, glory, and honor...

Obeys, serves, glorifies God the Father, extends mercy to others, forgives, and extends grace when grace is not deserved,

Who am I to refuse to do the things to God and my neighbor that my Lord and King has done?

> "For I have given you an example, that you also should do just as I have done to you." (John 13:15 ESV).

***

I am attending our BLAST studies that Campbell Rd church of Christ is hosting this weekend. Our Elders are part of the teaching.

Breck Lovinggood just made a statement that I find profound. Breck was given the topic "Tell of the years of His Labor."

Breck pointed out that serving in His role as Savior, Jesus' labor was in transforming people. We see it as a result of the fall of man in Genesis 3, and everything He did was to transform what was broken.

What wisdom in this observation about the years of His labor.

***

Terry Bennett reminded us yesterday that God made us in His image the way He wanted us to be. That means we have value.

We live in a world that tempts us to see ourselves as worthless, but God gave us an unspeakable gift in Jesus that proves we have more value than we can ever imagine.

As parents, teaching our children the value they have to God is the counter to the lie of Satan that causes much of the negative self-talk we all struggle with from time to time.

Thanks for sharing your wisdom, Terry.

***

I wonder what it would have been like to be a Jew in the days of Jesus.

If I saw Him heal, feed the multitude, or raise the dead, would that be enough for me to go against my Jewish leaders who hated Him?

Would I marvel but slowly distance myself from Him when it became apparent that I'd have to take an unpopular stand to follow Him?

Or would I quietly dismiss Him and hold on to my life as I knew it? Would I continue to attend synagogue and forget His call to me?

Today, Jesus calls to me. It's an unpopular call that will cause me to make a sacrifice to follow Him.

Today, will I marvel at the transforming, living Word but slowly distance myself from Him when it becomes apparent I'll have to take an unpopular stand?

Or will I quietly dismiss Him and hold on to my life as I know it? Will I continue to live my life and forget His call to me?

We all face the same choices when presented with the living Word of God.

***

Simple choices we make that will determine how hard or how easy our walk with Jesus will be:

Do we choose to spend time with godly people outside of public worship?

Do we spend time in His word daily?

Do we pray throughout the day?

Do we perform acts of service to others?

Do we look for ways to build up someone rather than tear them down with our tongues?

If we are purposeful with these choices, then our walk will be easier. If we are not, we make our walk harder each day than it needs to be. God equips us with everything we need if we only listen to Him and follow His wisdom.

***

What would you think if I told you I planned on dropping by your house soon without warning?

What would you do?

Would you worry and be filled with anxiety because I did not tell you when I was coming to visit you?

Would you stop what you're doing and make preparations for my eventual visit?

What would you do, what would you think, how would you feel if I told you I was going to visit you at any time?

Most likely, you wouldn't give it a second thought. You probably wouldn't go out of your way to accommodate me, especially if I didn't tell you when I was coming.

In the big scheme of things, I'm sure I am not important enough to you to cause you to center your time and energy on making preparations for my eventual arrival.

The real question is, do we treat the eventual return of Jesus the same way we'd treat the unexpected, eventual visit of someone like me?

I understand that I'm not worthy of people rearranging their lives in preparation for meeting me when my imminent visit comes without warning...

But do we treat Jesus as unworthy in the same way?

***

Patience With God

We live in a world that is increasingly determined to get what it wants right now. We no longer have to wait weeks for packages to arrive. Most will be delivered in 2 days, and some will deliver in hours.

If we're hungry, we can find food 24/7 to satisfy any appetite. The Internet allows us to get instant entertainment and instant gratification, to talk in real-time to someone, by video, on the other side of the globe, and to engage in the darkest sins instantly and in the privacy of our own homes.

For good or bad, we can do much of what we want in an instant. While the conveniences of instant gratification can make our lives easier, it can also help us to develop a short attention span. If we can't get what we want now, we can move on to the next thing that captivates our interests.

Patience is a virtue that many may no longer deem relevant. But God uses patience and develops it in us for our benefit. Patience requires trust and faith. What we can't get now teaches us to trust. Waiting can build character while we deny ourselves and still persevere.

When Moses was 40 years old, he thought he would be Israel's savior from God, as Stephen tells us in his sermon:

> "He supposed that his brothers would understand that God was giving them salvation by his hand, but they did not understand." (Acts 7:25 ESV).

Yet Moses would have to wait another 40 years before God would call him to be Israel's savior and lead them from Egyptian bondage to the promised land:

> "Now when forty years had passed, an angel appeared to him in the wilderness of Mount Sinai, in a flame of fire in a bush." (Acts 7:30 ESV).

When most men would be contemplating retirement, or more likely, deep into it, Moses was just about to embark upon his most amazing adventure as an eighty-year-old man. He became Israel's savior in God's time, not his time.

And we know what Abraham had to endure for the birth of his promised son, Isaac. Twenty-five years passed before this hundred-year-old man became a father. But during the waiting, Abraham learned to trust in God, even when he didn't understand how God would deliver on his promise. And Abraham never gave up believing God would be true to His word.

And yet, we are often like Saul, aren't we? Samuel told the king to wait seven days for him to come and sacrifice to the Lord before going into battle against the Philistines. But the people became afraid and began to desert Saul.

On the cusp of having the patience that God demanded, Saul instead took things into his own hands and offered the sacrifice himself:

> "He waited seven days, the time appointed by Samuel. But Samuel did not come to Gilgal, and the people were scattering from him. So Saul said, "Bring the burnt offering here to me, and the peace offerings." And he offered the burnt offering." (1 Samuel 13:8-9 ESV).

If Saul only had a little more patience and had put his trust in the Lord when things looked bleak, he would have benefited from the rewards patience produces. But instead, moments later, Samuel arrives and asks, "What have you done?" (vs. 11).

After making excuses, Samuel tells the king what his lack of patience would cost him:

> "And Samuel said to Saul, "You have done foolishly. You have not kept the command of the LORD your God, with which he commanded you. For then the LORD would have established your kingdom over Israel forever.
> But now your kingdom shall not continue. The LORD has sought out a man after his own heart, and the LORD has commanded him to be prince over his people, because you have not kept what the LORD commanded you." (1 Samuel 13:13-14 ESV).

As we look at these men and their experiences with patience, it's important for us to remember a few things as we endure or struggle with patience ourselves.

1. Serving God often requires faith that we learn when we have to wait. When we don't get the promised son now or become the savior at age 40, we learn that God is still God and His promises are still true. And when we refuse to take things into our own hands when life gets scary, our faith will make us stronger, and we will grow closer to our God.
2. Cultivating a godly life often requires years of planting and tending. To become the person we want to be, the person conformed to the

image of God's dear Son (Romans 8:29), we need to let Him make His impressions upon us through the experiences He sends as we put His living Word into our lives and live it.
3. God wants us to be people who learn how to endure. This is where our society will make it harder on us. Becoming godly doesn't happen by taking a pill or placing an order online. It takes work, determination, dedication, and resilience when we stumble. Endurance doesn't happen overnight; rather, it's a long road traveled by putting one foot in front of the other, over and over and over. Endurance happens when we realize that we are not spinning our wheels or missing out but that we are making progress in our walk with Jesus every day.

Patience is often something we long to have while we hate the things we have to endure to get it. But God is a rewarder of those who put their trust in Him, even when we have to wait 25 years, 40 years, or even a lifetime. Patience and endurance demonstrate to God that we believe Him no matter what is, or is not, going on in our lives. We will always wait on Him.

"And let us not grow weary of doing good, for in due season we will reap, if we do not give up." (Galatians 6:9 ESV).

***

It's January 18th, 2023, at 5:35am.
What if the Father is ready to send the Son back to earth at 1:45 pm today?
How would you spend the next 8 hours?
Are you ready to kneel before the King in 8 hours?
One day, 8 hours will be all we have.

"Behold, he is coming with the clouds, and every eye will see him, even those who pierced him, and all tribes of the earth will wail on account of him. Even so. Amen.
"I am the Alpha and the Omega," says the Lord God, "who is and who was and who is to come, the Almighty." (Revelation 1:7-8 ESV).

***

Giving thanks to God is an act of submission to His sovereignty.

We thank Him because we know what we thank Him for is given by Him, for all blessings flow from Him.

Inherent in this is the understanding that, as our sovereign God, He can also withhold blessings if He chooses.

We eat today only because God gives us our daily bread.

We work today only because God gives us work.

We live today only because God gives us breath.

We may not always get what we want when we want it, but when we do, it is from a sovereign God.

> "For although they knew God, they did not honor him as God or give thanks to him, but they became futile in their thinking, and their foolish hearts were darkened." (Romans 1:21 ESV).

***

Let us not let anyone lead us astray.

Salvation is not found in any church.

Salvation is not found in any creed.

Salvation is not found in any teacher.

Salvation is only found in Jesus.

When we are saved in Him, let us seek His word, earnestly strive to read it, and let it live in our hearts.

It will guide our speech.

It will guide our actions.

It will enable our continual walk with Him.

> "And there is salvation in no one else, for there is no other name under heaven given among men by which we must be saved." (Acts 4:12 ESV).

***

This isn't meant to be a political statement,

But it seems crazy that there are people who are more concerned about the potential return of Donald Trump to Twitter- whether for or against it-

Then they are concerned about King Jesus' imminent return to the earth.

***

One thing I find amazing and comforting is that the Lord will wipe away all tears from our eyes when we get to heaven.

> "He will wipe away every tear from their eyes, and death shall be no more, neither shall there be mourning, nor crying, nor pain anymore, for the former things have passed away." (Revelation 21:4 ESV).

No pain.
No Sorrows.
No death.
But even more amazing: we can grieve God, who lives in heaven.

> "And do not grieve the Holy Spirit of God, by whom you were sealed for the day of redemption." (Ephesians 4:30 ESV).

Imagine... God loves us so much that He will wipe away tears from the same people who grieve Him, whose throne is in heaven, so that we may never grieve again.
That's grace.
That's selflessness.
That's love with no limits.

***

In addition to worshipping our God this Lord's day, what can we do to:
Glorify His name?
Confess His Son before men?
Serve our neighbor?
Encourage a brother?
Reconcile a broken relationship?
Only the Kingdom of God can accomplish these things. The kingdoms of men have rulers who lord over their subjects.

> "But Jesus called them to him and said, "You know that the rulers of the Gentiles lord it over them, and their great ones exercise authority over them.
>
> It shall not be so among you. But whoever would be great among you must be your servant,
>
> and whoever would be first among you must be your slave,

even as the Son of Man came not to be served but to serve, and to give his life as a ransom for many." (Matthew 20:25-28 ESV).

***

What was it that Paul taught Felix about Jesus?
He taught Felix about righteousness.
He taught Felix about self-control.
He taught Felix about the resurrection.
When we wonder what to speak to others about when we share the story of Jesus with them, these are wonderful things for us to share too.
Teach people what is right-living according to the Word of God.
Teach them repentance and the need to live a moral life rather than continuing to pursue evil habits and manners.
Teach them of the coming resurrection and judgment of Jesus.
How they respond is not within our power.
We simply teach and then turn the situation over to Jesus and the person we teach.

"And as he reasoned about righteousness and self-control and the coming judgment, Felix was alarmed and said, "Go away for the present. When I get an opportunity I will summon you." (Acts 24:25 ESV).

***

How Can A Loving God Send People To Hell?

A question I often hear is, "How can a loving God send people to hell?" To many people, it doesn't seem fair that we can be punished for eternity in torment because of how we lived our lives in what is a blip compared to eternity. Does the punishment really fit the crime, or are we at the mercy of an intolerant God whose anger is out of control when He doesn't get His way or when people cross Him?

How is it fair that a powerful God can punish the "good" people who may not be perfect but don't commit sins against others like stealing, murder, or committing predatory acts of all kinds? How can this be the way that God determines the eternal destiny of people?

I understand how we can look at punishment this way. Depending on how we frame it, we can easily conclude that God really won't punish people for eternity or if He will, then He is not the kind of God that we would want to worship. Isn't this the conclusion many arrive at when considering heaven and hell?

May I suggest that this isn't how we should frame the discussion of heaven and hell, reward and punishment? The way we just laid out doesn't represent the reality of what the Bible teaches. Heaven and hell isn't about a grossly unfair form of justice and reward. In fact, I put forth for your consideration that what the Bible teaches about hell and our judgment magnifies God's great love for us and how He will literally sacrifice the most precious thing He has to keep us from going there.

First things first... The Bible indeed teaches that many will be sentenced to hell for an eternity on the Day of Judgment. In fact, Jesus spends much more time teaching about hell than He does about heaven. Consider these verses:

> "Then he will say to those on his left, 'Depart from me, you cursed, into the eternal fire prepared for the devil and his angels. ...
> And these will go away into eternal punishment, but the righteous into eternal life." (Matthew 25:41, 46 ESV).

And

> "And you, Capernaum, will you be exalted to heaven? You will be brought down to Hades. For if the mighty works done in you had been done in Sodom, it would have remained until this day. But I tell you that it will be more tolerable on the day of judgment for the land of Sodom than for you." (Matthew 11:23-24 ESV).

And

> "while the sons of the kingdom will be thrown into the outer darkness. In that place there will be weeping and gnashing of teeth." (Matthew 8:12 ESV).

So, Jesus indeed teaches that many will be condemned to an eternal hell. In fact, He says that there will be many "religious" people who will end up there as well"

> "Not everyone who says to me, 'Lord, Lord,' will enter the kingdom of heaven, but the one who does the will of my Father who is in heaven.

On that day many will say to me, 'Lord, Lord, did we not prophesy in your name, and cast out demons in your name, and do many mighty works in your name?'

And then will I declare to them, 'I never knew you; depart from me, you workers of lawlessness." (Matthew 7:21-23 ESV).

So, what are we to make of this? Can a loving, good God really send people to hell for eternity?

May I reframe the question and circumstance in a way I believe more accurately presents the situation we all face? I don't think asking, "How can a loving God send people to hell?" accurately reflect the reality of our perilous condition. You see, God isn't waiting as an angry, jilted supreme being Who is ready to enact His vengeance and ensure we get what's coming to us. Rather, God is a loving being who earnestly desires that not one of us perish.

"The Lord is not slow to fulfill his promise as some count slowness, but is patient toward you, not wishing that any should perish, but that all should reach repentance." (2 Peter 3:9 ESV).

And

"This is good, and it is pleasing in the sight of God our Savior, who desires all people to be saved and to come to the knowledge of the truth." (1 Timothy 2:3-4 ESV).

And

"Say to them, As I live, declares the Lord GOD, I have no pleasure in the death of the wicked, but that the wicked turn from his way and live; turn back, turn back from your evil ways, for why will you die, O house of Israel?" (Ezekiel 33:11 ESV).

All of these passages tell us that God is not a mean, vindictive supreme Being who is waiting to fling mortals into hell if they step out of line or cross Him. These passages, and more, paint the picture of a God who truly loves us and wants us all to be saved and that no one be condemned to eternal hellfire as punishment.

But here is our reality. Here is the proper way to frame our current condition.

"as it is written: "None is righteous, no, not one; ... for all have sinned and fall short of the glory of God," (Romans 3:10, 23 ESV).

And

"I was once alive apart from the law, but when the commandment came, sin came alive and I died." (Romans 7:9 ESV).

These verses and others teach us that we are all under the condemnation of spiritual death because we all have sinned. It's not that Jesus will judge good people as unworthy and send them to hell. We are already under that condemnation because of our sins.

In fact, if it were not for the sacrifice that Jesus made on the cross, we all would be staring at a death sentence on the Day of Judgment. But the Father loved us so much that He was not willing to give up on us and resign us to the condemnation that we deserve.

"For God so loved the world, that he gave his only Son, that whoever believes in him should not perish but have eternal life." (John 3:16 ESV).

You see, the question isn't, "How can a loving God send people to hell?"
We are all already headed there because of our sins and the choices we made. We are dead men walking.
The question is, "How can a loving God condemn men to hell with no way, no choice, no possibility of breaking free of the condemnation we deserve?"
The answer: "He didn't."

"but God shows his love for us in that while we were still sinners, Christ died for us." (Romans 5:8 ESV).

If Jesus sentences us to hell on the Day of Judgement, it's not because He doesn't love us or because He is being unfair or overly harsh. He is simply proclaiming the condemnation we are already under because of our sins.
Jesus has given us everything we need to avoid the judgment we deserve and the condemnation we are already under. He longs for us, He pleads with us, and He knocks at the door, begging us to accept His salvation.
Where we spend eternity will depend on our choice to receive Him and His way of escape. But if we reject Him and choose to stay in our condemned state, that is on us, not God.

**

In my daily Bible reading, I'm in Acts. An interesting and comforting observation is in reading the messages that Paul preached about Jesus.

His messages were not deep word studies or a dive into theological ideas.

They were simple messages of Jesus and what He did.

Of Jesus and what He offers to us.

They were messages that gave simple instructions to believe and be baptized.

Perhaps, sometimes we make evangelism much more difficult than it needs to be.

Perhaps we fear evangelism because we have greater expectations of ourselves than Jesus has of us.

Can I tell people the story of Jesus?

Can I let the Word do its job and find the good and honest hearts?

Can I let go of my expectations and trust in the power of God's word?

This changes our experience with evangelism and frees us from unrealistic expectations, doesn't it?

Let's just tell people the story of Jesus, just like Paul did.

If a man who writes difficult things preaches in such a simplistic manner when he shares the good news of Jesus,

Then why would we want to put an undue burden on ourselves when we share the gospel?

***

"I tell you, on the day of judgment people will give account for every careless word they speak," (Matthew 12:36 ESV).

I fear that this most likely also refers to every word we post on social media and every comment we author.

***

Life is too short to hold grudges.
Don't carry them with you into Judgement Day.
It will come when we least expect it, as a thief in the night.

***

Job made a covenant with his eyes not to look upon a woman to prevent him from lusting and sinning against God.

"I have made a covenant with my eyes; how then could I gaze at a virgin?" (Job 31:1 ESV).

What other covenants could we make as well? Perhaps...

A covenant with our hands not to remain idle so we can use them for useful things instead of vain things that produce no value and waste the time God has given us?

A covenant with our feet not to walk to places that Christians shouldn't be instead of places where God is worshiped and honored and places where we can help those in need?

A covenant with our mind to think on things that will make us spiritually stronger rather than things that let blasphemies and the garbage of the world into our hearts?

A covenant with our mouths to say things that encourage and edify rather than things that tear down and discourage?

What other covenants would we be wise in making today?

***

I finished the book of Acts in my daily Bible reading. This time through, I had an observation I had never considered before.

In Acts, we see Paul's conversion account on the Road to Damascus recited three times...

1. When Luke recounts the event to Theophilus in Acts 9.
2. When Paul defends himself to the people in Jerusalem after being arrested in the Temple in Acts 22.
3. And before king Agrippa in Acts 26.

In each case, the account of the conversion is to set up the authority by which Paul will preach. The things he teaches are based on Jesus and He being the Messiah and the resurrected and exalted King.

When we teach the Word to others, this must be the basis of our appeal. It must start with Jesus.

We don't make our appeal based on church doctrine.

We don't make our appeal based on family religion.

We don't make our appeal based on human reasoning.

When I read Acts, it seems to me that our appeal should start with Jesus, who He is, and what He has done.

Maybe I need to make a better point of mentioning what Jesus has done for me in my conversion to Him... my "testimony," if you will, as Paul did.

It all begins and ends with Jesus. That is the basis on which people should accept or reject my testimony and evangelism.

Just like it was with Paul in the book of Acts.

***

I'm in Romans in my Daily Bible reading. It's not an easy book, but it is not an overly complicated one, either. Reading it brings hope and encouragement.

For example, in Romans 5, we see that through one man, death entered the world, and through one man, life came to all men.

> "For if, because of one man's trespass, death reigned through that one man, much more will those who receive the abundance of grace and the free gift of righteousness reign in life through the one man Jesus Christ." (Romans 5:17 ESV).

And because of this, men were made sinners through Adam's disobedience, and men were made righteous through Jesus' obedience.

> "For as by the one man's disobedience the many were made sinners, so by the one man's obedience the many will be made righteous." (Romans 5:19 ESV).

So, what is the wonderful message Paul is preaching?

Because Adam sinned, the consequences of sin passed into the world. The paradise in Eden, where man and God walked together, was destroyed. The world that was made to serve man was corrupted because of sin and was cursed by God.

Access to the Tree of Life of taken away from man. Creation was broken because of the sin of one man, and because of one man, Adam, sin entered the world, and all of his descendants would live in a world where sinned dwelled.

But the good news is that God did not leave us at the mercy of a sin-stained world. Just as sin entered the world through one man, One man would also bring justification from sin.

> "Therefore, as one trespass led to condemnation for all men, so one act of righteousness leads to justification and life for all men." (Romans 5:18 ESV).

Through Jesus, God has fixed what man broke. God made that terrible sacrifice by sending His Son to be the propitiation for sin.

We now have a hope and an avenue by which to pursue life and to pursue God. Even in a world where sin still reigns, through one Man who conquered sin, we find victory and life through Jesus.

Sin can no longer keep us from God. Fellowship with the Creator has been restored.

Praise God for His unspeakable love!

***

What Went Through Saul's Mind When He Was Blind?

The apostle Paul went from being one of the most ardent opponents of the early church to one of its most staunch leaders. In doing so, he gave up everything. He was well-respected and yielded authority within the Jewish nation and religion. But when he converted to Jesus, he lost everything and counted it as rubbish.

We are first introduced to Paul (his Roman name) as Saul (his Jewish name). Saul appears in the New Testament by name in Acts 7. His name is mentioned after the Jewish people argue with Stephen over his preaching of Jesus. Stephen gives his defense, and they stone him, laying their garments at the feet of Saul, who gave his consent to the stoning of Stephen.

> "Then they cast him out of the city and stoned him. And the witnesses laid down their garments at the feet of a young man named Saul." (Acts 7:58 ESV).

But the argument with Stephen started before his defense. In Chapter 6 we read,

> "Then some of those who belonged to the synagogue of the Freedmen (as it was called), and of the Cyrenians, and of the Alexandrians, and of those from Cilicia and Asia, rose up and disputed with Stephen." (Acts 6:9 ESV).

Paul was a Jew from Cilicia. He would have been one of the men who argued with Stephen even after the Spirit, through Luke, tells us:

> "And Stephen, full of grace and power, was doing great wonders and signs among the people." (Acts 6:8 ESV).

Imagine, the man who would become one of the strongest defenders of Jesus and would suffer more than most, argued with a preacher who was doing great wonders and signs. Yet, in the end, the people laid their garments at his feet when they stoned the man Saul believed was a blasphemer.

This was a turning point for Saul. No more would he sit idly by as this sect continued to preach Jesus as God and Messiah. He made it his personal mission to destroy these people and defend the one true God of Israel.

> "And Saul approved of his execution. And there arose on that day a great persecution against the church in Jerusalem, and they were all scattered throughout the regions of Judea and Samaria, except the apostles.
>
> Devout men buried Stephen and made great lamentation over him.
>
> But Saul was ravaging the church, and entering house after house, he dragged off men and women and committed them to prison." (Acts 8:1-3 ESV).

We learn later from Ananias that word of Saul's bloodlust against the Christians spread even beyond Israel (Acts 9:13-14). In fact, it wasn't enough for Saul to confine his mission to cleanse the land of these blasphemers,

> "But Saul, still breathing threats and murder against the disciples of the Lord, went to the high priest and asked him for letters to the synagogues at Damascus, so that if he found any belonging to the Way, men or women, he might bring them bound to Jerusalem." (Acts 9:1-2 ESV).

And it was on the road to Damascus where the Lord Jesus appeared in person to Saul. We know the story. A blinding light appeared, and Jesus revealed himself to Saul. He told Saul to go to Damascus and he would be told what to do. When Jesus left, Saul was blind.

For three days, he waited for Ananias to come to him. For three days, he remained blind. That's a long time for him to think about what he had done. He was the catalyst for murder, persecution, and ultimately blasphemy against the Messiah he had been waiting for.

What do you suppose when through his mind during the three days of blindness? We don't know for sure because we're not told. However, we know some things...

We know he persecuted the disciples with a clear conscience, believing he was obeying God.

Jesus even said,

> "They will put you out of the synagogues. Indeed, the hour is coming when whoever kills you will think he is offering service to God." (John 16:2 ESV).

Could there be anyone who exemplifies this verse more than Saul?

We know he came face-to-face with Jesus and the truth about himself and his relationship with Jesus. Do you suppose he wrestled with godly sorrow in the three days of blindness as he played his sins over and over in his mind, having been told by Jesus that he was persecuting Him?

In his blindness, did he wonder, as the people on the day of Pentecost wondered, "What shall I do?" For three days, he wrestled with his sins and the reality of who he was and who Jesus was.

Then came a time to make a decision. When his blindness left and he could see, Saul heard the Gospel. Ananias told him how to obey. How did the three days of blind contemplation affect him?

He repented and submitted to Jesus in baptism.

He didn't argue with the man Jesus sent to tell him what to do. He didn't ask, "Why baptism?" Nor did he become so overcome with godly sorrow that he felt God could never forgive his sins, as bad as he was.

He simply obeyed the Gospel as Ananias taught him.

If we have not called upon the name of the Lord and have been baptized for the remission of sins, then we are contemplating something in our spiritual blindness today.

Have we been convicted of our sins?

Do we see our need for a Savior?

Do we cry out, "What should I do?"

Is our heart ready to repent?

If you are wrestling in your spiritual blindness with your sins, I leave you with the words of Ananias to Saul,

> "And now why do you wait? Rise and be baptized and wash away your sins, calling on his name." (Acts 22:16 ESV).

**

The angels told us that we are closer than ever to the return of Jesus, our King.

Get ready.

It's going to happen.

"And while they were gazing into heaven as he went, behold, two men stood by them in white robes, and said, "Men of Galilee, why do you stand looking into heaven? This Jesus, who was taken up from you into heaven, will come in the same way as you saw him go into heaven." (Acts 1:10-11 ESV).

***

As we study the word of God, let's use the reason that God endowed us with to think through the things the Spirit leaves us.

Our ability to reason is a gift of God that is part of the way we are made in His image.

But it is incumbent upon us to be aware of when we are employing our reason as we study.

The danger is not in using our reasoning, but in treating our conclusions and inferences as equal to the word of God.

It's good when we make a conclusion based on what we read. That shows we are striving to apply the word in our hearts. But we must always be willing to examine our conclusions.

Whether we eat meat offered to idols or whether we abstain can both be reasoned from how we apply God's word.

But to state that my reasoning and conclusions are elevated to God's word is a dangerous and presumptuous usurping of God's authority.

"Food will not commend us to God. We are no worse off if we do not eat, and no better off if we do." (1 Corinthians 8:8 ESV).

We should be more concerned about not letting our inferences and conclusions hurt our brothers.

"But take care that this right of yours does not somehow become a stumbling block to the weak." (1 Corinthians 8:9 ESV).

It is one thing to temper our conclusions, inferences, and reasoning for the sake of our brothers. It is another thing to elevate our conclusions, inferences, and reasoning to be equal to God.

If we condemn what God has not condemned or if we require what God has not required, we will have to give account to the author of the word on judgment day for our presumption.

> "This people honors me with their lips, but their heart is far from me; in vain do they worship me, teaching as doctrines the commandments of men." (Matthew 15:8-9 ESV).

Let us always approach God's word with the reverence and honor it deserves and not debase it by elevating our reasoning to be equal to God's.

***

It's sad that in our advertisements, we have normalized sin so much that it's becoming innocuous.

I used to worry about the movies and television shows I watched where sex, language, blasphemies, and violence were present.

Now, Satan has figured out how to get his evil into my mind in a 30-second commercial while I'm only paying half attention.

The devil is shrewd and opportunistic. If he can't get us to spend 90 minutes with him, he'll take 30 seconds at a time.

It's never been more important to guard our hearts and minds from sin.

It may take more work now that we have to guard against even 30-second commercials found on television and online,

But the alternative can affect our hearts before we realize what just happened.

> "Keep your heart with all vigilance, for from it flow the springs of life." (Proverbs 4:23 ESV).

***

The same Messiah that told the Samaritan woman that the time is coming when those who worship God will worship Him in spirit told her we will also worship Him in truth.

If we worship in spirit but not the truth, or in truth but not spirit, then we are not worshiping God as Jesus said we should.

The living truth will make us alive with its transforming power. Let's not be bewitched into worshiping God in spirit or truth only.

Let us worship God the way Jesus said we would when the time came because this is what our Father wants.

The time has come, and now is.

"But the hour is coming, and is now here, when the true worshipers will worship the Father in spirit and truth, for the Father is seeking such people to worship him. God is spirit, and those who worship him must worship in spirit and truth." (John 4:23-24 ESV).

***

God's sovereignty is amazing and beyond what we can ever imagine.
For example, when God wants to exercise His sovereignty over a nation, He has more arrows in His quiver than we can imagine to accomplish His purposes.
He doesn't have to bring in another nation to conquer in order to exercise His sovereignty.
Sometimes He may choose to just make a nation's leaders stupid and therefore make stupid decisions.

"therefore, behold, I will again do wonderful things with this people, with wonder upon wonder; and the wisdom of their wise men shall perish, and the discernment of their discerning men shall be hidden." (Isaiah 29:14 ESV).

As an American, I'm not sure which is the more scary way God can exert His sovereignty.

***

Interesting historical note...
Annas, the patriarchal High Priest of his family, was in his 1st to 3rd year as High Priest when Jesus was 12 years old and impressed the leaders in Jerusalem (depending in what year Jesus was born).
Annas served as High Priest from 6 AD to 15 AD. All five of his sons eventually served as High Priest, as did his son-in-law Caiaphas.
It is very likely that one of the people Jesus impressed at age twelve in the Temple was the patriarch of the family that would put him to death by crying out to the Romans, "Crucify Him!" 2 decades later.

"After three days they found him in the temple, sitting among the teachers, listening to them and asking them questions. And all who heard him were amazed at his understanding and his answers." (Luke 2:46-47 ESV).

***

Today is the Lord's Day.
Wouldn't it be wonderful if we could worship together and then greet Jesus together as He returns today, His day?

***

Paul is an amazing convert. His life was 100% converted to the Messiah he once persecuted.
After all he lost for the sake of Jesus, he said this to the brethren at Philippi:

> "I am hard pressed between the two. My desire is to depart and be with Christ, for that is far better. But to remain in the flesh is more necessary on your account." (Philippians 1:23-24 ESV).

He thought it far better to be with Jesus.
He wanted to be with the One he once despised, fought against, and rejected.
I pray that no matter what our past, our present can also say to depart and be with Jesus is far better than anything we have today.

***

The Silence Of Jesus

> "and like a sheep that before its shearers is silent, so he opened not his mouth." (Isaiah 53:7b ESV).

The contrast between Isaiah and John couldn't be more pronounced. Isaiah prophesied about a gentle, silent servant who refused to defend

Himself when the time came. John talked about Jesus being the embodied Word.

Jesus, Who commanded light to come into existence and commanded souls to return to their bodies, stood in silence when the High Priest and Pilate questioned Him before His execution. It is unimaginable that the One who could speak the universe into existence by His word chose to remain silent when His word could have put a stop to the greatest injustice of all time.

Why?

Why did my Savior, like a sheep before its shearers, refuse to open His mouth?

Why did He stay on the cross when men clucked their tongues and wagged their heads saying, "Come off the cross and we'll believe You!"

When the power of His word could do all that He pleased, why did our Savior remain silent?

When we are forced to think about the answer to that question, we are led face-to-face with our own corruption, our own need, and our own helplessness. Our sins caused Jesus to remain silent as evil men did their worst to their God and Creator.

We had lost paradise. We had lost fellowship with God. We had all fallen under condemnation because we all chose to sin and rebel against God. There was only one penalty due our error.

We were helpless and needed a Savior. We needed someone who could pay the price to redeem us back to the Father and offer a gift so precious it could wipe the guilt of sin away, leaving us pure and innocent before the Father.

When Jesus knew the flogging was coming and His back and sides would be split open and his muscles and bones would be exposed when leather straps with embedded rocks and bones tore into His flesh, He remained silent.

When Jesus knew His face would be disfigured when vile men blindfolded Him and beat Him, He remained silent.

When Jesus knew that evil men would press a crown of thorns into His head and beat it into His scalp with the reed they gave Him as a mock scepter, He remained silent.

When they put Him on trial and demanded He give a defense, He remained silent.

When they placed the nails on His hands and feet, drew back the mallet, and pinned Him to the tree, He remained silent.

One word from Him could have called 12 legions of angels.

One word from Him could have opened the ground to swallow His tormentors.

One word from Him could have caused the people He created to cease from existing.

> "and like a sheep that before its shearers is silent, so he opened not his mouth." (Isaiah 53:7b ESV).

Why?
Because He saw you and me as He remained silent. He saw us and loved us. He knew that the awful deed had to be done, and He was willing to do it silently so He could become the sacrifice that appeased the Father's wrath and redeemed us back to Himself.

His silence wasn't a silence of weakness, but one of incredible strength.

The Creator of the universe, the sovereign God of all, the great I AM, stayed His mighty power and remained silent because of a love for you and me that we may never be able to truly understand.

Our sins led Him to the cross so His blood could cleanse us and give us hope. And the Word became flesh so He could face the day when He would be silent for you and for me.

***

Free will is a wonderful gift from a sovereign God who made us in His image.

It is true power and sovereignty to create another being, endow him with true free will, and still maintain Your sovereignty.

We often want to give God a crutch to help Him maintain His sovereignty as we consider our free will and how He accomplishes all His purposes in the presence of our free will.

But it's not God who needs a crutch. We are the ones who can never understand the depth and riches of God.

Let's not trip over our inability to fully understand God and project our inadequacies upon Him.

> "But Jesus answered them, "You are wrong, because you know neither the Scriptures nor the power of God." (Matthew 22:29 ESV).

***

In my daily Bible reading, I read through the letters Paul wrote to Timothy and Titus and the letter he wrote to Philemon.

Reading these letters as a whole, we see a few things that may be lost when we dissect his letters line by line in our studies.

These are some of my takeaways.

1. Paul was concerned with building up brethren. The reason he wrote to these men was to lift them up in the Lord and send a message of encouragement to them as they labored in the Lord's vineyard. Who do we know who labors in the vineyard, whether a minister of the Gospel, an elder, or a fruitful worker? Sometimes a letter, a call, or a text can be just the thing to lift their spirits, encourage them in their work, or give them relief when they are facing struggles and even discouragement.

2. Paul's focus was on building up, not tearing down. Over and over, Paul urged these men to labor out of love and treat others with the respect they would show their own families. Very rarely does Paul encourage harsh treatment, and then only when it's needed to preserve the peace in the church. When we interact with God's people, do we do so like a bull in a china shop, or do we first desire to build up, encourage, and foster peace?

3. Paul underlays his letters with an encouragement to live with a servant's heart. Throughout his letters, Paul encourages the men to approach others in a spirit of service. He asks them to approach older men, younger men, older women, younger women, and even a slave as people they should serve. Everything Paul writes that we often parse out is done for their benefit and service. I wonder how the local church we are part of would be if everyone approached everyone else with a spirit of service.

Paul said many things in his letters that are worthy of deep study, but only if we remember the spirit in which he wrote these things. Sometimes that is lost when we read sentences and paragraphs when the letter was meant to be read as a whole.

***

When you try to please everyone, you usually please no one.

Best to just please God and let the chips fall where they may.

It makes sleeping at night much sweeter and pleasing God usually ends up pleasing others in ways that really matter.

***

Growing in the faith is not just about learning what we need to know, it's also about being willing to unlearn the false things we have been taught.

"See to it that no one takes you captive by philosophy and empty deceit, according to human tradition, according to the elemental spirits of the world, and not according to Christ." (Colossians 2:8 ESV).

***

I'm reading Hebrews in my daily Bible reading. It is quickly becoming one of my favorite books for strength, faith-building, and confidence.

In it, the writer shows the preeminence of Jesus, showcasing His deity and His humanity in a chorus that only God Himself could compose.

As the book starts, I zeroed in on this verse:

"For surely it is not angels that he helps, but he helps the offspring of Abraham." (Hebrews 2:16 ESV).

This verse has buried in it so many things that should help us gain strength, confidence, and a hope built in expectation.

From the beginning, when God said, "Let us make man in our image, after our likeness," we realize that there is something different from man than any other part of creation.

We were not made to be simply a display of his glory as the rest of creation, but we were created to be much more. We were made to be His children.

God created us to be sons and daughters. God created us to share in aspects of His nature.

He endowed us with free will, a portion of His dominion and sovereignty, the ability to think and reason, and an eternal nature.

Because we are more than part of His creation, a part that He has made in His image to be His children, His love and longsuffering have been demonstrated to us to redeem us from sin.

In fact, God went to extreme lengths as a Father to redeem that which sin has taken away. The lengths He went to for us are unlike anything He has done for anything else He has made.

"For surely it is not angels that he helps, but he helps the offspring of Abraham." (Hebrews 2:16 ESV).

We are His children.
We are His offspring.
We have an inheritance worth more than we can imagine.

And our God desperately desires us to choose Him and to have a relationship with Him.

And so He helps us in ways He helps no other part of creation.

***

Here's a question I've been wondering...

Is the United States on the path to severely persecute Christians?

I'm not sure the answer is an absolute foregone conclusion.

But the answer to that question is not nearly as important as the answer to this question:

Am I ready and prepared in my faith if it is?

***

I am beginning to shift the way I see a New Testament passage based on an Old Testament verse.

> "And at the ninth hour Jesus cried with a loud voice, "Eloi, Eloi, lema sabachthani?" which means, "My God, my God, why have you forsaken me?" (Mark 15:34 ESV).

I had always thought that this was Jesus crying out because of our sins He had taken upon Himself and the darkness represented the Father having to turn away from Jesus because He could have no fellowship with sin.

But in Psalm 22, we read,

> "For he has not despised or abhorred the affliction of the afflicted, and he has not hidden his face from him, but has heard, when he cried to him." (Psalm 22:24 ESV).

It seems that the Father was always there for His Son.

The Gospels seem to show us this event through the suffering Savior's perspective. In pain and anguish, Jesus makes this guttural cry. Even though His head knew better, this is the way He felt.

We can understand this. In times of tremendous anguish, our head knows God is with us, but it doesn't always feel that way. Don't we often make a similar cry to God from our purest emotional heart when we hurt?

That is our perspective. But Psalm gives the Father's perspective. He doesn't turn His head from us or hide His face from our pain. He still hears us even when it doesn't feel like He does.

Truly, Jesus experienced everything we did. He understands us more than we can imagine. And this is where His grace comes from. He gives it freely because He knows us and understands exactly what we endure and what we need.

***

Another Perspective On Luke 16: The Rich Man And Lazarus

In this post, I want to offer a perspective on the story Jesus tells in Luke 16 about the rich man and Lazarus. This post will seek to provide the following as a *possible* interpretation to the story Jesus told:

1. The primary audience was the High Priest Caiaphas.
2. Jesus was shooting a "warning shot" across the bow of the chief shepherd of His people.
3. The rich man in Jesus' story represented Caiaphas.
4. The application, though primarily aimed at Caiaphas, can also be appropriate for us as well.

To lay out this perspective, it is important to understand the history of Annas' family in the first century and how it intersected with the work and mission of Jesus.

The History and Wealth of Annas

Annas became the High Priest in 6 AD and served until 15 AD, when the Romans deposed him. Rome was wary of letting anyone serve a lifetime appointment to such a powerful position. However, Annas must have found favor with the Romans because he was able to spend the next half of a century positioning his five sons into the office of High Priest, along with his son-in-law, Caiaphas.

Having first taken up the role of High Priest in 6 AD, it is likely that Annas was one of the religious officials who marveled at the 12-year-old Jesus when He astounded the teachers of the law with his teachings:

"After three days they found him in the temple, sitting among the teachers, listening to them and asking them questions. And all who heard him were amazed at his understanding and his answers." (Luke 2:46-47 ESV).

Jesus was born between 6 BC and 4 BC, according to most scholars. That would put the twelve-year-old Jesus teaching in the Temple during the first to third year of Annas' appointment as High Priest. This would have likely been the first time that Israel's chief shepherd to God's people first met the Messiah, and the first encounter seemed to be a promising one.

But as the years passed, Annas used his position and influence to amass tremendous power and wealth for his family. According to the Jewish historian Josephus,

> "Now the report goes, that this elder Ananus proved a most fortunate man; for he had five sons, who had all performed the office of high priest to God, and he had himself enjoyed that dignity a long time formerly, which had never happened to any other of our high priests" (Ant 20:198).

And

> "for he was a great hoarder up of money:" (Ant 20:205).

How wealthy was Annas, and how did his family secure this wealth? In addition to the annual salary he would have been paid, the High Priest would have collected a 12.5% commission on the money changers as people came to Jerusalem for the Passover and other feast days. They also levied a fee for inspecting animals people brought with them for sacrifices. And for the people who didn't bring animals for sacrifice, they could visit the **Bazaars of the Sons of Annas** and secure an animal, often at exorbitant prices when Holy Days drew near. Together, these sources of income would bring in millions of dollars in today's value each year for the High Priest's family, making them one of the most powerful and wealthy families in Israel. Is it no wonder Jesus was filled with rage when he cleansed the Temple from the moneychangers, charging that they had made His Father's house a den of thieves? (Luke 19:45-46).

By the time the Messiah started His public ministry, Annas was the patriarch of one of the most influential, powerful, and wealthy families in the region. Though Jesus, as God, had appointed them to be the chief shepherds of His people, Annas and his children had abused their role to make themselves rich and powerful. And when they came face-to-face with the promised Messiah, instead of being ready to welcome Him, they sought at every turn to defeat Him and put Him to death. Jesus proved to be a threat to their twin idols of wealth and power.

Luke 16:19-31- The Rich Man And Lazarus

As we pick up Luke's account in chapter 16, Jesus tells a story that seems out of place in the context of His teachings. In Chapter 15, we see that Jesus starts to tell a string of parables and teachings aimed at the Pharisees and religious teachers:

"Now the tax collectors and sinners were all drawing near to hear him. And the Pharisees and the scribes grumbled, saying, "This man receives sinners and eats with them." So he told them this parable:" (Luke 15:1-3 ESV).

What follows are the teachings of

· The Lost Sheep (Luke 15:4-7)
· The Lost Coin (Luke 15:8-10)
· The Prodigal Son (Luke 15:11-32)
· The Dishonest Manager (Luke 16:1-13)
· The Law and the Kingdom (Luke 16:14-17)
· Divorce and Remarriage (Luke 16:18)
· Rich Man And Lazarus (Luke 16:19-31)

Lest we forget that these teachings are still aimed at the religious leaders, Luke tells us:

"The Pharisees, who were lovers of money, heard all these things, and they ridiculed him. And he said to them," (Luke 16:14-15a ESV).

When Luke recounts the story of the *Rich Man And Lazarus*, Jesus narrows in on the love for money these religious leaders had. This is the story where Jesus tells about the rich man who dies and ends up in torment. Because of the details Jesus uses in this story, I believe this story may be aimed primarily at Caiaphas, the reigning High Priest in Israel and the son-in-law of Annas.

If so, then the story of the *Rich Man And Lazarus* would not be a parable or a true historical event, but a story meant to fire a warning shot from God over the bow of His chief shepherd, who was letting wealth and power get in his way of making ready the people for the coming Messiah. Consider these details:

The rich man's clothing: "There was a rich man who was clothed in purple and fine linen and who feasted sumptuously every day." (Luke 16:19 ESV).

Colors are often used as identifiers. If we watch the Olympics and someone says, "Here comes the Red, White, and Blue," we know they mean, "here come the American athletes." Purple and fine linen would have conjured up an image of the High Priest in the first century Jew's mind because they would have been familiar with Exodus 28-32, which went into great detail about the clothing of the High Priest. Speaking about Aaron's garments:

> "They shall receive gold, blue and purple and scarlet yarns, and fine twined linen. "And they shall make the ephod of gold, of blue and purple and scarlet yarns, and of fine twined linen, skillfully worked." (Exodus 28:5-6 ESV).

And the Jews would have already known that the High Priest was one of the wealthiest people in Israel.

I have five brothers: "And he said, 'Then I beg you, father, to send him to my father's house-- for I have five brothers--so that he may warn them, lest they also come into this place of torment.'" (Luke 16:27-28 ESV).

It's interesting that Jesus drops in this detail in the story. The man says he has five brothers that he is concerned with. As the current High Priest, Caiaphas has five brothers-in-law, all sons of the patriarch Annas, who has engineered the family's wealth and power.

They have Moses and the prophets: "But Abraham said, 'They have Moses and the Prophets; let them hear them.'" (Luke 16:29 ESV).

When this rich man pleads for Abraham to send back Lazarus to warn his five brothers, Abraham tells him that they have everything in the Law they need to avoid coming to this place. Of all people, it should be the chief shepherd of God's people who knew the Law well enough to see signs of the coming Messiah. But the rich man argues,

> "And he said, 'No, father Abraham, but if someone goes to them from the dead, they will repent.'" (Luke 16:30 ESV).

To which Abraham responds,

> "He said to him, 'If they do not hear Moses and the Prophets, neither will they be convinced if someone should rise from the dead.'" (Luke 16:31 ESV).

If this is Jesus sending a warning shot across the bow of Caiaphas, then perhaps He is setting up something big that He wants the High Priest to consider. There is one detail in the story we have not mentioned. Jesus gives the name of the beggar who died: Lazarus.

> "And at his gate was laid a poor man named Lazarus, covered with sores," (Luke 16:20 ESV).

When we look at the chronological events of the Gospels, what do you suppose comes immediately after Jesus's story of the **Rich Man And Lazarus** in Luke 16?

It's John 11. You know, the chapter with the shortest verse in the Bible: "Jesus wept." (John 11:35 ESV).

Right after the story in Luke 16, Caiaphas and a man named Lazarus are introduced. The name should have been on the top of Caiaphas' mind after hearing the story of the rich man and Lazarus. While this man was not the poor beggar in Luke 16, a man named Lazarus would, indeed, come from the dead. And the reaction was exactly as Jesus said it would be.

As we start into chapter 11, Jesus gets word that his friend Lazarus is sick. But Jesus says something interesting and waits two days before heading to His sick friend:

> "But when Jesus heard it he said, "This illness does not lead to death. It is for the glory of God, so that the Son of God may be glorified through it." (John 11:4 ESV).

This is for the glory of God. Well, we know the story. Lazarus dies, and Jesus raises him to life. Everyone who saw and heard about this miracle was amazed. Well, almost everyone:

> "but some of them went to the Pharisees and told them what Jesus had done. So the chief priests and the Pharisees gathered the council and said, "What are we to do? For this man performs many signs. If we let him go on like this, everyone will believe in him, and the Romans will come and take away both our place and our nation." (John 11:46-48 ESV).

And guess who is there? Guess who heard about a man named Lazarus raised from the dead? I'll give you a hint: He was a rich man clothed in purple and fine linen, who fared sumptuously, and someone who had five brothers who should have known Moses and the prophets more than anyone else:

> "But one of them, Caiaphas, who was high priest that year, said to them, "You know nothing at all. Nor do you understand that it is better for you that one man should die for the people, not that the whole nation should perish." (John 11:49-50 ESV).

In fact, Caiaphas was so blind to the truth of the Messiah, he even decided that Lazarus should die too:

> "So the chief priests made plans to put Lazarus to death as well, because on account of him many of the Jews were going away and believing in Jesus." (John 12:10-11 ESV).

Application for Caiaphas And For Us

So, what does this mean? If Luke 16 was a warning shot that God fired over the bow of His chief shepherd of Israel for letting wealth and power blind him to the coming of the Messiah, how careful must we be about the idols we hold tight to? Whether money, power, work, family, or anything we hold more precious than God, if we are not careful, we will walk away from the Messiah even though His truth is so plain to us today.

We can't serve two masters. We will love the one and hate the other. Is there anything in our way of fully devoting ourselves to our Savior and King? If so, learn the tragic lesson of Israel's High Priest, who was uniquely in a position to welcome the promised Messiah. If Caiaphas could be blind to Jesus when the truth was plain to see, then let us all examine the things in life we hold dear and ensure nothing causes us to be blind to the truth before us.

***

In my daily Bible reading, I am in 1 Peter. Peter talks about the suffering that we must endure for the name of Jesus. That suffering will vary from person to person.

But in some way, we all will endure something for the name of Jesus. For some, it will be a lot. For others, it will be less. But the focus shouldn't be on how much you suffer versus how much I suffer.

Rather, we must ask ourselves, "What will I do when I face suffering for Jesus, rather little or much?"

Will I endure little? Will I endure much? Whatever I endure, it is for the glory of God.

Satan would have us adjust our faith, lay down our beliefs, or compromise our hearts to lessen the suffering. It is our endurance that brings glory to God, not our compromises.

Let me leave you with a verse from Peter to pray over today. As our society changes, which it is, more of us will start to suffer "little." When this testing of our faith comes, how will we react?

"If you are insulted for the name of Christ, you are blessed, because the Spirit of glory and of God rests upon you." (1 Peter 4:14 ESV).

Insults are the "less" of suffering. Let us be prepared for them before we are asked to endure the "more" of suffering.

***

Matthew 24 speaks to the coming of the Lord. Whether you think this is the coming of the Lord for the destruction of Jerusalem or the Second Coming, there are similar principles that apply.

In fact, the Bible talks about many "coming of the Lord" when the Lord comes in judgment. Matthew 24 talks about two conditions that usually exist when the Lord comes in judgment.

"For as were the days of Noah, so will be the coming of the Son of Man. For as in those days before the flood they were eating and drinking, marrying and giving in marriage, until the day when Noah entered the ark, and they were unaware until the flood came and swept them all away, so will be the coming of the Son of Man." (Matthew 24:37-39 ESV).

Ignorance and Indifference.
"they were eating and drinking, marrying and giving in marriage" - This represents indifference.
"they were unaware"- This represents ignorance.
Take stock of our world today. Do we see ignorance of and indifference toward God?

We do not know when the Lord will return, and it is futile to try to nail down a date or time, but God is well aware of the ignorance and indifference of His creation today.

Whenever the Son of Man returns for His bride, let us be prepared and watching, full of concern and discernment as we trim our lamps for His impending return, so we are not found indifferent or ignorant.

***

Daily Bible Reading... This is one of the best ways to get the Word into your heart. It's better than watching videos of sermons and better than reading spiritual posts. Nothing is better than listening to the Spirit speak to your heart directly as you read the inspired word.

Have you ever wondered if there were other ways to read the word, rather than starting with Genesis and reading through Revelation, and then starting over? Well, there are several ways to mix up your routine and keep it fresh. Here are a few ways I do it.

1. **Read in order**- Genesis through Revelation.

2. **Read randomly**- Pick out a book, and when you are done, randomly pick another book.

3. **Change up the translations you use**- Sometimes, you can gain insights from comparative reading. Read through the word in one translation, and then choose another translation the next time.

4. **Read the books in chronological order by when they were written**- This will look at the date the book was written so you can read them in the order the Spirit inspired them to be written.

5. **Read a chronological Bible**- This differs from the above method because it will break out pieces of a book and place the word in chronological order. This means you may have verses from one book next to verses from another book. For example, rather than read the books of history back-to-back that tell similar events, you will read excerpts of all the books in the order that the events happened. LaGard Smith has *The Narrated Bible In Chronological Order* I plan on reading one day: https://www.amazon.com/dp/0736902392/.

If you want a start on mixing up your daily Bible reading, here is a list of the books of the Bible in chronological order as they were written (I have included a link to the source I used to grab this order).

Have fun mixing up your daily Bible readings!

Genesis
Exodus
Leviticus
Numbers
Deuteronomy
Joshua
Psalms
Judges
Ruth
Proverbs
Song of Solomon
1 Samuel
2 Samuel
Ecclesiastes

Job
Jonah
Amos
Hosea
Joel
Micah
Isaiah
Nahum
Zephaniah
Habakkuk
Jeremiah
Daniel
Ezekiel
Lamentations
Obadiah
1 Kings
2 Kings
Haggai
Zechariah
1 Chronicles
2 Chronicles
Ezra
Nehemiah
Esther
Malachi
Galatians
1 Thessalonians
2 Thessalonians
1 Corinthians
2 Corinthians
Romans
Mark
James
Ephesians
Philippians
Colossians
Philemon
Matthew
Luke
Acts (of the Apostles)
1 Peter
Titus
1 Timothy

2 Timothy
2 Peter
Hebrews
Jude
John
1 John
2 John
3 John
Revelation

https://connectusfund.org/books-of-the-bible-in-chronological-order

**

What do you suppose God thinks about us exploring the oceans or the universe? What does He think about us seeking empirical knowledge?

"It is the glory of God to conceal things, but the glory of kings is to search things out." (Proverbs 25:2 ESV).

Could it be that God delights in His creation searching after and striving to understand the things He conceals?
I'd like to think so.

**

Tomorrow, I begin the last book of my Bible reading this time around before I start over by going through the Bible chronologically. Sunday and Monday, I will be reading the book of Revelation.
I've already read the spoiler...
God wins.
But I'm looking forward to seeing Him win again in the reading!

**

If we could always see our spouse through the same selfless eyes that Jesus sees the church, it would go a long way to mending many problems that couples face.

> "Husbands, love your wives, as Christ loved the church and gave himself up for her," (Ephesians 5:25 ESV).

> "In the same way husbands should love their wives as their own bodies. He who loves his wife loves himself." (Ephesians 5:28 ESV).

***

Well, I started the book of Revelation, and something that has always bothered me reared its head again. I see the heavenly creatures seemingly worshipping God non-stop. I cannot imagine an existence where I would be able to worship God without ceasing.

Would I have the stamina? Would I know how to do something like that?

But then it occurred to me that I am making a lot of assumptions and not giving God nearly the credit due Him.

I know that most of my eternal existence will be in praise and worship to Him. That is what my spirit here on earth wants.

I need to trust that God will equip me to do what I have been created to do. He will give me the body made to carry out my purpose.

Today, I become disillusioned or disappointed because I fail to do in the flesh what my spirit earnestly desires to do. In heaven, I will be given a body that will enable me to finally do all my spirit wants to do when it comes to praising and worshiping God.

I'm not sure we understand everything about how our existence will be in heaven, but whatever it is, God will equip me with all that I need to do it without...

Growing tired

Feeling overwhelmed

Being inadequate

Or getting distracted.

God is good, and in eternity, He will equip me to finally be able to do all that my spirit desires.

> "Watch and pray that you may not enter into temptation. The spirit indeed is willing, but the flesh is weak." (Matthew 26:41 ESV).

In eternity, God will equip me to finally do all that my spirit is willing to do.

***

I know not everyone will agree with this, but I love seeing posts and pics of people being baptized. For me, it is encouraging to see evidence that the Word is flourishing more than we may realize.

What better thing than to see a new brother or sister in Jesus make the commitment that will alter their eternal destiny!

***

I am reading Revelation. What a powerful book. It tells us that no matter when the enemy rises against the Lamb and His kingdom, it will not prevail. And those who choose to side with the enemies of God will share in their punishment.

As we move away from God as a society, remember that there are followers of the Lamb sprinkled throughout the land. He is our shield, our redeemer, and our Lord and King.

Just keep on keeping on. Have patience and remember that we are citizens of a kingdom that shall not fall. Even when the dragon hurls its fury at the people of God, let us stay in the palm of our God's hand.

There will be a time when war with God's enemies will be done. We will witness our King cast the devil in the Lake of Fire. We will be clothed with an incorruptible body and be given honor as children of God made in His image.

We must stay true to our Savior when the war is waged against us in its full fury. Victory for us is ensured.

The message of Revelation is that God will win. Let us remember that when the heat of the war arrives at our doorsteps.

Praise God, the sovereign creator of all things!

> "Then the dragon became furious with the woman and went off to make war on the rest of her offspring, on those who keep the commandments of God and hold to the testimony of Jesus. And he stood on the sand of the sea." (Revelation 12:17 ESV).

***

What point of prophecy do you see in Micah 5:2?

"But you, O Bethlehem Ephrathah, who are too little to be among the clans of Judah, from you shall come forth for me one who is to be ruler in Israel, whose coming forth is from of old, from ancient days." (Micah 5:2 ESV).

Yes, it says that the Messiah will be born in Bethlehem from the tribe of Judah. But what else does it say?

Does it not also say that this Messiah, who is born in Bethlehem from the tribe of Judah, whose coming is from old, from ancient days?

Not only will the Messiah be born in Bethlehem and be of the tribe of Judah, but He will also be God coming to be with man. Is it no wonder that Matthew writes this concerning the birth of Jesus:

"Behold, the virgin shall conceive and bear a son, and they shall call his name Immanuel" (which means, God with us)." (Matthew 1:23 ESV).

***

Preparing My Heart For Kingdom Living

Let me preview what I have planned for the next few weeks on my Facebook posts. For years, I have struggled in my walk with God. I approached my relationship with Him in a self-centered, checklist fashion that had my duties on one side of the ledger and God's duties on the other side of the ledger.

But if you've shared my experiences, you know that sometimes we can work, and work and work, but it doesn't seem that God responds the way we expect Him to respond. Pretty soon, we begin to think God is not being fair or that He's more concerned about helping others than He is about helping me.

This can lead to frustrating questions for God and even accusations against Him and His actions or inactions in our lives. Have you ever been there in your life? If not, I am so thankful because it is a heartbreaking place to be.

This is where I was. And I stayed there for a long, long time. But Jesus patiently waited for me to align myself with Him. I had sinned so much and so badly that it was a challenge for me to get to where I needed to be. Not because of any difficulties that Jesus laid before me but because of the difficulties I laid before myself.

But here is where things started to come into balance for me. I had been trying to serve God with a bad heart. I tried to do it on my own terms. I didn't seek His grace, I set up a system of transactions between what I would do and what He would do.

The problem is that this system does not work. It is doomed to fail, and it is not biblical. I realized that I needed His grace in order for me to live the life Jesus has in store for me.

I began to understand that Jesus didn't lay a heavy burden on me and say, "You better get this right, or I'm going to condemn you!" Rather, Jesus says, "Put your trust in Me and accept my grace, take my light yoke, and I will transform you into a man you could never become on your own."

So, instead of focusing on being a man of works, I surrendered to His grace. And an amazing thing happened. I became a man who began to do more than I have ever dreamed I'd be able to do. By focusing on getting my heart right, it prepared the soil for the Word to work in me mightily. And that mighty work was changing my nature where the spiritual me claimed dominance over the carnal me.

Over the next few weeks, I will share things I put into place to help me, as James says, "establish my heart". These things are practical tips that anyone can do. You don't need a certain level of knowledge or minimum experience as a Christian to do these things. You can simply choose to do them or choose not to do them.

But I can tell you that having made them a part of my life, they helped my heart be what it should be, and I began to see the issues of life flow from it (Proverbs 4:23). And when I am diligent in keeping my heart where it needs to be, living a Christ-centered life just happens. But when I neglect my heart, I struggle greatly.

I pray that the things I share with you can help you as richly as they have helped me. I look forward to meeting with you next week as we discuss the first thing I do to prepare my heart for Kingdom living.

> "Keep your heart with all vigilance, for from it flow the springs of life." (Proverbs 4:23).

***

Our nation has taught us to be prideful. And while there is nothing wrong with feeling the satisfaction that comes with using our God-given talents to achieve accomplishments, let us not be quick to forget God in the "God-given" aspect of our accomplishments.

Do we open our pantry and see the overflowing blessings that God has given and think, "Look at what I have provided for myself and my family?"

Do we see our home with its full multicar garage, furnishings, and pool and think, "Look at what I have been able to provide for myself and my family?"

Do we look at our job title and think, "Look at how I have navigated myself through my career to achieve my accolades?"

Do we look at our paychecks and think, "Look at what I earn because of my value?"

Before we are too quick in looking at the things we have done for ourselves and assume they will continue forever because of our greatness, let us remember the words of an ancient king who thought much the same way when He forgot to acknowledge God:

> "and the king answered and said, "Is not this great Babylon, which I have built by my mighty power as a royal residence and for the glory of my majesty?"
>
> While the words were still in the king's mouth, there fell a voice from heaven, "O King Nebuchadnezzar, to you it is spoken: The kingdom has departed from you," (Daniel 4:30-31 ESV).

***

Sometimes, I fear we put more of a burden on our shoulders than God puts upon us. How often have we stressed over decisions we must make, hoping we make the choice God wants us to make?

Do we approach these major decisions as though there are two doors, and as long as we choose the door God wants us to choose, we will be blessed? But if we choose the wrong door, do we think we will miss out on the blessings of God?

I'm not sure that this is how God expects us to approach our decisions as we use the free will He has endowed us with. While we always need to pray for wisdom when making decisions because we want God to partner with us as we navigate life, as long as the choices before us are honorable, I'm not sure God is too concerned about our decisions.

Could it be that God's disposition is, "If you choose path A, obey and honor Me, and I will be with you; but if you choose path B, obey and honor Me, and I will be with you."

The anxiety we feel over making the "right" choice which is before us can be eased if we approach it not as, "Lord, please help me make the right choice"; but rather, "Lord, give me wisdom as I consider the choices before me and bless me in the choice I make."

I choose to see my loving God as someone who will aid me in whatever honorable choice I make rather than as a game show host who says, "Oh, you choose door A. Let's see what you would have received if you chose door B."

My God is my Father, who wishes to bless me as I walk with Him. I will concern myself with walking with Him, regardless of my choices, rather than stress over making the "right" decision.

Isn't it amazing that we serve a sovereign God Who can bless our path regardless of our choices?

***

I'm back in Genesis in my daily Bible reading, this time going through the Bible in the chronological order the books have been written. It never ceases to amaze me how many things you learn when you read God's word.

This time, I noticed something interesting in chapter 32. Jacob, who had deceived his older brother Esau and taken his birthright, has returned home after 20 years of fleeing Esau's rage.

During the time he was with his uncle Laban, God had made Jacob a wealthy man. Jacob was learning to trust in God, especially when he faced circumstances that caused him fear.

The time had come when God told him to go back home. But this is where Esau lived. Jacob followed God, even though he feared for his life. Jacob literally put his life in God's hands.

Listen to how Jacob comes to God in prayer as he casts his anxiety on God:

> "I am not worthy of the least of all the deeds of steadfast love and all the faithfulness that you have shown to your servant, for with only my staff I crossed this Jordan, and now I have become two camps." (Genesis 32:10 ESV).

Say what you want about this man, who had problems and personal character flaws, but we must admire his humility in the eyes of God. Oh, that we all see ourselves this way in God's eyes.

In his deepest anxiety, Jacob laid it all on the Lord. Rather than disobeying the word of the Lord, he was determined to return home as God instructed him. And so, he prays this to God:

> "Please deliver me from the hand of my brother, from the hand of

Esau, for I fear him, that he may come and attack me, the mothers with the children." (Genesis 32:11 ESV).

This deceiver knew one thing... when he faced danger and the unknown, there was only one place to go for comfort and protection. Despite his character flaws, Jacob gets it right in the matters that really count.

***

As I start the book of Exodus, I am amazed as I see God's providence play out in Israel. He looked among the nations and created a people to be His own possession. He started with one old man and created a nation that formed within Egypt.

By the time the book of Exodus begins, Israel had become a mighty nation, just like God promised Abraham. The rest of the world followed after other gods, but Yahweh would make His name known throughout the world through this nation.

In truth, over the next 40 years, God would take these people with Him kicking and screaming. He would provide for them, defend them, and show His glory to them. Yet this new nation would constantly complain and yearn for the days when they lived in a land ruled by idols.

Perhaps the greatest gift God gave the people, aside from His direct providence, was a leader like Moses. Someone trained by Egypt with leadership but one who would be willing to lay down his life for the people.

Through Moses, Exodus declares the glory of God in a manner that makes God's name known for thousands of years. We're still making movies today about the things God did in Exodus.

Exodus is about the making of a nation as God's possession within a world dominated by false gods. There is no better book to read that shows us God's power, glory, great love, and grace for a people who didn't deserve it.

***

"And Pharaoh sent..."

This is an amazing phrase found in Exodus 9:7. This follows the fifth plague of the Egyptian livestock that died.

God said He would strike the Egyptian livestock but leave Israel's livestock alone. This is precisely what happened. To be sure,

"And Pharaoh sent, and behold, not one of the livestock of Israel was dead. But the heart of Pharaoh was hardened, and he did not let the people go." (Exodus 9:7 ESV).

"And Pharaoh sent..."
Why is this amazing to me? Not only was God able to target His plagues, but God protected His people's livestock from Pharaoh.

To me, it's amazing that Pharaoh didn't confiscate Israel's livestock to replace theirs that God killed in the plagues when he sent people to see if Israel's livestock was, indeed, untouched.

God's providence is often seen in subtle ways in our lives that we may be quick to overlook.

Isn't it amazing that God can protect us from the evil of others in ways we may never pick up on?

Praise the name of God seen in the little phrase, "And Pharaoh sent...!

***

Preparing My Heart For Kingdom Living: Read The Bible Daily

Last Tuesday, I said I would share with you the things I did to help create in me a heart prepared for kingdom living. I talked about how I had hit rock bottom spiritually and had a choice to make. Sin had taken over my life so much. Insecurity and a feeling of worthlessness had been my daily refrain, and it wasn't as easy as flipping a switch to get to where I wanted to be spiritually.

After reading what I wrote last Tuesday, you may have been expecting some deep revelation that has been hidden from the masses for eons. I mean, this one seems like a no-brainer, right? Of course, we need to read the Bible. But I can tell you that there were years when I spent very little time reading His Word. I would nibble at it, maybe reading a few words at a time, or a few verses here and there. But listen to how God has always revered His Word and instructed man to imbibe it.

"Your word is a lamp to my feet and a light to my path." (Psalm 119:105 ESV).

"This Book of the Law shall not depart from your mouth, but you shall meditate on it day and night, so that you may be careful to do according to all that is written in it. For then you will make your way prosperous, and then you will have good success." (Joshua 1:8 ESV).

"Like newborn infants, long for the pure spiritual milk, that by it you may grow up into salvation--" (1 Peter 2:2 ESV).

"So faith comes from hearing, and hearing through the word of Christ." (Romans 10:17 ESV).

"but his delight is in the law of the LORD, and on his law he meditates day and night." (Psalm 1:2 ESV).

So, why spend so much time in the Word? (And yes, I strongly suggest daily). Because everything comes from the living Word of God. From Matthew through Revelation, they are all the words of Christ. In it, we learn who Jesus is, what He did for us, and why He needed to do it. Through it, we learn everything we need to live in the presence of God and how to live with our fellow man. And it is the means by which God can begin to create in us a new heart.

It is in the Word that we draw near to God. It instructs and comforts. It showers us with wisdom, and it shows us the way in a dark and crooked world. It is breathed by the Spirit of God Himself, and because of that, it has the strength to do what no other words can do. And don't stop at the New Testament. The Old Testament teaches us about God. In it, we learn of Him and see His finger on all things. We see His power, His mercy, His grace, and His promises.

Doesn't it stand to reason that if we want to have a heart that is tender toward God and trained to hear His voice, then we need to spend time listening to what He is speaking to us? And there are so many ways to drink in the Word of God.

We can open a physical Bible and read it in the quiet of our day.

We can listen to an audio reading of the Scriptures. In fact, that's how it was done in the 1st century while the Spirit was working on writing it down for the ages- Christians listening to it being read to them.

I combine reading and hearing, and my comprehension and the quantity of what I read daily have skyrocketed. I open a YouTube video of the ESV dramatized Bible being read while following along in the free Blue Letter Bible online.

And I am very intentional in my reading of God's Word. I schedule it so that I always have time. 7 days a week, I am up between 4 or 5 am, and I read Scripture for about an hour a day. I choose my own personal reading schedule and go through the Bible from cover to cover over and over. After prayer, it is the way I must start each day if I am to prepare my heart for the day to come.

I can tell you from experience that when I start my day in God's Word, it helps set the tone for the rest of my day. And as the carnal man in me looks for every opportunity to sin, having the day start with a reading of God's Word gives my spiritual man a boost and sets him up for success throughout the day.

Is it no wonder that in resisting Satan in the wilderness, Jesus responds by saying:

> "It is written, "'Man shall not live by bread alone, but by every word that comes from the mouth of God.'" (Matthew 4:4 ESV).

If it is by every word that comes from the mouth of God that we live, shouldn't we spend time daily in His word?

If you do not have a significant commitment to daily Bible reading, can I suggest that there will be few things that will better help you establish your heart and move you toward becoming the spiritual man or woman that I'm confident you want to be? Let reading His Word become so ingrained in you that it becomes second nature.

And here's the great thing. If you are committed to this, you will start seeing an amazing change in your life. You can't spend this much time with God and it not have an amazing effect on you.

If you are like me, you may find a time in your life when you have to do so much to prepare your heart for kingdom living that it may seem overwhelming. It's okay. I took things one day at a time and focused on making one change at a time in my life. Daily Bible reading is something we all can do no matter how lost we have become or no matter how worthless or insecure we feel. Do this until the habit is set and you begin to draw strength from His words. Then consider the next thing I did to prepare my heart for kingdom living, which we will discuss next Tuesday.

> "For the word of God is living and active, sharper than any two-edged sword, piercing to the division of soul and of spirit, of joints and of marrow, and discerning the thoughts and intentions of the heart." (Hebrews 4:12 ESV).

> "I have stored up your word in my heart, that I might not sin against you." (Psalm 119:11 ESV).

***

God has extended His longsuffering today. Perhaps we will see Him in the clouds today, or perhaps He will bless us with another day of stewardship to Him. Whatever His sovereign choice may be, to Him be glory and honor today.

***

When Israel made the golden calf idol, it wasn't just that that turned from God to another god. Israel fashioned the calf to represent Yahweh. In their minds, this golden calf represented their God.

> "And he received the gold from their hand and fashioned it with a graving tool and made a golden calf. And they said, "These are your gods, O Israel, who brought you up out of the land of Egypt!" (Exodus 32:4 ESV).

Whenever we fashion God after our minds, we do the same thing the people of Israel did. We may not make a representation of God with gold, but if we fashion Him in our image, then we are idolaters.

Let us approach God in His holiness and see Him as He is. A god fashioned after our image is not the God we shall stand before in judgment.

***

In my daily Bible reading, I came across an interesting verse that shows us that if we put our faith in the Lord, He will have our back.

> "For I will cast out nations before you and enlarge your borders; no one shall covet your land, when you go up to appear before the LORD your God three times in the year." (Exodus 34:24 ESV).

God told the people that when they all traveled to Jerusalem three times a year to serve Him, making them vulnerable to attack from their neighbors, God would protect them.

What a wonderful trust to put in God. He will be our security when we obey Him. While God never promises that we will never see persecution, God does promise that He will take care of us when we are persecuted for doing what He asks us to do. He will always have our back.

We should never wonder if it's worth it to serve the Lord. It is always worth it. He will not allow our enemies to triumph over us when we lay down our lives to Him in service and obedience.

***

I am in the book of Leviticus in my daily Bible reading. When you see all the sacrifices in this book, you see just how far above man God is.

You have a system of blood sacrifices to cleanse people of their uncleannesses. Some were unclean because of sin, and some were ceremonial uncleanness that had nothing to do with personal sins.

But where the tabernacle was, so was the presence of God. It was holy ground. And God went to great lengths to show the Israelites that our uncleanness cannot exist in the presence of a holy God.

So, God made a way for impure man to exist in the presence of a holy God. This is what the sacrifices did for the people.

What we read in Leviticus also teaches us who live under Jesus how necessary His sacrifice is for us. His blood cleanses us and makes us pure before God. Jesus makes it possible for unclean sinners to approach His Father, Who is holy and pure.

Without His blood sacrifice for us, we cannot approach the Father. Jesus knew this. And this is why...

> "Jesus said to him, "I am the way, and the truth, and the life. No one comes to the Father except through me." (John 14:6 ESV).

***

In my daily Bible reading, I came across this passage about the aid that God would give His people:

> "You shall chase your enemies, and they shall fall before you by the sword. Five of you shall chase a hundred, and a hundred of you shall chase ten thousand, and your enemies shall fall before you by the sword." (Leviticus 26:7-8 ESV).

Isn't that amazing? God would fight for His people and send ten thousand fleeing when a hundred Israelites would chase them. That got me thinking about what Jesus said about the church He would build:

> "And I tell you, you are Peter, and on this rock I will build my church, and the gates of hell shall not prevail against it." (Matthew 16:18 ESV).

Our traditional interpretation of this verse often goes something like this: When the gates of hell, the forces of darkness and evil, when the principalities strike out against the church, they will not be able to conquer the church. The church will survive the attacks.

One of the reasons that we think this way is because of the word "against" in this passage. But this word is not in the original text. The translators added it to help us better understand the meaning of the text. But I wonder if they may have watered down the true strength of what Jesus is saying.

Literally, the text says that the gates of hades will not prevail it. So, one way we can translate it is the way we talked about it- that the church will be able to survive against the powers sent against it.

But another way that we can read this when we remove the added word "against" is that the gates of hell will not prevail it; will not withstand it. This changes the thrust of what Jesus is saying.

Instead of the church surviving the attacks of the forces of evil and death, Jesus is saying that the forces of evil and death will not endure the onslaught that Jesus is about to unleash upon it through the victory He makes possible on the cross.

His church will lead a charge into the evil powers that reign in death, but no matter how hard they fight, no matter how viciously they fight back to defend themselves against the armies of Jesus, they will not prevail it; they will not withstand it. His church will lead an offensive battle that they will not be able to survive.

Jesus will lead His people and take the battle to His enemies. He will give us the ability to send 10,000 fleeing with 100 in His army. Our strength is in Him, and He tells Peter the church He will build will be such a force in the spiritual realm that His enemies will not prevail it; will not withstand it.

> "For we do not wrestle against flesh and blood, but against the rulers, against the authorities, against the cosmic powers over this present darkness, against the spiritual forces of evil in the heavenly places.
>
> Therefore take up the whole armor of God, that you may be able to withstand in the evil day, and having done all, to stand firm." (Ephesians 6:12-13 ESV).

God has always given His people a supernatural ability to take the battle to His enemies. As members of the church He built, we are part of an invading army that brings light to darkness and sends His enemies fleeing on a death march that will lead to utter victory through Jesus.

This is the power of the God we serve.

***

Have you ever wondered what it was like for someone who heard Jesus teach in person to accept Him as the Messiah?

He or she would have to go against the religious leaders of their days. They would have to choose between following their beliefs and possibly being put out of the synagogue.

Everything in their life was on the line with the decision they would have to make. As it became increasingly clear that Jesus claimed to be more than a man, they would have to decide if the Messiah they believed in was truly God or a blasphemer, especially after His death and resurrection, as that claim became crystal clear.

We take this decision for granted because we are surrounded by people who, for the most part, either believe Jesus is God or don't have a problem with someone believing this.

My point is this... if you came to an understanding from Scripture that your church or traditions were inaccurate, would you stand for the Truth you uncovered, or would you be more concerned about being put out of your church or your denomination?

Would you fear the words of the religious leaders in your life or the Lord more?

Standing on the Truth is not easy to do when everyone important in your life believes something else and threatens to excommunicate you if you do not conform to their way of thinking.

It is the same decision the people in the first century faced. It is not an easy one. But would you be willing to walk away from everything you were brought up to believe, knowing that everyone you love and respect would excommunicate you from a relationship with them?

When the man who was born blind was healed by Jesus and refused to condemn Jesus as a sinner before the religious leaders, he had to pay the ultimate social price:

> "Never since the world began has it been heard that anyone opened the eyes of a man born blind.
> If this man were not from God, he could do nothing."
> They answered him, "You were born in utter sin, and would you teach us?" And they cast him out." (John 9:32-34 ESV).

Even his parents refused to stand by him because they feared being put out of the synagogue:

> "(His parents said these things because they feared the Jews, for the Jews had already agreed that if anyone should confess Jesus to be Christ, he was to be put out of the synagogue.)" (John 9:22 ESV).

What about us? Are we willing to be excommunicated for standing on the Truth we uncover from Scripture? It's a real decision that people have always had to face. What is the payoff if we do? It is the same payoff for the man born blind who refused to walk away from the Messiah:

> "Jesus heard that they had cast him out, and having found him he said, "Do you believe in the Son of Man?"
> He answered, "And who is he, sir, that I may believe in him?"
> Jesus said to him, "You have seen him, and it is he who is speaking to you."
> He said, "Lord, I believe," and he worshiped him." (John 9:35-38 ESV).

***

In my daily Bible reading, I am in Numbers. In one sense, it is a sad book in that the people constantly rebel against God, and God brings judgment on them. They seem never to learn their lesson.

In chapter 15, God instructs the people to put tassels on the corner of their garments and explains why He wants them to do this:

> "And it shall be a tassel for you to look at and remember all the commandments of the LORD, to do them, not to follow after your own heart and your own eyes, which you are inclined to whore after.
> So you shall remember and do all my commandments, and be holy to your God." (Numbers 15:39-40 ESV).

The problem that kept getting the Israelites into trouble is, at its root, the same problem that often gets us into trouble. We take our eyes off the commandments of the Lord and follow after our own hearts and eyes.

We are blessed when we seek God's Word with our hearts, but when we start to replace His Word with what is good in our own eyes, we start to walk a dangerous walk.

When we usurp God's Word with our own reasoning and desires and follow those, we kindle the Lord's wrath against us.

Israel was told to make tassels as a visible reminder to revere God's Word above all and not start down the path of teaching as doctrine the commandments of men. This is vain worship to God. He did not put up with it in the days of Moses, and He will not put up with it today.

Quoting from Isaiah, Jesus says,

> "This people honors me with their lips, but their heart is far from me; in vain do they worship me, teaching as doctrines the commandments of men." (Matthew 15:8-9 ESV).

Let us all approach God's Word with reverence and resist following after our own eyes, which we are inclined to whore after.

***

A question to meditate on today: Do we seek glory cloaked in garments of humility?

***

Preparing My Heart For Kingdom Living: Pray Without Ceasing

Last Tuesday, I discussed the importance daily Bible reading had in helping me establish my heart. But communication is a two-way street, and communicating with God is no different. Reading the Word allows us to hear His voice, Him speaking to us. Praying is our end of this conversation. This is us speaking to Him. And our God greatly desires to hear from His children. That's why Paul admonishes us to:

> "pray without ceasing," (1 Thessalonians 5:17 ESV).

We see in how Jesus responds to the Pharisees it is not the act of prayer that is so important to Him, but rather the heart behind the prayer. In Luke 18, Jesus contrasts two different prayers. One from a man who, in pride, extols His own virtues to God and prays to be heard by men more than by

God. Then there was the other man.

> "But the tax collector, standing far off, would not even lift up his eyes to heaven, but beat his breast, saying, 'God, be merciful to me, a sinner!'" (Luke 18:13 ESV).

Jesus said that this man went away justified. And He, God, would know. Then we read the Lord's prayer to learn how to pray a Kingdom-focused prayer. And Peter tells us to cast our burdens on Him, for He cares for us. But it is so easy for my prayers to become rote. I can't tell you how many times I sat down to eat, uttered a prayer, and as I took my first bite, knowing I prayed but not being able to recall the thoughts or the words I just uttered.

What made a difference for me was to focus on what I was actually doing in prayer. I was approaching the throne of God, and He was giving me His undivided attention. He, the Creator of the universe, the all-powerful, all-knowing God, was listening to me with His angels standing in dead silence as I spoke to my Protector and Provider.

When I pray, my presence is in the throne Room of God. It is an awesome image I have in my mind, and I always see myself bowed down to His feet in humble submission as I pray. I know He hears every word I say in prayer. I know He has all the time I want to spend with Him, speaking my heart to Him. He never glances at His watch as I pray. It is never too early or too late to talk to Him. He will hear me when I speak to Him for 30 minutes just as intently as when I speak to him for 30 seconds.

Before you pray next time, read Revelation 4 and 5 to prepare you for your next conversation with the Almighty, and then let that image burn into your mind's eye so you can see it as you kneel before the throne. I can honestly tell you that now, I eagerly wait for my prayers to the Lord. When I know I am about to go before the throne of God, a deep anticipation builds within me as time draws near.

For me, this anticipation has happened because I have established my heart to walk through what is actually happening as I pray. Sometimes I am overjoyed, wanting to share an awesome experience with my Creator. Sometimes, my heart hurts, and He is the first One to whom I turn to share my pain. And yes, sometimes I can't even lift my eyes to heaven when I plead with Him to be merciful to me, a sinner, because I just lost a battle to the carnal man.

If you can start to see God sitting on His throne, in all His glory and majesty as you pray to Him, it will affect everything about your prayer. I know it does mine. And your prayers will become your personal standing meetings between you and God where you have access to the most powerful being in existence. You will fiercely covet your time with Him in prayer.

When you can see God as you pray and not just utter rote words in His direction, your life will change. Couple this with the daily Bible reading we discussed last week, and you will start to see Him work on your heart. It cannot help but happen. Next Tuesday, I look forward to sharing another thing I do to help prepare my heart for Kingdom living.

***

Some of the hardest things to do as a Christian:
Let God control our lives.
Revere God when our prayers are not answered the way we want.
Trust God when we suffer due to no fault of our own.
Believe God when we don't understand what is happening or we don't know what will happen.
See others who are blessed more than we are without envy.
Turn the other cheek.
Wait on God.
We must have faith that when we do the things above, it will always lead to God's glory and Him transforming us into the image of His dear Son.

"For those whom he foreknew he also predestined to be conformed to the image of his Son, in order that he might be the firstborn among many brothers." (Romans 8:29 ESV).

"And we all, with unveiled face, beholding the glory of the Lord, are being transformed into the same image from one degree of glory to another. For this comes from the Lord who is the Spirit." (2 Corinthians 3:18 ESV).

***

I'm finishing up the book of Numbers in my daily Bible reading. One thing that amazes me is when God sent men into battle, He was with them in a way that proves God's presence with them.
No man fell in battle when God was with them.
Not one.
Isn't that amazing? No arrow, spear, or sword found its mark on the Israelites. Listen to what Moses writes after 1,000 men of war from each tribe went against Midian, killing all its men:

"and said to Moses, "Your servants have counted the men of war who are under our command, and there is not a man missing from us." (Numbers 31:49 ESV).

Not a man missing.
That's why, later under Joshua, when 36 men died before the small city of Ai, it sent the Israelites into full lament. 36 losses in any other circumstance would be a resounding victory. But when God wasn't with them, they had no divine protection.

> "So about three thousand men went up there from the people. And they fled before the men of Ai,
> and the men of Ai killed about thirty-six of their men and chased them before the gate as far as Shebarim and struck them at the descent. And the hearts of the people melted and became as water.
> Then Joshua tore his clothes and fell to the earth on his face before the ark of the LORD until the evening, he and the elders of Israel. And they put dust on their heads." (Joshua 7:4-6 ESV).

No man lost his life in battle when God was with the Israelites. No matter how fierce the battle was, men were safe when God was their shield.

We are in a fierce battle against the forces of darkness. God arms us and protects us with His armor. He is our shield, and King Jesus is the Captain who leads us in battle.

When we fight in His army, He knows how to protect us. The enemy cannot- hear this- CAN NOT defeat the servants of our sovereign King Jesus.

But when we fight the battles of life without Jesus, we are as vulnerable as the 36 men who fell at the hands of the people of Ai.

The enemy will try to scare us, engender fear, and paint a hopeless picture in our hearts. The enemy does this for one reason. The powers of darkness have no power over us when we are in the presence of our Creator and Savior. Evil's only hope over us is if we separate ourselves from our Lord. Then, we become easy prey for the evil one.

Numbers show us tangible evidence of the power of God. Let us take up the whole armor of God and remain safely in the Lord's presence.

If we do, we will be eyewitnesses of our God's final victory over all enemies, and we will stand safely at His right hand as we witness Him casting all His enemies into the Lake of Fire.

***

I love this. In my daily Bible reading, the stubborn, complaining, short-sighted people with a short memory regarding God gets it right on this occasion.

Moses reminds them about the time when they revered and feared God. He reminded them about the time when they encouraged Moses to speak to God for them, and they would do all He spoke to Moses.

This attitude touched God's heart.

> "And the LORD heard your words, when you spoke to me. And the LORD said to me, 'I have heard the words of this people, which they have spoken to you. They are right in all that they have spoken.
>
> Oh that they had such a heart as this always, to fear me and to keep all my commandments, that it might go well with them and with their descendants forever!" (Deuteronomy 5:28-29 ESV).

My takeaway: I need to approach God in reverence.

I need to seek His purpose for me.

I need to have a heart that fears God and loves Him with everything in my being.

For God also says to me, "Oh that you have a heart as this always, that it might go well with you forever!"

My Lord and King Jesus, help me have this heart.

Father, finish your work in me to create me in the image of your dear Son.

May the Spirit rest in me and give me wisdom, discernment, and understanding that I may have a heart that touches God's heart.

***

God made man and set him in a perfect paradise to live in His presence forever.

But man separated from God, and sin tarnished the paradise and relationship man was intended to share with His Creator.

Man grew further away from His Creator and began to seek after his own selfish interests.

God watched man drift away from Him so far that, without His intervention, man would be hopelessly lost.

So God chose one man from among an idolatrous nation and started from scratch to create a nation, and He would begin to redeem all nations back to Him.

God grew this nation, revealed His holiness to them, and taught them how to represent Him and His character to others.

He taught them how much they needed Him, and He provided a system of blood sacrifices to show the cost of their sins.

As they struggled to stay faithful to Him, God promised to send a Savior Who would carry their burdens and free them from the shackles that bound them.

But when the Savior came, they rejected Him and put Him to death.

In doing this, the Savior did the one thing that had to be done to redeem His people from the bondage they were under.

The Savior became the sacrifice and the appeasement to God for our sins.

He rose from the dead to conquer death.

The Savior did what we could not do. He brought grace to save all nations.

He became the only way to the Father and began to restore the Edenic relationship that we had lost.

He became our King and High Priest to restore our place in God's presence forever.

He calls all men everywhere to partake in His mission and very being.

He works continually to transform us into a new creature fashioned after Himself and the example He left.

He creates a new priesthood, a new nation, and a new people who takes His light into the darkness to overcome evil.

Day by day, we become more like Him, we live more like He lived, we do more of what He did, and we tell others how our Savior can be their Savior too.

And we live for the promise that one day, He will return and transform His followers' bodies into perfect, spiritual bodies equipped for eternal living.

We believe that Eden will be restored, death will be destroyed, and we will once again walk with Him in His presence.

This is the Gospel that we live, believe, and share with others.

***

Yesterday, I was talking to my neighbor. We realized early on that we both believe in Jesus as Lord and King, so we have a lot of good conversations when we talk.

A few weeks ago, his house had a major leak, and the insurance company moved his family into a house while the restoration company fixes the mess. I have been checking his mail and helping his family as needed.

Yesterday, when he picked up his mail, we began talking about how God can do amazing things when bad things happen to us. In fact, we shared stories about lessons God taught us during struggles in our lives.

We both said that we didn't like the struggle, but we were so thankful for the blessings that came through them. We knew if it weren't for the struggle, we'd miss the blessings.

He recounted an ad hoc trip that he and his wife took to Michigan, where his wife grew up. They visited the house she grew up at, the schools she went to, the church her father was a pastor of, and the summer camp she spent time at each year.

All stops had good memories mixed with struggles. Yet she left their trip down memory lane, knowing each place had a profound impact on her that made her the woman she is today.

Her husband told me she referred to this trip they took together as "trace the grace."

I love that.

Too often, we focus on the bad things in our past to the neglect of seeing the good that God might have given to help us through the struggles.

Perhaps it was strength or wisdom He gave us from the struggles.

Maybe it was bringing in the right person into our lives at the right moment to be our support.

Whatever it is, hindsight often helps us see God's goodness in the midst of the pain and struggles we endure.

And hindsight is the best blessing to help us, in our own life's journey, "trace the grace."

***

Jesus taught when He was popular
Jesus taught when He was unpopular
Jesus taught when He was persecuted
Jesus taught when He was victorious
What does it mean to be His disciple?
Jesus sought to live in the Lord's will when He was popular
Jesus sought to live in the Lord's will when He was unpopular
Jesus sought to live in the Lord's will when He was persecuted
Jesus sought to live in the Lord's will when He was victorious
What does it mean to be His disciple?
Paul was a disciple of Jesus, which is why he could say this:

> "Not that I am speaking of being in need, for I have learned in whatever situation I am to be content.
>
> I know how to be brought low, and I know how to abound. In any and every circumstance, I have learned the secret of facing plenty and

hunger, abundance and need.

I can do all things through him who strengthens me." (Philippians 4:11-13 ESV).

***

I'm pretty sure, as much as I have read and studied the Scriptures about living on the new Earth in the presence of God with my immortal, glorified body...

I am not even close to understanding the joy that awaits me.

"For I am already being poured out as a drink offering, and the time of my departure has come.

I have fought the good fight, I have finished the race, I have kept the faith.

Henceforth there is laid up for me the crown of righteousness, which the Lord, the righteous judge, will award to me on that day, and not only to me but also to all who have loved his appearing." (2 Timothy 4:6-8 ESV).

***

I am finishing up the book of Deuteronomy in my daily Bible reading. The more I read, the more I see how little has changed between people who lived 3500 years ago and us today.

The problem the Israelites had to struggle with was having a bad heart. Their struggles sprang from a heart issue. Deuteronomy 28:18 says,

"Beware lest there be among you a man or woman or clan or tribe whose heart is turning away today from the LORD our God to go and serve the gods of those nations. Beware lest there be among you a root bearing poisonous and bitter fruit," (Deuteronomy 29:18 ESV).

This heart issue caused them to turn away from God when they felt like they could live however they wanted without regard for God. Listen to how this bad heart speaks:

"one who, when he hears the words of this sworn covenant, blesses himself in his heart, saying, 'I shall be safe, though I walk in the stubbornness of my heart.' This will lead to the sweeping away of moist and dry alike." (Deuteronomy 29:19 ESV).

What a bad place for us to be. Do we say in our hearts, "I will be safe," while we walk in the stubbornness of our hearts? This isn't someone who is learning and growing but one who consciously disregards God and feels safe with this choice.

May we have a heart that seeks God and feels safe when we rest in Him and seek a relationship with Him in all we do.

***

Preparing My Heart For Kingdom Living: Put Good In

Last Tuesday, I talked about how prayer has been an important part of how I am preparing my heart for Kingdom living. Having an avenue to speak to the Creator is an awesome and powerful tool for me. But today, I want to share the next thing I started to focus on to prepare my heart for Kingdom living. It's the practice of purposefully filling my mind with good things.

This aspect of Kingdom living is too important to leave to the whim of the environment we live in. Even if we do not actively go after evil thoughts, unless we are strategic in what we put into our minds, the evil thoughts will find their way in. Paul addresses this as he instructs,

> "Finally, brothers, whatever is true, whatever is honorable, whatever is just, whatever is pure, whatever is lovely, whatever is commendable, if there is any excellence, if there is anything worthy of praise, think about these things." (Philippians 4:8 ESV).

So, how do I strategically put good things into my mind while limiting the opportunity for evil things to come in? For me, it's a two-pronged plan. First, I fill my idle time with constructive or wholesome thoughts. When I am in my car, I listen to a select few podcasts by Christians who speak on spiritual things. When I go for my walks, I listen to encouraging audio books or sermons on YouTube.

Second, I limit empty-calorie entertainment. While there might not be anything wrong with watching TV shows or YouTube videos of cute kittens doing silly things, I often found myself letting hours slip away before realizing the day was already spent. Now, I am very judicious with the good things I let pass into my mind. Proverbs 23:7 says, "For as he thinks in his heart, so is he." What we think about are the things that we let occupy our minds.

Here are some other activities I guard against. I'm not saying that they are wrong, but for me, they get in the way of me putting good things in if they take control of my time or my thoughts: mobile games, binge-able TV show seasons, any movie or show with questionable content or language, click-bait websites that send me mindlessly from one site to another, 24/7 news programs, and the list goes on and on. Yeah, I let a lot of empty content take up way too much of my brain's real estate.

What I learned is that Satan is not too concerned about me putting lewd and evil thoughts into my mind. He is content with me filling my mind with worthless thoughts so that there is no room for the things that Paul encouraged me to think about in Philippians 4.

This idea of putting in good and keeping out bad is beautifully taught by Jesus as he describes the role that the eye plays as the mind's gatekeeper:

> "The eye is the lamp of the body. So, if your eye is healthy, your whole body will be full of light, but if your eye is bad, your whole body will be full of darkness. If then the light in you is darkness, how great is the darkness!" (Matthew 6:22-23 ESV).

So here's the conclusion that I have learned on how to prepare my heart for Kingdom living:

1. I am in control of what I let into my mind and what I will think about.
2. What I choose to let in will affect the kind of heart I have.
3. Choosing what to think about is a purposeful action. Good things won't just happen to come into my mind on their own, though evil things will.

If you want to have a good heart that will prepare you for Kingdom living, then fill your heart with good and think on things that give it the building blocks it needs. This has been vital for me. When I take control of what I let into my mind, it is easier for my spiritual man to win his battles. When I grow lax and let evil or empty thoughts dominate, my carnal man inevitably launches a strong battle against me as he is fed by the sin I let in.

So far, I have talked about the importance of Bible reading, prayer, and putting the right things into my mind. These things have been so important for me to take my bad heart and prepare it for Kingdom living. Next week, I will discuss something that involves other people. This has been so important to me in preparing my heart for Kingdom living I dare say it might be a deal-breaker if I had never spent the time cultivating this within my heart.

***

In my daily Bible reading, I am in Joshua. It is a wonderful book of faith as we witness God doing amazing things for the Israelites.

I love the story of the Israelites crossing the Jordan river. What a sight! The children of the generation who crossed the Red Sea were privileged to experience what their parents experienced.

But I have always read this crossing from the perspective of the Israelites... until today.

God told Moses that He would make His name great before all nations and glorify his name through the Exodus and His power over mighty Egypt.

Imagine the sight from the Canaanites' perspective when they saw the water of the mighty Jordan heap by the city of Adam and the Israelites walk on dry land toward their city.

Truly, their hearts would melt within them.

God's name would be glorified. The Canaanite's sins were now full, and God would judge them through the Israelites who walked with their God across the Jordan on dry ground, and there was nothing they could do to stand against this God.

***

I'm finishing up the book of Joshua in my daily Bible reading. In chapter 20, God talks to Joshua about setting up the cities of refuge that He talked to Moses about.

These were cities where someone who accidentally killed a man could flee for refuge. Here is the thing that just struck me as I read this today:

God had the foresight to see all the circumstances the Israelites would need in a government. We set up a legislature and a system of amendments to adjust as we learn better ways to govern.

But when God wrote the Law for the people, there was no legislator, no new laws as they learned new needs, and no amendments.

Isn't it amazing how God is so much higher than man? He gets it right the first time. We see His wisdom in the creation of the cities of refuge.

Truly, God created a government for people with zero experience in governing, and for thousands of years, it needed no amendments.

The giving of the Law of Moses is evidence of God's existence, love, and grace for His people, and it is underscored in the establishment of the cities of refuge.

"Say to the people of Israel, 'Appoint the cities of refuge, of which I spoke to you through Moses,

that the manslayer who strikes any person without intent or unknowingly may flee there. They shall be for you a refuge from the avenger of blood." (Joshua 20:2-3 ESV).

***

I have started reading Psalm in my daily Bible reading. What a wonderful book to find comfort and to find words for a troubled soul when words are hard to find.

I love the words in the tenth Psalm. It speaks to men when we forget about the Lord's all-seeing eyes.

"He says in his heart, "God has forgotten, he has hidden his face, he will never see it."

Arise, O LORD; O God, lift up your hand; forget not the afflicted.

Why does the wicked renounce God and say in his heart, "You will not call to account"?" (Psalm 10:11-13 ESV).

Why should I do good? It's because the eyes of the Lord are always upon us. He sees all and is never fooled. This is the help we need to choose right and never wrong.

"But you do see, for you note mischief and vexation, that you may take it into your hands; to you the helpless commits himself; you have been the helper of the fatherless." (Psalm 10:14 ESV).

Amen.

***

I don't care what you think the divine council is...
I don't care who you think the sons of the Most High are...
You can't read this Psalm and walk away from these facts:
1. God the Father is the Most High.
2. He expects others to administer justice to the weak, the destitute, and the orphans.
3. Those who don't will answer to Him.

"A Psalm of Asaph. God has taken his place in the divine council; in the midst of the gods he holds judgment:

"How long will you judge unjustly and show partiality to the wicked? Selah

Give justice to the weak and the fatherless; maintain the right of the afflicted and the destitute.

Rescue the weak and the needy; deliver them from the hand of the wicked."

They have neither knowledge nor understanding, they walk about in darkness; all the foundations of the earth are shaken.

I said, "You are gods, sons of the Most High, all of you;

nevertheless, like men you shall die, and fall like any prince." (Psalm 82:1-7 ESV).

***

I need to remind myself of this important fact,

God wishes me to do less study and more living what I study.

Study is to equip me for good and not a means unto itself.

When I stand before the righteous Judge, I will not answer a quiz to assess my knowledge to determine my eternity.

My Judge will ask,

"When I was naked, did you clothe Me?" He will not ask, "Did you know you were supposed to clothe Me?"

My Judge will ask,

"When I was hungry, did you feed me?" He will not ask, "Did you study that you should feed Me?"

My Judge will ask, "When I was sick and in prison, did you visit Me?" He will not ask, "In all your Bible reading, did you read that you should visit Me?"

My Judge will ask,

"When I was thirsty, did you give Me something to drink?" He will not ask, "When you taught Bible classes or wrote Facebook posts, did you tell people to give Me something to drink?"

Study is not the end. Study is to equip me to live the Gospel message of grace and to prepare me to stand before my King and Judge as His disciple.

In the end, disciples study to know how to follow. We don't study to profess our knowledge.

"Then they also will answer, saying, 'Lord, when did we see you hungry or thirsty or a stranger or naked or sick or in prison, and did not minister to you?'

Then he will answer them, saying, 'Truly, I say to you, as you did not do it to one of the least of these, you did not do it to me.'" (Matthew 25:44-45 ESV).

***

In my daily Bible reading, I'm in Psalm. David wrote the 51st Psalm after He committed adultery with Bathsheba and murdered her faithful husband, Uriah.

In this Psalm, David owns his sin and lays it before God, asking for a new, clean heart which he pleads for God to create in him. Haven't we all felt this longing at times?

Listen to what David says as he zeros in on the crux of the situation:

"For you will not delight in sacrifice, or I would give it; you will not be pleased with a burnt offering.

The sacrifices of God are a broken spirit; a broken and contrite heart, O God, you will not despise." (Psalm 51:16-17 ESV).

It is a consistent theme in both the Old Testament and the New Testament that God wishes us to do "the weightier matters of the Law" (judgment, mercy, and faith- Matthew 23:23) before the lesser things. In fact, Jesus also says,

"Go and learn what this means: 'I desire mercy, and not sacrifice.' For I came not to call the righteous, but sinners." (Matthew 9:13 ESV).

But as people, we have always set sacrifices up as preeminent. While they are important, they are not what the Lord desires most from us.

When we put sacrifices first, we start down the road of legalism and self-justification. David knew this. Sacrifices must come from a clean heart that seeks the weightier matters. Without the weightier matters, sacrifices are nothing. They are just a checklist of tasks we do to make us feel better because of our own deliverance.

That's why David goes on to say,

"Do good to Zion in your good pleasure; build up the walls of Jerusalem;
then will you delight in right sacrifices, in burnt offerings and whole burnt offerings; then bulls will be offered on your altar." (Psalm 51:18-19

ESV).

Sacrifices will not help us if we do not perform them from a clean heart that seeks the weightier matters first.

***

If our King returned in 30 minutes, how would that affect your schedule?
Would He be an inconvenience?
One day, He will be 30 minutes away from returning.
Are you ready to greet Him today?

***

Preparing My Heart For Kingdom Living: Seek Out Daily Service Moments

Last Tuesday, we showed how important it is to take control of our thoughts and to control what we choose to let into our minds in order to prepare our hearts for Kingdom living. Today, I want to share another thing I learned to do that helped prepare my heart for Kingdom living. It's all about putting others before ourselves and seeking moments to serve our fellow brothers and sisters in Christ.

This is a message that Jesus kept hitting hard during his ministry. In fact, every time His disciples argued over who would be the greatest in the kingdom, Jesus answered that the greatest would be the servant of others. To nail this point home, Jesus left us an example of service by washing His disciples' feet and then explaining His expectations for all of us:

> "If I then, your Lord and Teacher, have washed your feet, you also ought to wash one another's feet. For I have given you an example, that you also should do just as I have done to you." (John 13:14-15 ESV).

I am humbled every time I realize that the Creator of all, the God of heaven, washed the dirty feet of His creation. I cannot fathom how I can ever make excuses for not having to serve others and put them before myself. How can I justify that when I stand before Him on the day of Judgement?

And so I began to look for opportunities to serve. And Matthew 6 really hit me hard. Jesus teaches us to do our good deeds in secret and not before men:

> "Thus, when you give to the needy, sound no trumpet before you, as the hypocrites do in the synagogues and in the streets, that they may be praised by others. Truly, I say to you, they have received their reward.
> But when you give to the needy, do not let your left hand know what your right hand is doing,
> so that your giving may be in secret. And your Father who sees in secret will reward you." (Matthew 6:2-4 ESV).

There is something about seeking out opportunities to serve others that changes the way you think about what is important. And this results in cultivating a heart ready for the Kingdom of heaven. Listen to what the Spirit says about our service to others:

> "But if anyone has the world's goods and sees his brother in need, yet closes his heart against him, how does God's love abide in him?" (1 John 3:17 ESV).

> "Let each of you look not only to his own interests, but also to the interests of others." (Philippians 2:4 ESV).

> "Bear one another's burdens, and so fulfill the law of Christ." (Galatians 6:2 ESV).

> "Contribute to the needs of the saints and seek to show hospitality." (Romans 12:13 ESV).

And the examples in James 2 and Matthew 25 continue to show how our God teaches us to adopt a posture of service. Unless we do, we cannot develop the character that Jesus wants us to develop. It's hard to live a selfless life and harbor a selfish heart. The key is to guard against seeking glory through the service. As we learned in Matthew 6, once we covet the praise for our service, we lose out on the transforming power it will have on us.

So, how can we cultivate a servant's heart? For me, it is happening with purpose. Service rarely occurs by happenstance. I purposefully determined to develop a servant's heart. Whether it's an opportunity to take care of a monetary need within my ability, provide food or clothing, be ready to help when illness strikes, volunteer for opportunities that come through our local congregation, or offer a word of encouragement when given a chance, I am opening myself up to service in whatever way I can offer it.

And this kind of service goes beyond just helping fellow Christians. If we develop the heart of a servant, we will humble ourselves whenever we see the need. We will be like the Good Samaritan who helps his neighbor when he sees someone in need. This was Jesus' answer to the question, "Who is my neighbor?"

> "Which of these three, do you think, proved to be a neighbor to the man who fell among the robbers?"
> He said, "The one who showed him mercy." And Jesus said to him, "You go, and do likewise." (Luke 10:36-37 ESV).

A heart prepared for Kingdom living is a heart that shows mercy to those created in the image of God.

I am nowhere close to being the servant I want to be, but I seek the opportunity each week. It might be something as small as a cup of cold water given in the name of the Lord, but my goal is not to let the week come to an end without having offered at least one distinct act of service. I'd encourage you to make this part of your Christian life.

> "For God is not unjust so as to overlook your work and the love that you have shown for his name in serving the saints, as you still do." (Hebrews 6:10 ESV).

***

I am in the Psalm in my daily Bible reading. As the collection ends, we are reminded not to trust man but God. In the 146 Psalm, we read:

> "Put not your trust in princes, in a son of man, in whom there is no salvation.
> When his breath departs, he returns to the earth; on that very day his plans perish." (Psalm 146:3-4 ESV).

In a political nation, I wonder if we put too much trust in the princes of men. Every election seems to be the most crucial, the last grasp to get things the way we want them to be.

For those who serve in the Kingdom of God, it is never too late for things to turn out the way God wants them to turn out.

Rather than wring our hands over the election of princes, we need to sleep peacefully in the presence of the Lord. That's what the Psalmist says:

"The LORD watches over the sojourners; he upholds the widow and the fatherless, but the way of the wicked he brings to ruin.

The LORD will reign forever, your God, O Zion, to all generations. Praise the LORD!" (Psalm 146:9-10 ESV).

Let us pray for goodness, righteousness, justice, wisdom, and that God will be honored. If we pray for these things and not just for a political party or our prince to be elected, our God may answer our prayers regardless of who gets elected.

Let's pray to God for the eternal blessings we want, which will survive beyond the grave of our princes.

***

Be not dismayed...

When things happen to us beyond our control, God is there to pick us up.

When things happen to us because of our actions, God is there to pick us up.

When we sin, God is there to pick us up.

There is never a time beyond God's ability or inclination to help us when we need His help.

"fear not, for I am with you; be not dismayed, for I am your God; I will strengthen you, I will help you, I will uphold you with my righteous right hand." (Isaiah 41:10 ESV).

***

I just finished up the book of Ruth in my daily Bible reading. This book drips with messianic shadows of the great redeemer God would send to Israel and the Gentiles, making one people from many.

While I see an overarching type woven into this story, today it struck me that there is also a personal story in Ruth. This story belongs to Naomi. It is a personal story we all need to hear and remember when our lives are shattered and upended.

This godly woman had to leave her land with her husband and two sons because of a famine. While in a foreign land, her sons married two Moabite women. Life was as good as it could be under the circumstances.

But then her life began to shatter. First, her husband died, leaving her a widow. A few years later, her two sons also died. Naomi was left a widow and childless, lost in a strange land. But by the grace of one of her daughter-in-laws, Ruth, she was not alone.

She and Ruth make the trek back to Israel. Although she has land, she is impoverished and cannot redeem her family's inheritance and is on the verge of losing everything. While her relatives were happy to see her back, Naomi wasn't feeling blessed:

> "She said to them, "Do not call me Naomi; call me Mara, for the Almighty has dealt very bitterly with me.
> I went away full, and the LORD has brought me back empty. Why call me Naomi, when the LORD has testified against me and the Almighty has brought calamity upon me?" (Ruth 1:20-21 ESV).

Have we ever felt this way? We suffer a great loss, and it seems that the foundation of our lives crumbles beneath us, leaving us exposed and stripped of joy.

In times like these, we feel the way Naomi felt when she returned home. It's hard to see any good when our heart breaks from a loss. It's hard to see how the pain can ever go away or how joy can ever find its way back into our lives.

Naomi is grieving. But the book of Ruth shows us that God can restore joy, even when we cannot see how it is possible. He tenderly wraps us in the healing balm of time and helps us slowly start to see the joys He still has for us, even in the wake of our pain.

Naomi ends up with a daughter-in-law who loves her, a redeemer who will protect her family's inheritance, and a great-great-grandson who will be her people's greatest king.

God didn't remove Naomi's pain, but He did help her find life again when the world she knew died around her.

Ruth is an amazing messianic story foreshadowing the redemption of Jesus, but it is also the amazing story of Naomi that teaches us of God's deep love and His power to put shattered lives back together again with hope.

***

Forgiveness is easier when people come prostrate before us, begging for forgiveness.

It's easy to show grace when people deserve it.

It's natural for us to serve people who can return the service to us.

But Jesus calls for us to be spiritual, not natural.

"But love your enemies, and do good, and lend, expecting nothing in return, and your reward will be great, and you will be sons of the Most High, for he is kind to the ungrateful and the evil." (Luke 6:35 ESV).

"Be kind to one another, tenderhearted, forgiving one another, as God in Christ forgave you." (Ephesians 4:32 ESV).

"Be merciful, even as your Father is merciful." (Luke 6:36 ESV).

***

It's Saturday.
The Lord will probably not come today.
If He returns soon, it will likely happen on the Lord's Day.
Today will likely be a safe day to party and put off doing what we know we should do.
Tomorrow, we can prepare for the return of the Lord.
Tomorrow...

"For as were the days of Noah, so will be the coming of the Son of Man.
For as in those days before the flood they were eating and drinking, marrying and giving in marriage, until the day when Noah entered the ark,
and they were unaware until the flood came and swept them all away, so will be the coming of the Son of Man." (Matthew 24:37-39 ESV).

***

I'm in the book of Proverbs in my daily Bible reading. It's amazing how often the author advises us to spend less time talking and more time remaining silent.
Wisdom is in the man who judiciously chooses his words without rushing to be heard.

***

King David always sought the Lord before going into battle. For the most part, so did the Israelites under Joshua. When they did not, they faced needless defeat.

When we go into a spiritual battle or face someone to whom we must deliver a tough message, do we seek the Lord's help first?

Seeking the Lord's help first is wisdom. Trusting in our own ability to succeed is folly.

***

We are much more gluttons for punishments than we are gluttons for goodness.

We watch things on TV that we know will make us angry, yet we still watch them.

We hang with people we know will bring us down, yet we still hang with them.

We waste hours away with useless activities when we know they will stress us out when we see how unproductive we have been, yet we still waste away the hours.

We spend too much time in our heads, practicing pitched battles with others when someone does or says something that offends us, knowing it turns up the heat, yet we still simmer in anger, letting it fester.

We take too many things personally rather than looking at disagreements objectively, knowing it will cause us to dig in our heels and act out of defensiveness. Yet, we continue to react to disagreements personally.

Rather than continuing to be gluttons for punishment, what would it do to our lives and experiences if we became gluttons for goodness?

What would happen if we could identify the punishments we put ourselves through and replace them with spiritually productive habits?

"Keep your heart with all vigilance, for from it flow the springs of life." (Proverbs 4:23 ESV).

***

Preparing My Heart For Kingdom Living:

Build Relationships

Last Tuesday, we discussed how important it is to seek out daily service moments to help prepare our hearts for Kingdom living. That is one way we can make a difference in the lives of others. But to better prepare our hearts for Kingdom living, we must also learn to build relationships with others who share our same goals, values, and hopes. We must seek out relationships to help us learn to support those in need while finding people who can lift our hearts as we travel through rough roads.

> "And day by day, attending the temple together and breaking bread in their homes, they received their food with glad and generous hearts, praising God and having favor with all the people. And the Lord added to their number day by day those who were being saved." (Acts 2:46-47 ESV).

From the beginning, early Christians knew the importance of seeking each other out. God never intended us to be islands trying to make it through this world alone. No, Jesus has brought together men and women to encourage, uplift and cheer each other on. He has given us the ability to walk with people who understand what our commitment to Him is. This is a wonderful jewel in the treasure Jesus has provided us.

But for me, that meant I would have to take the initiative to seek out others and get to know them. After all, Christians are still people. They only know what we need if we share our needs with them. They will only understand who we are if we drop our guard and appear authentic before them. And the powerful thing I have realized is that other people are just as eager and open to wanting to find someone like me as I want to find someone like them. Not that I am such a great, interesting, or entertaining person, but because I love the same God they love, and I am walking down the same road they are walking down. People do not want to build a relationship simply because they think I can overcome the same challenges they face. They want to build a relationship because I sometimes fail, but I am determined to get back up, just like them.

I learned that the idea of reaching out to others is such a powerful part of preparing my heart for Kingdom living that Satan doubles down on convincing me this is either a waste of time or that no one would be interested in building a relationship with me. After all, it will be just a matter of time before I say something stupid or embarrassing.

And yes, I sometimes say stupid things. I sometimes tell an awkward joke that is taken wrong. Sometimes I hurt someone without realizing it because I say something insensitive without thinking. Sometimes I embarrass myself and want to crawl under a rock. And Satan keeps whispering into my ear, "It's not worth pursuing relationships with God's people. They are ready to pounce and to judge. It's best to keep to yourself."

Sometimes I listen. But the more I listen to that kind of thinking, the lonelier and more isolated I become, and Satan starts to get leverage on me. The truth is, Satan understands that his job gets exponentially tougher when I build relationships with others. He's not stupid. He knows:

> "Two are better than one, because they have a good reward for their toil.
>
> For if they fall, one will lift up his fellow. But woe to him who is alone when he falls and has not another to lift him up!
>
> Again, if two lie together, they keep warm, but how can one keep warm alone? And though a man might prevail against one who is alone,
>
> two will withstand him--a threefold cord is not quickly broken." (Ecclesiastes 4:9-12 ESV).

> "Therefore encourage one another and build one another up, just as you are doing." (1 Thessalonians 5:11 ESV).

What I am talking about goes beyond just attending church services with each other, though I think this is a powerful and needed thing for us all. No, I am talking about getting to know our brothers and sisters. Spending time with them outside the assembly strengthens our bond of worship when we come together. It's the way we become excited when we see a friend and long to catch up with them. Isn't this what we all really want?

But we are people. This kind of relationship will not happen automatically, nor will it develop deeply without the commitment of time and an investment of service. So I learned I must start down a long road to cultivate these relationships. They are not built overnight, and not all will grow to the depth of others. And that's okay. Building these kinds of relationships isn't done in a sprint, they are cultivated over a marathon.

I love to set up an hour to meet with someone over coffee just to get to know them outside church services. Sometimes this leads to many other meetings, phone calls, or messages. Sometimes, not so many. But you know what? There is no one whom I reached out to that I don't feel closer to. And after that first awkward meeting takes place, the rest is downhill.

But it involves me taking that first step. This has become such a powerful part of preparing my heart for Kingdom living. This process of building relationships teaches me to love, invest in others, and stop looking at things only through my eyes. When we go through the process of building relationships, we learn how to become better servants of the Lord. We learn to be more like Jesus.

Who knows how deeply these relationships will grow? But as I engage in trying to build them, I become a better person. After all, isn't this the purpose of Kingdom living; having a heart that learns to have more of others and less of me?

> "Do nothing from selfish ambition or conceit, but in humility count others more significant than yourselves. Let each of you look not only to his own interests, but also to the interests of others." (Philippians 2:3-4 ESV).

***

I am in 1 Samuel in my daily Bible reading. We read about the rise and fall of a great man as king.

Saul had everything going for him as king, including the support of God. In fact, it was God who choose Saul as King. Yes, he was the hand-picked leader who God Himself chose.

We often hear that David was chosen as a man after God's heart and assume that the people chose Saul. But that wasn't the case.

God chose both men. But God chose Saul after the people's hearts; that is, He chose someone who was "kingly" in the way people thought a king should be. Saul was an impressive specimen of a man, standing head-and-shoulders above other men.

But he was still a man chosen by God to be king. However, when God was ready to replace Saul as king, He chose someone after His heart who was "kingly" in the way He thought a king should be. David had a shepherd's heart, and that's just the kind of person God wanted to be king over His people.

God's first choice of king didn't live up to his potential though God loved him and gave him every opportunity to thrive. He sinned against God and was more concerned about his appearance in the eyes of the people than repenting before the Lord.

Because of this, we read one of the most tragic verses in the Bible:

> "And Samuel did not see Saul again until the day of his death, but Samuel grieved over Saul. And the LORD regretted that he had made Saul king over Israel." (1 Samuel 15:35 ESV).

"The Lord regretted that he made Saul king over Israel." What a terrible place to be. Yet this was because Saul refused to walk with God. It wasn't because Saul made mistakes, for God is full of mercy and grace to imperfect people who humble themselves in repentance. We see this in God's next choice as king, David.

I don't want God to have any regrets about me. If He does, it will be because I quit walking with Him, not because I make mistakes.

***

In 1 Samuel 2, we read Hannah's prayer. God had opened her womb in response to her pleading for a child. She told the Lord that if He gave her a son, she'd devote him to His service all his life.

The prayer in 1 Samuel 2 is her prayer of praise to God. It's amazing to me that Hannah is full of praise to God, knowing she would have to send her son away.

Do you think that Hannah wanted to send her firstborn away? She could have been distressed, but instead, she found a way to rejoice in what the Lord did for her.

It shows us that even when things happen we don't want, we can still praise the Lord. It shows us we can still praise even when we must sacrifice something precious to the Lord. Hannah found joy in the Lord's promise, even when it meant she had to fulfill her vow and release her son to the Lord.

Sometimes, we have to find joy in serving the Lord, even when it means sacrificing to the Lord. Hannah had to sacrifice what she loved most to the Lord, yet she did so gladly.

I want to be like Hannah. I want to be able to sacrifice to God without resentment for doing so.

***

I'm in the book of 2 Samuel in my daily Bible reading. King David had such a rollercoaster of a life.

He started as a fearless youthful shepherd boy, killing lions and bears to save his sheep. Then, God killed a giant by His hand, and David served in the king's court.

God gave him victories in battle and favor in the people's sight. But Saul's jealousy burned against him, and David found himself running from Saul with only a step between him and death.

During these days, David experienced deep depression and anxiety, yet he leaned on the Lord to work through it.

Even when David became king, he allowed sin to come between him and

God. God killed the first son Bathsheba bore him, and then God raised a sword in his house.

David had to flee from his son Absalom, and eventually mourn the third death of one of his sons.

Through all of this, David was an imperfect man. But what made him a man the Lord loved was that he never stopped walking with God. He stumbled, but he did not go his own way.

When we stumble, God still loves us. We may have to endure our own rollercoasters in life, but let us have the same heart David had. Let's get back up and continue walking with God when we stumble.

God is gracious to imperfect people. But He will let us go our own way if we quit walking with Him. In this, let us follow in David's steps and not in Saul's steps.

***

I finished up 2 Samuel in my daily Bible reading. It tells of Absalom's rebellion against his father, King David.

In this rebellion, sides are taken. One person who leaves David and places his loyalty with Absalom is Ahithophel. This counselor's advice was credited as coming from God by both David and Absalom.

I often wonder why Ahithophel was so quick to change his loyalty. He was Bathsheba's grandfather. Perhaps he never forgave David for killing his granddaughter's husband and bringing disgrace upon his family when David committed adultery with Bathsheba. We don't know for sure, but this wise man took the first chance to betray king David.

The first advice he gives Absalom when the rebellion happens is to run after David immediately to strike him while David is still confused. But another adviser, who secretly works for David to thwart Ahithophel's counsel, condemns Ahithophel's advice and offers his counter-advice. Absalom rejects Ahithophel's advice and follows Hushai's advice instead. This is how Ahithophel responds:

> "When Ahithophel saw that his counsel was not followed, he saddled his donkey and went off home to his own city. He set his house in order and hanged himself, and he died and was buried in the tomb of his father." (2 Samuel 17:23 ESV).

Have you wondered what caused Ahithophel to take such drastic actions when his advice wasn't followed? The Bible doesn't say for sure, but remember, this wise man was sought after because he understood things that others didn't. God had given him a spirit of wisdom that no one denied.

It is likely that Ahithophel understood what was going on and realized that Absalom's rebellion was doomed by God. That left him in a no-win situation. He had cast his lot against the Lord's anointed king, and he knew it was a matter of time before he'd have to answer for this betrayal.

Each of us faces a similar choice. At some point, we come to terms with the fact that we have cast our lot against the Lord, and it is a matter of time before we will have to face the music and be held accountable for our rebellion.

But our Lord is rich in mercy and grace. All we need to do is repent and kneel in submission to Him, and Jesus will take us back and remember our rebellion no more.

But many of us will commit spiritual suicide rather than repent and turn to Jesus. What a sad state to be in when forgiveness and life are choices we have before us.

Will we set our house in order and receive the wages of our rebellion against God, or will we turn to Him and receive his mercy and grace today?

***

When Jesus stood before Pilate, Pilate responded to the Jews by saying he found no fault in Him:

"Then Pilate said to the chief priests and the crowds, "I find no guilt in this man." (Luke 23:4 ESV).

This is important in so many ways.

Perhaps one of the most beloved purposes for this statement is in Jesus being declared the pure, perfect lamb without blemish.

God only accepted the perfect lamb for sacrifices, and Pilate declared Jesus a fitting lamb for the terrible deed that was about to happen.

Jesus was the spotless lamb who would lay His life down for each one of us.

***

God is held to no moral standard.
God IS the moral standard.
Good is good because God defines what good is.

Evil is evil because God defines what evil is.
God can hold anyone accountable to His standard.
God answers to no authority.
This is precisely what it means to be sovereign.
We get no say in the matter.
We get no vote.
We simply choose to submit to His sovereignty today,
Or we will submit on the Day of Judgment.
We can not rebel against God's sovereignty forever with impunity.

***

Preparing My Heart For Kingdom Living: Confess Jesus Daily

Well, we have come to the end of a seven-week journey. I have endeavored to share with you what I do to prepare my heart for Kingdom living. As you recall, nearly two months ago, I shared with you that I came from a place where I had ended a decade-plus-long struggle with God. I lived, then, in some of my darkest moments in life, and my family had to endure this dark age with me because of my rebellion against God.

But God was gracious to me. He didn't write me off. He didn't let me go my own way. There was always an ember in my heart with a faint glow. God blew on that ember and kept it alive. He left the safe ninety-nine sheep as He went into the wilderness with me to lead me home.

I still remember the moment when I broke and surrendered to God. I was driving to work on Sachse Road, and the culmination of years of questions, accusations, bitterness, hatred, obstinance, and rebellion melted away into surrender. God had worked His work in me and brought me to where I had to be. It was on that road that I determined to fully give myself to my Master for the rest of my days.

That was a few years ago, and each day I have only grown stronger in my resolve to live in Him. Today, I have a stronger relationship with God than I have ever had in my life. But it wasn't like that when I surrendered to Him on Sachse Road that day. God had broken me with a contrite spirit. My life was a shambles of broken pieces, and I had to begin the process of piecing things together again. I had a lot of consequences to face and a heart that needed attention if it were to survive the task ahead.

So, I determined to eat this elephant one bite at a time. My task was monumental. Left on my own, it would have been impossible. But for the first time in over a decade, I wouldn't be doing it alone. Jesus would be walking this road with me, and I placed my faith in Him to help me with my impossible task.

He was faithful, and together we rebuilt my faith and my life. As I have said in these last few weeks, I decided to work on one thing at a time to prepare my heart for Kingdom living and trust that God would be gracious and merciful to me, seeing me as a work in progress. As long as I was walking with Him each day, my faith was fully in Him, and I never let Satan convince me that I was a lost cause or that I was so far gone I might as well give up.

So I started with the easy things to do. I made commitments that only involved discipline. I knew I had to fill myself up with His Word.

So I committed to reading His word every day, on average, an hour or so a day.

Then I focused on my prayer life, speaking to God when I arose and when I went to bed. Within months, I found myself praying without ceasing, and I cannot imagine facing a day without being able to pray to Him. I greatly covet my one-on-one time with Him.

I then started to work on controlling the things I let into my heart. From the movies I watched to the empty time wasters, I began to limit things that were of little value and replace them with wholesome things that provided the building blocks of strong faith.

The next thing I tackled was developing a heart shaped by service. In my Bible readings, I could not escape the expectation Jesus gave me to become His disciple. That manifested itself in service. I knew that if I stopped growing, I would not have the heart I desperately wanted. So I sought ways to do something each day to serve others. In this, the Lord opened my eyes to the numerous service moments that were always around me.

Then that led me to focus on stepping out and purposely building relationships with others. I realized that God had never intended for me to walk through life alone. I had done this for over a decade and proved to be a miserable host of my own life.

All these things have taken years of purposeful deliberate planning and commitment. But they started with small steps that the Lord helped me take each day. I spend this time with you now, retracing the things we talked about over the last seven weeks because it helps bring context to this last thing that I focused on to help me develop my heart for Kingdom living:

Confess Jesus Daily.

Having built a foundation, I knew that I was ready to grow into the next step. I was committed to finding ways each day to confess my Savior to others. I began my days with a prayer for God to help me have the wisdom to know how to confess Jesus that day, and I ended with a prayer that God would accept my confession of His Son that day.

That led to conversations with people I worked with and friends I have known for years. When one of my elders encouraged me to share my insights on Facebook, I agreed only after I prayed to God and agreed with Him that if I did this, it would be for His glory and to further confess His Son daily.

I'm still developing this part of my heart for Kingdom living, and it's become a regular part of my prayer each night that God has accepted the confession of His Son that I make each day. When I stand before Jesus, I want no possibility of being denied by my Savior before His Father in Heaven:

> "So everyone who acknowledges me before men, I also will acknowledge before my Father who is in heaven,
> but whoever denies me before men, I also will deny before my Father who is in heaven." (Matthew 10:32-33 ESV).

As I close this series, I hope I have said something that can help you as you look to prepare your heart for Kingdom living. If you are like me, you might find it a daunting task at times. Satan will try to convince you that it is too hard.

But I can tell you from experience that Jesus will walk with you every step of the way, giving you His grace to succeed.

The Spirit will give you the wisdom you need to grow in the Lord each day.

The Father will work on you each day to conform you more and more into the image of His dear Son.

And along the way, you will surround yourself with others who are taking this journey with you.

One day, you will look back and be amazed at how far you have come, not because of your strength but because of what God has done in your heart. This is how I have begun to prepare my heart for Kingdom living here on earth and for the age to come.

All of God and none of me.

***

I am in the book of Job in my daily Bible reading. I have heard people say that Job didn't have a sense of an afterlife because he focused so much on the finality and futility of death.

But they miss the point that Job is making. Job is talking about serving God vs. not being able to serve Him if he is dead. He's talking about not being able to do anything good in this life when he is in Sheol.

On one hand, Job argues for what God will miss if he dies. On the other hand, he longs for death to bring a permanent end to his suffering.

But as the Ecclesiastes writer says, God has put eternity in man's heart. Even Job had a sense of eternity. As he struggled with his suffering, Job gave us a glimpse of his eternal perspective in chapter 19.

> "For I know that my Redeemer lives, and at the last he will stand upon the earth.
>
> And after my skin has been thus destroyed, yet in my flesh I shall see God,
>
> whom I shall see for myself, and my eyes shall behold, and not another. My heart faints within me!
>
> If you say, 'How we will pursue him!' and, 'The root of the matter is found in him,'
>
> be afraid of the sword, for wrath brings the punishment of the sword, that you may know there is a judgment." (Job 19:25-29 ESV).

I believe this core belief in something beyond death anchored Job. Eternity is the anchor we can also hold to when our life becomes a struggle and seems so futile to us.

Our Redeemer lives, and we shall also see Him after our skin is destroyed.

Yes, Job believed in life after death, even though his suffering invited death. And though his death would bring him before God, it would mean he would no longer be able to do any good on the earth forever.

This is the hopeless permanence of death that Job laments.

***

We do what we want, thinking God will always bear with us while we rebel against Him.

Samson didn't even know the Lord left him after he continued to rebel against God.

The Jews didn't believe God would abandon His temple, even while they continued to rebel against Him.

God doesn't leave anyone who is striving to serve Him; He departs from us once we depart from Him.

> "Keep your life free from love of money, and be content with what you have, for he has said, "I will never leave you nor forsake you."
>
> So we can confidently say, "The Lord is my helper; I will not fear; what can man do to me?" (Hebrews 13:5-6 ESV).

***

When was the last time we confessed Jesus before others?
When was the last time we denied Him?
Confession is a purposeful action.
It happens more than one time in our lives, fulfilling our duty as disciples.
Confession is an everyday thing we do.
We confess Jesus with our mouth.
We confess Jesus with our actions.
We confess Jesus when it's convenient.
We confess Jesus when it brings us derision.
We cannot stay silent in our words or actions and still confess Him before men.
Silence is denial.
If Jesus returned today, can we stand on the confession we have been making of our Lord?
Our confession of Him will dictate the confession He makes of us.

> "So everyone who acknowledges me before men, I also will acknowledge before my Father who is in heaven,
> but whoever denies me before men, I also will deny before my Father who is in heaven." (Matthew 10:32-33 ESV).

***

I am in the book of Hosea in my daily Bible reading. This is a heartbreaking book. Israel is committing adultery with God, leaving Him for other gods.

God longs for them, but they laugh in His face as they seek others to replace Him. Yet, God still seeks to woo them back.

Listen to how God describes their utter spurning of Him:

> "Hear the word of the LORD, O children of Israel, for the LORD has a controversy with the inhabitants of the land. There is no faithfulness or steadfast love, and no knowledge of God in the land;
> there is swearing, lying, murder, stealing, and committing adultery; they break all bounds, and bloodshed follows bloodshed." (Hosea 4:1-2 ESV).

Can we really be considered a "Christian nation" anymore? To my brothers and sisters in Jesus, I plead and pray we never commit spiritual adultery with those in our nation, our world, who partake in the sinfulness that characterizes our world; the sinfulness that Hosea describes in chapter 4.

We have long moved past the point where we are a good nation with bad people in it.

We are now a sinful nation with good people in it. Let the righteous stay faithful to our God.

> "My people are bent on turning away from me, and though they call out to the Most High, he shall not raise them up at all." (Hosea 11:7 ESV).

***

I am in the book of Micah in my daily Bible reading. This time though, I am reading the books of the Bible in the chronological order in which they were written.

This gives me a unique perspective. When the people of Judah and Isreal hear from prophets, they hear messages of judgment with a call to repent.

Over and over, year after year, this is what they hear. As I look over the rest of the readings in store for me, the messages of judgment will only grow more intense for God's people.

> "Writhe and groan, O daughter of Zion, like a woman in labor, for now you shall go out from the city and dwell in the open country; you shall go to Babylon. There you shall be rescued; there the LORD will redeem you from the hand of your enemies." (Micah 4:10 ESV).

But the Lord still shows His grace to them. Unlike the judgments that come upon other nations, God promises grace and mercy to His people.

> "But you, O Bethlehem Ephrathah, who are too little to be among the clans of Judah, from you shall come forth for me one who is to be ruler in Israel, whose coming forth is from of old, from ancient days." (Micah 5:2 ESV).

This is the message that Israel and Judah will hear for decades to come.
This is the message I will read over and over for days to come.

***

The world is celebrating Easter today. That's a good thing. As Paul said, regardless of the motive, at least Christ is preached. Let's focus on the good today and not look for the bad. We will find what we are looking for.

***

I am in the book of Isaiah. It's passages like this that cause me to lose hope for the direction of our country today:

> "Woe to those who call evil good and good evil, who put darkness for light and light for darkness, who put bitter for sweet and sweet for bitter!
> Woe to those who are wise in their own eyes, and shrewd in their own sight!
> Woe to those who are heroes at drinking wine, and valiant men in mixing strong drink,
> who acquit the guilty for a bribe, and deprive the innocent of his right!" (Isaiah 5:20-23 ESV).

In the next chapter, Isaiah has his lips purified and his guilt taken away. This prepares him to live among the wicked people of his days and answer the Lord's call:

> "And I heard the voice of the Lord saying, "Whom shall I send, and who will go for us?" Then I said, "Here I am! Send me."
> And he said, "Go, and say to this people: "'Keep on hearing, but do not understand; keep on seeing, but do not perceive.'" (Isaiah 6:8-9 ESV).

May our lips be pure and our guilt be taken away so we, too, can answer the Lord's call from the midst of a wicked people.

***

Wisdom Is Not Always Found With The Aged

The Bible often points us to aged men and women as we look for wisdom, and for good reason. With age comes life experience. This experience can often help young men and women see traps and pitfalls that are hard for the naive to see. In fact, Proverbs is full of the wisdom of seeking advice from others rather than relying on our own wisdom.

"The way of a fool is right in his own eyes, but a wise man listens to advice." (Proverbs 12:15 ESV).

And the more counselors we have, the more sound the advice may be. This gives us a chance to hear a broad perspective of advice as we weigh them out before we take action.

"Where there is no guidance, a people falls, but in an abundance of counselors there is safety." (Proverbs 11:14 ESV).

But specifically, we see the Bible point to older people as sources of wisdom and counsel.

"Likewise, you who are younger, be subject to the elders. Clothe yourselves, all of you, with humility toward one another, for "God opposes the proud but gives grace to the humble." (1 Peter 5:5 ESV).

And

"Honor your father and your mother, that your days may be long in the land that the LORD your God is giving you." (Exodus 20:12 ESV).

In all of this, there is respect that we should show toward those who are aged:

"Do not rebuke an older man but encourage him as you would a father, younger men as brothers, older women as mothers, younger women as sisters, in all purity." (1 Timothy 5:1-2 ESV).

But there is a difference between showing this respect for and seeking counsel from those who have age on us and taking their words as the final authority for our lives. I wonder if sometimes we put too much authority into the words of people older than us.

While this may have minimal effect on our lives when it comes to making a life decision, it can be devastating if we take the advice of an older person when it comes to how we should serve the Lord. Just because someone has lived much longer than us doesn't make them the final word on how we should serve God.

While I see the wisdom in approaching our elders on spiritual matters, it is vital we continue to study ourselves and live the way we understand that God wants us to live. On the Day of Judgment, it will not be our elders we have to answer to about life choices and the discipleship we choose to live.

It will not be our parents to whom we can appeal when we stand before Jesus as our Judge. We cannot abdicate our responsibility to live for God the way He wants us to live by submitting to the aged people in our lives, our leaders, our families, our church, or our creeds. Advice is only as good as the truth that backs it up.

In the book of Job, we are introduced to five main characters. Job, his three friends, and a fourth, younger man. Job was a wise, older man whom people sought out before the plagues brought disaster upon him. His three friends that we are introduced to early on seem to be aged men of wisdom as well.

Then we are introduced to a young man named Elihu. Out of respect for his elders, Elihu waits until his elders finish their counsel before he speaks up. But as he listens to Job and the three other elders, his anger starts to burn against them all.

> "Then Elihu the son of Barachel the Buzite, of the family of Ram, burned with anger. He burned with anger at Job because he justified himself rather than God.
>
> He burned with anger also at Job's three friends because they had found no answer, although they had declared Job to be in the wrong." (Job 32:2-3 ESV).

When he opens his mouth, Elihu sets this perspective of wisdom and those older than him in perspective:

> "And Elihu the son of Barachel the Buzite answered and said: "I am young in years, and you are aged; therefore I was timid and afraid to declare my opinion to you.
>
> I said, 'Let days speak, and many years teach wisdom.'
>
> But it is the spirit in man, the breath of the Almighty, that makes him understand.
>
> It is not the old who are wise, nor the aged who understand what is right." (Job 32:6-9 ESV).

As Elihu continues to give wisdom from a younger person's perspective, he reminds these elders that wisdom comes from an absolute source and is not sourced simply from someone who may be older.

> "Bear with me a little, and I will show you, for I have yet something to say on God's behalf. I will get my knowledge from afar and ascribe righteousness to my Maker." (Job 36:2-3 ESV).

When this young man speaks to Job, a man he desperately wants to vindicate because of his great respect for him, Elihu goes to the source of wisdom:

> "Hear this, O Job; stop and consider the wondrous works of God.
> Do you know how God lays his command upon them and causes the lightning of his cloud to shine?
> Do you know the balancings of the clouds, the wondrous works of him who is perfect in knowledge,
> you whose garments are hot when the earth is still because of the south wind?
> Can you, like him, spread out the skies, hard as a cast metal mirror?" (Job 37:14-18 ESV).

In the end, God takes Job to the woodshed and condemns the wisdom of Job's older friends. It is only the young, respectful Elihu that God has no words of chastisement for. What can we learn from this?

First, there is wisdom in seeking counsel from others, but we must understand that age is no guarantee that advice will be sound.

Second, aged men cannot be a substitution for the will of God. Our elders can lead us astray, though they may do it with the best of intentions.

Third, we must continue to study God's Word ourselves. We will not be judged on the words of elders, parents, preachers, or church creeds, and we must not appeal to them as our final authority.

Fourth, it is ok to reject the counsel of our elders if we do not see their advice lining up with the Word of God. We must be responsible for our own souls and discipleship to Jesus.

Elihu was the only one God did not condemn in the book of Job. He escaped condemnation because he appealed to God and did not capitulate to the older men he had tremendous respect for. He did not stay silent. He took the lonely path of bucking against society to take his stand with God.

So must we.

***

Well, my week of Social Media/TV/Phone Games fast is over. This is something I suggest that everyone consider participating in periodically. I was surprised at all the time I spent on things that were not really important.

During my fast, I made this note during one of my readings that I want to share with you:

God will wipe away every tear. Perhaps this is even greater than we have thought. When our sins are laid bare on judgment, and we are pained over our sins, on that day, God will take away godly sorrow forever, and we will never again have to contend with godly sorrow over our sins. Our sins will forever be forgotten by us and by God, never to be thought of again.

***

Let us always put our trust in the one, unique, eternal, all-powerful, all-knowing God who sees all.

"All the nations are as nothing before him, they are accounted by him as less than nothing and emptiness.

To whom then will you liken God, or what likeness compare with him?" (Isaiah 40:17-18 ESV).

There is only one eternal God, one I AM. One Yahweh. There is none before the One who always existed. There will be none like Him after Him because He will have no "after." He has, is, and always will exist.

Because of this, there is no salvation found anywhere but in Him. Only the I AM can offer salvation, and salvation can only be offered in Him.

He will not be defeated.

He will not fade away.

He will not die.

"You are my witnesses," declares the LORD, "and my servant whom I have chosen, that you may know and believe me and understand that I am he. Before me no god was formed, nor shall there be any after me.

I, I am the LORD, and besides me there is no savior." (Isaiah 43:10-11 ESV).

***

Sometimes, when we watch society deteriorate, it tempts us to take our eyes off the Lord.

We worry about being canceled.

We worry about being sued.

We worry about being imprisoned.

We worry about being threatened with violence.

When society turns to utter disregard for God, let us not forget who God is.

Who are we to take our eyes off God, who is mightier, more trustworthy, and has us in His hand?

Let us not be full of dread when men become more evil; rather, let us rejoice in the steadfast love and protection of the Almighty!

> "I, I am he who comforts you; who are you that you are afraid of man who dies, of the son of man who is made like grass," (Isaiah 51:12 ESV).

***

I am in the book of Isaiah in my daily Bible reading. Wow, things never change. What God hated thousands of years ago, He hates today.

This is what Isaiah wrote in his day. Is it really much different in our day?

> "For your hands are defiled with blood and your fingers with iniquity; your lips have spoken lies; your tongue mutters wickedness.
>
> No one enters suit justly; no one goes to law honestly; they rely on empty pleas, they speak lies, they conceive mischief and give birth to iniquity." (Isaiah 59:3-4 ESV).

And a few verses later, Isaiah writes,

> "Justice is turned back, and righteousness stands far away; for truth has stumbled in the public squares, and uprightness cannot enter.
>
> Truth is lacking, and he who departs from evil makes himself a prey. The LORD saw it, and it displeased him that there was no justice." (Isaiah 59:14-15 ESV).

Oh, that we will always remember that God is not mocked, nor is evil ever hidden from His sight. We must always stand in His grace lest we become lulled into the soft seduction of the evil one and be led to our own destruction with the wicked people of our day.

***

I am in Jeremiah in my daily Bible reading. Jeremiah was the reluctant prophet who, in his youth, was chosen by God to preach judgment against the people of Judah.

We know that God sent the terrible and mighty people of Babylon against Judah, a people whom He personally raised up for this purpose.

Yet, God's love for His people was so great that, even as He spoke judgment against Judah, He was still straining to find a way to extend His grace and soften His hand.

> "Run to and fro through the streets of Jerusalem, look and take note! Search her squares to see if you can find a man, one who does justice and seeks truth, that I may pardon her." (Jeremiah 5:1 ESV).

But God found no repentance. He found no one who sought His grace, so judgment fell upon the people in full measure.

Today, the Lord is seeking people who will turn away from evil, people who will say "no" to the perversions in our society, and people who do justice and seek truth.

The Lord is earnestly seeking people to pour out His grace upon today, just like He sought people in the days of Jeremiah to pour His grace upon. As judgment was around the corner for the people of Judah, and they didn't know it, so is judgment coming for us as a thief in the night.

Let us all seek God, turn from our evil ways, and humble ourselves in the presence of our Creator so we may find grace in the day of judgment when it comes.

***

Well, my social media fast is over. One thing I learned is that we have too many distractions in life.

When I restricted the time I spent online, watching television, and playing game games on my phone, I was forced to find something to do to replace those activities. I could have chosen to replace them with low-quality activities, but I was purposeful in choosing things important to me.

I prayed a lot and spent time in His Word. I spent more time catching up on things I've been putting off.

Social media doesn't have to be a bad thing. I am learning, however, that I need to be judicious about how much time I spend on these activities at the expense of more important things in life.

I'll never get squandered hours back, so it's vital I do a better job at redeeming the time, for the days are, indeed, evil.

***

Here is an interesting post. As many of you know, I have been playing with Bard, Google's AI tool that creates posts and answers your questions. Artificial Intelligence is really coming along.

I decided to try an experiment. Tomorrow's Tuesdays With Tony post is entitled, "Be Thankful Every Day For The Lord's Providence." It deals with not taking God's daily blessings for granted. I will post it tomorrow morning.

But I wondered what Bard would write on this topic if I asked it to write a post. I was somewhat impressed. Here was my prompt for Bard:

Write a post about the importance of not taking God's blessings for granted each day.

What follows is from the mind of artificial intelligence. I'd be interested in what you think. Without further ado, here is Bard's post:

{Begin Post}

God has blessed us with so many things, both big and small. We often take these blessings for granted, but it is important to remember that they are not ours by right. They are gifts from God, and we should be grateful for them.

One of the most important things we can do is to **express our gratitude to God**. We can do this through prayer, worship, and simply taking the time to think about all the ways He has blessed us. When we express our gratitude, it helps us to remember how much we have to be thankful for, and it also helps us to build a stronger relationship with God.

Another important way to **not take God's blessings for granted** is to **use them to glorify Him**. When we use our blessings to help others, it shows that we are grateful for what we have, and it also brings glory to God. There are many ways to use our blessings to glorify God, such as volunteering our time, donating to charity, or simply being kind to others.

Finally, it is important to **remember that God is always with us**. Even when we are going through tough times, God is there for us. He loves us unconditionally, and He wants to help us through whatever we are facing.

When we remember that God is always with us, it gives us strength and hope.

So, how can we **make sure we don't take God's blessings for granted**? Here are a few tips:

* **Express your gratitude to God.**
* **Use your blessings to glorify Him.**
* **Remember that God is always with you.**

When we follow these tips, we can live a life that is full of gratitude and joy. We can also show God that we appreciate all the blessings He has given us.

{End Post}

Note: Even the **bold text** was created by Bard.

https://bard.google.com/

***

Be Thankful Every Day For The Lord's Providence

Most of the people who read my posts live in the most wealthy country that has ever existed. In the United States, people we call poor would be wealthy in many parts of the world. We eat ourselves to excess, house ourselves to excess, clothe ourselves to excess, and we often play and travel to excess. But when we compare ourselves to others in this country, we are often blind to just how well-off we really are.

That is both a blessing and a potential curse. It's a blessing because we have tangible things we can thank the Creator for. He is the source of every good blessing.

> "Every good gift and every perfect gift is from above, coming down from the Father of lights, with whom there is no variation or shadow due to change." (James 1:17 ESV).

It is certainly a blessing when we know that our family will eat, will be clothed, and will have shelter. But the danger comes when we have those blessings in such abundance, we wake up each morning expecting them to be there. When God blesses us that much, do we wake up assuming that the blessings will still be there?

If we do, we risk enjoying God's blessings without being truly thankful for what we have. Even worse, we start to lose appreciation for the truth that we only have what we enjoy because God allows us to keep our blessings each day.

Without God's daily providence, we will wake up with everything taken away from us. We may think, "Yeah, I know that's true, but it's not likely to happen. I mean, I have so much stored up, the chance I will not be able to enjoy my abundance is extremely remote."

That may be true, but it harbors a heart that diverts its eyes from the Creator to our own selves for security. Jesus tells a parable of just such a man.

> "And he told them a parable, saying, "The land of a rich man produced plentifully,
> and he thought to himself, 'What shall I do, for I have nowhere to store my crops?'
> And he said, 'I will do this: I will tear down my barns and build larger ones, and there I will store all my grain and my goods.
> And I will say to my soul, "Soul, you have ample goods laid up for many years; relax, eat, drink, be merry."'
> But God said to him, 'Fool! This night your soul is required of you, and the things you have prepared, whose will they be?'
> So is the one who lays up treasure for himself and is not rich toward God." (Luke 12:16-21 ESV).

This man woke up every day rich and yet forgot to keep God in mind. In this case, God required his soul, and the man enjoyed none of what he stored up. This man forgot that all blessings flowed from God, and God alone was sovereign over who had what. The Lord gives, and the Lord takes away (Job 1:21).

There is a story in 2 Kings that shows just how much we need to appreciate God's daily providence. No matter what the daily reality is, nothing is certain when God is concerned. In 2 Kings, the Syrians lay siege to Samaria, and the people are scared and hungry. Food was scarce.

> "And there was a great famine in Samaria, as they besieged it, until a donkey's head was sold for eighty shekels of silver, and the fourth part of a kab of dove's dung for five shekels of silver." (2 Kings 6:25 ESV).

But the prophet Elisha makes this bold proclamation:

> "But Elisha said, "Hear the word of the LORD: thus says the LORD, Tomorrow about this time a seah of fine flour shall be sold for a shekel, and two seahs of barley for a shekel, at the gate of Samaria." (2 Kings 7:1

ESV).

The next verse tells us how the king's captain scoffed at Elisha's prophecy.

> "Then the captain on whose hand the king leaned said to the man of God, "If the LORD himself should make windows in heaven, could this thing be?" But he said, "You shall see it with your own eyes, but you shall not eat of it." (2 Kings 7:2 ESV).

The captain looked at their current circumstances and did not ascribe the power to God to give and take away. His faith was in what he saw. Thus, Elisha told him that he would see the fulfillment of this word, but he would not taste the food. And that's exactly what happened. God scared away the Syrian army, and they left everything behind, including the food.

When the people of Samaria learned this, they made a stampede to the plentiful bounty, trampling the captain to death before he had the opportunity to take a bite.

> "Now the king had appointed the captain on whose hand he leaned to have charge of the gate. And the people trampled him in the gate, so that he died, as the man of God had said when the king came down to him.
>
> For when the man of God had said to the king, "Two seahs of barley shall be sold for a shekel, and a seah of fine flour for a shekel, about this time tomorrow in the gate of Samaria,"
>
> the captain had answered the man of God, "If the LORD himself should make windows in heaven, could such a thing be?" And he had said, "You shall see it with your own eyes, but you shall not eat of it."
>
> And so it happened to him, for the people trampled him in the gate and he died." (2 Kings 7:17-20 ESV).

These biblical stories teach me a powerful lesson. When I wake up and open my full pantry, I thank God that His province for me and my family extended another day. I truly wake up each morning without expecting anything so I can be thankful for everything.

When my children wear warm clothes, I thank God for clothing my family that day because I know that at any time, He can withdraw His providence from me and nothing I plan for will mean a thing if He does.

When I wake up with a roof over my head, I thank God that day for His providence because I know that any day, in His sovereignty, He could choose to take away my house.

I didn't always approach my daily prayers this way. I used to assume that I would have the things I built and saved by my own hands. But God has taken things away from me that I thought were safe. He has taught me that I need to rely each day on Him regardless of how much He blessed me with yesterday.

I counsel that we learn to be thankful every day for the Lord's providence, that we fight the urge to assume we will always have tomorrow what we had yesterday, and that we always respect God's power and ability to give and to take away at His will.

Let us be thankful for the overflowing blessing that pours from God into our cups, but let us truly be thankful and never take them for granted.

***

The time had come. Judgment was at hand.

God had sent prophet after prophet to warn Judah, but they refused to listen.

The people's heart was so cold they persecuted the prophets sent to them.

But even as judgment was imminent, God still had compassion upon the people. He still wished to extend grace and not judgment.

Though His anger was kindled, it was not enough to quench His love.

To the bitter end, the Lord desired to save and not to condemn.

Today, judgment is imminent. The Lord's anger is kindled against those who rebel with no desire to repent.

But His love desperately wishes to extend grace to us and not condemnation.

Yet, with a heavy heart, our God will let us walk into the condemnation we seek if we refuse to turn to Him with all our hearts.

Satan has a strong grip on our society. Today is the day we must choose which side we are on.

Let us take our stand with Jesus and accept His grace, unlike the people of Judah, who accepted condemnation and not salvation.

> "Take a scroll and write on it all the words that I have spoken to you against Israel and Judah and all the nations, from the day I spoke to you, from the days of Josiah until today.
>
> It may be that the house of Judah will hear all the disaster that I intend to do to them, so that every one may turn from his evil way, and that I may forgive their iniquity and their sin." (Jeremiah 36:2-3 ESV).

***

Every generation has its moment to stand for Jesus and His kingdom. Change is in the air. Perhaps this generation of kingdom disciples is about to take up a new mantle.

Lines are being drawn. Those in power from the local to the national level are adopting philosophies that run counter to the teachings of Jesus.

While I do not equate this with the mark of the beast in Revelation, many of us may soon find it difficult to buy and sell unless we renounce our Lord and confess a doctrine of diversity that accepts all sorts of evil.

Historically, we see the persecution of the church come in waves. We have lived in relative peace and safety for generations, but that is changing.

The wheat shall be separated from the tares. The sheep from the goats. The devoted from those who pay lip service.

We see the signs. Unless good people can curb the trajectory, it doesn't take a prophet to see what is coming.

Now is the time to ground our faith.

Now is the time to make our faith our own.

Now is the time to draw close to Jesus and draw on His strength and the strength that the Spirit promises to believers.

Now, the choice we make is ours. But the day is coming when we may be forced to publically take a stand and choose a side.

God, in His graciousness, has given us this time of peace to prepare for possible hard times ahead.

I pray that I am wrong and God extends our time of peace. But when we look at the rest of the world, we see our brothers and sisters suffering tremendously already.

May we all work to be the salt and light this world needs as the powers of darkness tighten their grip on our society.

No matter how dark the days may get, let us always remember Jesus has already secured victory for us on the cross.

We must never forget.

***

I have plenty to worry about on the day of judgment.
The only hope I have is the grace of God.

***

The "I will" statements of God in Jeremiah 51 showcases God's sovereignty. Throughout the chapter, God repeatedly mentions, "I will {do this or that}..."

No one can make so many deterministic statements with impunity unless that Being has absolute sovereignty. God controls all, and His purposes will always be fulfilled.

I challenge you to read Jeremiah 51 and focus on all the times God says He will do something. These are big, massive "I wills" that cannot come to pass unless the One declaring them has absolute power to fulfill His declarations.

The nations would thwart God's "I wills" if it were in their powers.

The spiritual powers that war against God would stop His "I wills" if it were in their power.

Yet God boldly and openly declares what He will do as if daring anyone to try to stop Him if they could.

Because of God's "I wills" in Jeremiah 51, we get to see if God is all He claims to be or if He is a being whose bark is bigger than His bite.

Well, history vindicates God's sovereignty. The nations could not stop one "I will" of God.

None of the spiritual principalities or powers could keep one "I will" of God from coming to fruition.

The next time the power of evil in our society plays its seductive song to us, read Jeremiah 51 and remember, when God says, "I will," then it will come to pass.

> "And if I go and prepare a place for you, I will come again and will take you to myself, that where I am you may be also." (John 14:3 ESV).

***

I believe God cares about the "little" things we pray for more than we often think.

***

I believe God loves watching us grow, explore all aspects of His creation, and see the wonderment in our eyes as we experience the unexpected joys that come our way.

***

I believe when we are hurting, it breaks God's heart, and He desperately wants us to crawl into His arms and trust fully that He will not let us go through it alone.

***

I believe God is very forgiving of our missteps, very patient as we grow, and very supportive as we transform into the new creature He wants us to become.

***

I believe when we pray to God, we have His undivided attention for as long as we wish to speak to Him.

***

I am in the book of Ezekiel in my daily Bible reading. Judah is in captivity, and the Lord is still prophesying to the people. But the people are not listening to the prophecies. In fact, they claim that the prophecies are false.

> "Son of man, what is this proverb that you have about the land of Israel, saying, 'The days grow long, and every vision comes to nothing'?
> Tell them therefore, 'Thus says the Lord GOD: I will put an end to this proverb, and they shall no more use it as a proverb in Israel.' But say to them, The days are near, and the fulfillment of every vision." (Ezekiel 12:22-23 ESV).

This sounds a lot like the people of our day concerning the return of our King. Peter says that we have the same problem that the people of Judah had in the days of Ezekiel.

> "knowing this first of all, that scoffers will come in the last days with scoffing, following their own sinful desires. They will say, "Where is the

promise of his coming? For ever since the fathers fell asleep, all things are continuing as they were from the beginning of creation." (2 Peter 3:3-4 ESV).

But to the people of Judah in captivity, God says His words are coming to pass much sooner than they realize.

"For I am the LORD; I will speak the word that I will speak, and it will be performed. It will no longer be delayed, but in your days, O rebellious house, I will speak the word and perform it, declares the Lord GOD." (Ezekiel 12:25 ESV).

Peter tells us the same thing today:

"But the day of the Lord will come like a thief, and then the heavens will pass away with a roar, and the heavenly bodies will be burned up and dissolved, and the earth and the works that are done on it will be exposed." (2 Peter 3:10 ESV).

God gives us warning today. His words may seem distant because it has been thousands of years since the promise of His return was made. But that is not because God is slack concerning His promises. Rather, it is because of God's love. He is longsuffering, not willing that any should perish but that all come to repentance.

But the day of the Lord will come...

***

I am in Ezekiel in my daily Bible reading. Boy, things are not much different today than in Ezekiel's day. Even then, people found fault with God. They ignored their own sin and made charges against God that He was not just.

"Yet your people say, 'The way of the Lord is not just,' when it is their own way that is not just." (Ezekiel 33:17 ESV).

Have you heard it today? I have. People who turn their hearts away from God claim that if there is a God, He is not a just God. They point to His justice and His expectation of moral living. To many people, God is an overbearing, restrictive God.

We tend to blame God when our lives run counter to His will. Rather than submit to Him, we cast blame on Him. We make Him the evil one while we justify ourselves.

In our eyes, it is not us who is unjust. God is not just. He is the one Who isn't fair. He is the one Who unfairly discriminates.

But the truth always vindicates God. Man makes excuses while God speaks truth. Man points the finger while God judges in righteousness. In the end, no amount of blaming God will move the needle in favor of the rebellious person.

God is just, and God is gracious. God is fairer than what we deserve. We seek to do what we want without answering to our Creator.

So we claim that it is God Who is not just.

***

The day is coming when the proud will quake in the presence of Jesus.

Those who speak arrogant words against God will be silent when awed in His presence.

I do not think the rebellious will truly understand how overwhelming the presence of the mighty God will be.

No words can truly prepare us to stand in the presence of God.

But Ezekiel tries...

> "The fish of the sea and the birds of the heavens and the beasts of the field and all creeping things that creep on the ground, and all the people who are on the face of the earth, shall quake at my presence. And the mountains shall be thrown down, and the cliffs shall fall, and every wall shall tumble to the ground." (Ezekiel 38:20 ESV).

***

Choosing God

What do we learn about God's judgment by reading the Old Testament? Even then, God sought to give grace and forgiveness. God did not seek to condemn. He sought that all would repent and live.

But when men refused to repent and instead set their faces against God, there came a moment, a line in the sand, where God moved against them in judgment.

In a word, His longsuffering came to an end. Men had set their way, and no repentance was found in them. God would not let them continue in their rebellion and evil in perpetuity.

I don't know when the Lord will return to judge this world. He first came to save and offered His grace to all His image bearers, including you and me.

And He is patiently waiting for whosoever will to claim His grace and live. He has not come to judge the world yet because He is waiting for you and me to repent.

But once we no longer repent, once we decide to go our own way, then the longsuffering of God will no longer benefit us.

Ezekiel speaks of this truth throughout his book. God wanted to extend grace to all who would accept it, but His judgment reluctantly came for those who did not accept His salvation. I say reluctantly because He prefers to extend grace to judgment.

He is the same God today. He wants a relationship with us. He has given us a way to Him through His Son. He offers His grace that will build our faith, leading to obedience because of our faith.

He promises to create in us a new heart, to make us a new creature, to renew and strengthen us as we give ourselves wholly to Him.

But if we have one foot on the cross and the other foot in the world, we become whores who break our Lord's heart. Like a faithful husband, He wants us to be fully devoted to Him and no other.

If we continue to conform to this world rather than being transformed, we walk away from the royal inheritance we are promised. We give up the grace that He offers. We lay down our saving faith.

If we cast our lots with the damned, we will be damned. If we choose those who have rejected His grace, we will reject His grace.

When judgment comes, we will have nothing. We will have traded our birthright for a mess of pottage, and God will give us what we truly want- an existence without Him.

Let us be wholly devoted to our Lord and King. Let His grace be the foundation of our faith, and let our faith cause us to live lives as His disciples, not out of compulsion, but out of love for Him because He first loved us.

He offered Judah and Israel the same thing, but they refused His offer. Let us embrace Him while His longsuffering is extended. Let us be fully His when our King comes again in judgment against those who refuse Him. Let us be in His grace and claim our royal promise from Him.

***

Read Lamentations. It is a book of weeping, sadness, and despair. The nation that was the apple of God's eyes is now despised in the eyes of the nations.

Once rich in wealth and food, its people now grope about for a morsel of food and drink. Rich and poor, old and young alike suffer because of the judgment of God against them.

I can only imagine what it will be like for many of us on the Day of Judgment when we realize that we have given up a prince's inheritance for a meager existence without God for eternity, that we have traded our birthright for a mess of pottage.

Perhaps for those of us who turn away from the Lord, we will understand the heart-wrenching lamentations of Jeremiah. The big difference is that Jeremiah speaks of repentance and restoration. On the Day of Judgment, there will be no more repentance or salvation.

May we never experience that lamentation.

> "For if we go on sinning deliberately after receiving the knowledge of the truth, there no longer remains a sacrifice for sins,
>
> but a fearful expectation of judgment, and a fury of fire that will consume the adversaries." (Hebrews 10:26-27 ESV).

***

I am in the book of 1 Kings in my daily Bible reading. This is the book where God blesses Solomon with tremendous wealth and wisdom. Yet, Solomon took these blessings, and instead of using them to bring glory to God, the king forsook God and used His blessings for his own glory and sinful purposes.

King Solomon broke the commands that God gave to the kings through Samuel. Among these commands was not to marry foreign wives because they would turn away the king's heart. This is precisely what happened to Solomon.

> "Now King Solomon loved many foreign women, along with the daughter of Pharaoh: Moabite, Ammonite, Edomite, Sidonian, and Hittite women,
>
> from the nations concerning which the LORD had said to the people of Israel, "You shall not enter into marriage with them, neither shall they with you, for surely they will turn away your heart after their gods." Solomon clung to these in love." (1 Kings 11:1-2 ESV).

But Solomon followed his heart and walked away from the Lord Who had shown tremendous kindness to him, and just as the Lord had warned, his wives turned his heart away from God.

"He had 700 wives, who were princesses, and 300 concubines. And his wives turned away his heart." (1 Kings 11:3 ESV).

God, Who had given Solomon wisdom, wealth, peace, and a long life, was angry and heartbroken. King Solomon chose to walk his own way and not with his Lord.

"And the LORD was angry with Solomon, because his heart had turned away from the LORD, the God of Israel, who had appeared to him twice" (1 Kings 11:9 ESV).

What a lesson for us. God will not give us nearly what He blessed King Solomon with, but will we choose to walk away from the Lord for far less than Solomon had? Will we turn our hearts away from God over our small mess of pottage?

Let us be careful where we put our hearts. Let us be careful to have the discernment to see the true treasure we have.

"Do not lay up for yourselves treasures on earth, where moth and rust destroy and where thieves break in and steal,
but lay up for yourselves treasures in heaven, where neither moth nor rust destroys and where thieves do not break in and steal.
For where your treasure is, there your heart will be also." (Matthew 6:19-21 ESV).

***

This is one of my favorite verses in the Bible:

"This is a light thing in the sight of the LORD. He will also give the Moabites into your hand," (2 Kings 3:18 ESV).

"This is a light thing in the sight of the LORD." Isn't that amazing? In this context, the armies of Israel, Judah, and Edom were going after the rebellious army of Moab, but the soldiers did not have water and would die unless water was found.

In this context, God told the kings that giving them water would be a light thing for Him to do. In fact, God would deliver the Moab army into their hands.

Sometimes, we see the impossible and forget that the impossible to us is a light thing to God. Sometimes, we put God in a box and determine what He can or cannot do before we even ask Him.

Sometimes, we don't ask because we have already determined what God will or won't do.

When we do this, we do not act in faith but in doubt. We forget that everything is a light thing in the eyes of our Almighty Creator.

James teaches us the same principle when we pray to God for wisdom:

"If any of you lacks wisdom, let him ask God, who gives generously to all without reproach, and it will be given him.

But let him ask in faith, with no doubting, for the one who doubts is like a wave of the sea that is driven and tossed by the wind.

For that person must not suppose that he will receive anything from the Lord;" (James 1:5-7 ESV).

May we remember that anything we ask of the Lord our God is always a light thing in His sight. Always.

***

2 Kings 6 talks about the angels of God and chariots of fire. Elisha could see them, but his servant could not until Elisha prayed that his servant's eyes be opened.

I believe that there is an unseen realm all around us. Angels, sent to minister to God's children who have accepted Jesus as our Savior and King, are here, doing their divinely appointed duty (Hebrews 1:14).

We do not know much about God's unseen realm, but ignorance does not mean that it is any less real. It is amazing that God has brought together the seen and unseen realms for the benefit of His children.

Just like the servant of Elisha was amazed to see God's protection in the form of mighty angels waiting in chariots of fire, I believe we would be overwhelmed to see what God has provided for us in the unseen realm.

Let us praise God for using all at His disposal to benefit His adopted children, those of us who have a divinely appointed inheritance made possible through our King Jesus.

***

I sometimes wonder if we spend too much time on the less weighty spiritual matters and not enough time on the weightier matters.

***

We Can Do Right Wrong

We are often too quick to condemn with broad strokes without thinking through the logic of our condemnations. How many times, for example, have we heard about the dangers of situational ethics? While I generally believe that we need to be careful not to let the situation dictate our ethics, we need to be pragmatic enough to understand sometimes situations precisely dictate our ethics and the Bible is actually pretty clear about that.

In a lot of these cases, it's the heart that is the deciding factor of what is right and what is wrong and not the action itself. Sometimes we can, indeed, do right wrong. What do I mean?

The Pharisees were really good at doing right wrong. They would often do many things to be pleasing to God, but they sometimes did those things without the right heart. Sometimes they were hypocritical when they did the things they were supposed to do.

> "Beware of practicing your righteousness before other people in order to be seen by them, for then you will have no reward from your Father who is in heaven.
>
> "Thus, when you give to the needy, sound no trumpet before you, as the hypocrites do in the synagogues and in the streets, that they may be praised by others. Truly, I say to you, they have received their reward." (Matthew 6:1-2 ESV).

Here is an example of people doing right wrong. The hypocrites practiced good deeds, which is right, but they did it with a wrong heart. They practiced right to receive praise and not from a position of humility to honor God. Jesus said the praise these people receive will be the only reward they will get.

Paul also talked about people who did right wrong.

> "Some indeed preach Christ from envy and rivalry, but others from good will.
>
> The latter do it out of love, knowing that I am put here for the defense of the gospel.

The former proclaim Christ out of selfish ambition, not sincerely but thinking to afflict me in my imprisonment.

What then? Only that in every way, whether in pretense or in truth, Christ is proclaimed, and in that I rejoice. Yes, and I will rejoice," (Philippians 1:15-18 ESV).

Here are two groups of people who preached Christ. One group did it from a good heart that was based on love. The other group did it for selfish, hypocritical reasons. They did right wrong. But what was Paul's reaction? He rejoiced that at least Christ was preached.

Sometimes it's easy to see when people do right wrong, but other times only God can see that. This is why Jesus, our Lord and Judge, tells us that when we stand before Him on the Day of Judgement, it won't just be the actions we are judged on, but the heart behind the actions. Doing right wrong is lawlessness.

"Not everyone who says to me, 'Lord, Lord,' will enter the kingdom of heaven, but the one who does the will of my Father who is in heaven.

On that day many will say to me, 'Lord, Lord, did we not prophesy in your name, and cast out demons in your name, and do many mighty works in your name?'

And then will I declare to them, 'I never knew you; depart from me, you workers of lawlessness.'" (Matthew 7:21-23 ESV).

Here were people who were doing right wrong. Jesus never denied they did these things, but He said that their works were lawless works. There are many ways we can do right wrong. As we have seen, we can do it with the wrong motives or with a bad heart. We can also ignore what Jesus says, and we can do things the way we want to do them. I suspect this is where the condemnation in Matthew 7 came into play.

What about doing good to others? Jesus said the two greatest commands are to love God and to love our neighbors. In fact, all the laws hang on these two. But can we do these two great commands right but in the wrong way? Sure. It's a heart thing.

I can give to the poor, visit the sick, and clothe the naked all without love for them. I am doing right wrong. Perhaps I am doing these things because others expect me to do them and I don't want to lose face with them. Perhaps I am doing these things because I know I can call in favors at a later time. Whatever the reason, we can do the right actions in the wrong way.

Why is it important for us to see this distinction? Because this is the basis of a works, or merit-based salvation. Doing right wrong gives us a sense of confidence that what we are doing will pave our way to heaven. This was the problem with the Pharisees. Doing right wrong gave them a sense of security in their relationship with God, though their divine Judge told them over and over that their actions were not the things that would save them in the end.

When we get caught in this system of doing right wrong, we find ourselves in a constant cycle of doing and doing and doing, just trying to do enough to keep us safe in the eyes of God. But it is not the doing that earns His grace for us. His grace is freely given, and it should be the catalyst for the good works we do.

Just like the men who preached Christ from goodwill, we do because of the love we have for others. We do it because of the grace that Jesus has given us. We do right, right; that is with a good heart and from the right motives. This is how Jesus will judge us on the last day.

When we struggle with sin, let us first address our hearts as we are led by our godly sorrow. We must first fix our hearts and ensure they are tender toward God. Otherwise, we will find ourselves in a constant cycle of trying to do better and then trying to do better, better. No amount of doing right will help us if we don't first ensure that our hearts are where they should be.

I counsel that we all continually examine our motives when we do right. Ask ourselves if we would do right for God and for our neighbor if no one else knew. Ask ourselves if we would do right because of the great love that God has shown us by giving us His grace, and we want to show our great appreciation by doing right for others.

It's easier than we think to do right wrong and feel secure in our works. But doing right wrong will not save us. Only the grace of God will save us. And that grace will be the catalyst of the faith we have in Him. And that faith will cause us to do right right.

If we are stuck in a rut of doing right wrong, let us not keep trying to do better, better. Instead, let us examine our hearts and motives, working on building our faith and spending time considering the grace Jesus has given us. This is the only way to break the cycle of doing right wrong.

***

I am in 2 Kings in my daily Bible reading. In chapter 17, God finally sends Israel into captivity:

> "And this occurred because the people of Israel had sinned against the LORD their God, who had brought them up out of the land of Egypt from under the hand of Pharaoh king of Egypt, and had feared other gods
> and walked in the customs of the nations whom the LORD drove out before the people of Israel, and in the customs that the kings of Israel had practiced." (2 Kings 17:7-8 ESV).

What a sad state for a people who had everything handed to them on a silver platter by God, the Creator of the universe. Yet,

> "And the people of Israel did secretly against the LORD their God things that were not right. They built for themselves high places in all their towns, from watchtower to fortified city." (2 Kings 17:9 ESV).

The people did secretly against the Lord. This is a warning for us today. God offers us everything on a silver platter. He offers His peace and an inheritance befitting a prince.

What will we do? Will we sin against God and give into the nations of the world? Will we follow their idolatry and evil? will we call what is good evil, and call what is evil good?

Will we try to have one foot in the world and one foot in the army of Jesus? Will we also do "secretly against the Lord our God things that are not right?"

If we do, we will be rejected by our King just like the people of Israel were rejected. Let us live wholly devoted to our God and King so that we may embrace the Day of Judgement where we will be vindicated by the grace of God.

***

As I read the story of David, a man after God's own heart, the Holy Spirit does not sugarcoat David's life. He had his sins he had to contend with.

In 1 Chronicles 21, David went beyond God's command and acted in pride when he numbered the people in his kingdom. Notice God's reaction to David's sin:

> "But God was displeased with this thing, and he struck Israel." (1 Chronicles 21:7 ESV).

Then, in the most famous of David's sins with Bathsheba which led to the murder of her husband, notice God's reaction to this sin:

> "And when the mourning was over, David sent and brought her to his house, and she became his wife and bore him a son. But the thing that David had done displeased the LORD." (2 Samuel 11:27 ESV).

In both cases, David's sins displeased God. Sin always displeases God.

This is why we must have the heart that David had. In both cases, David's heart was broken when confronted with his sins. His broken and contrite heart moved him to godly sorrow.

We live in a nation that prides self-reliance and self-indulgence. We "deserve" what we want and no one can tell us that what we want is wrong or should be withheld. This kind of thinking will mollify our hearts rather than break them.

God is rich in grace to all who want it. But if we spurn His grace, He will not force it upon us. I pray that when we sin (because we all sin- 1 John 1:8-10), our hearts are tender, just like David's was, and we see when we displease God.

I pray that when we displease God, it breaks our hearts and we respond like the man after God's own heart responded. May we never lose the ability to have a broken and contrite heart.

> "For you will not delight in sacrifice, or I would give it; you will not be pleased with a burnt offering.
> The sacrifices of God are a broken spirit; a broken and contrite heart, O God, you will not despise." (Psalm 51:16-17 ESV).

***

I love this verse. It is true even today:

> "And you, Solomon my son, know the God of your father and serve him with a whole heart and with a willing mind, for the LORD searches all hearts and understands every plan and thought. If you seek him, he will be found by you, but if you forsake him, he will cast you off forever." (1 Chronicles 28:9 ESV).

***

This is comforting to me.
The essence of my faith, which pleases God, is this,
I believe He exists.
I believe that He rewards those who diligently seek Him.
This is the basis of my faith.

> "And without faith it is impossible to please him, for whoever would

draw near to God must believe that he exists and that he rewards those who seek him." (Hebrews 11:6 ESV).

***

How do we look at our possessions? Do we see them as things we have labored for, things we have earned because of our work?

There is truth to that for sure, but there is an even greater truth we need to always be aware of. Even things we work for are still owned and given to us by God.

Nothing is truly ours, but all comes from God. He gives and He takes away as He wills. This is the heart we must always have toward the possessions God blesses us with.

David knew this. When he gave a great treasure to the Lord for the temple his son would build, and when the people contributed their riches to the temple as well, notice the observation King David made.

May it always be the same observation we make as we keep our possessions in perspective.

> "But who am I, and what is my people, that we should be able thus to offer willingly? For all things come from you, and of your own have we given you." (1 Chronicles 29:14 ESV).

***

What's the difference between having a best friend and loving our neighbor?

When we love our neighbor, we are willing to do anything we can for them because of love.

When we love a best friend, we have the inner drive to do whatever they need, whenever they need it, while hurting with them.

We love our neighbor because we want to to be like Jesus.

We love our best friend because they are a part of us, just like Jesus.

"A friend loves at all times, and a brother is born for adversity." (Proverbs 17:17 ESV).

***

God was not ashamed to be called their God.
Is God ashamed to be called our God?

"But as it is, they desire a better country, that is, a heavenly one. Therefore God is not ashamed to be called their God, for he has prepared for them a city." (Hebrews 11:16 ESV).

What do we truly desire?
How much of our desire rest upon our God?

***

We know the story about God granting Solomon both wisdom and knowledge. In 2 Chronicles 1, God grants this wisdom. In the next chapter, Solomon prepares to build the Temple his father was forbidden to build. Here is where we first see his wisdom displayed in the book of 2 Chronicles:

"The house that I am to build will be great, for our God is greater than all gods.
But who is able to build him a house, since heaven, even highest heaven, cannot contain him? Who am I to build a house for him, except as a place to make offerings before him?" (2 Chronicles 2:5-6 ESV).

Solomon understood something about God's nature that many people struggle with. This house he was to build for God could not literally contain a God who is limitless.

While God would "dwell" in the temple, giving His presence to this house, it wasn't God's literal and only dwelling place. As Solomon in his wisdom declares, "But who is able to build him a house, since heaven, even highest heaven, cannot contain him?"

This man understood God's true nature perhaps better than anyone. God gave him insights and understanding that we often spend a lifetime pursuing in our studies and prayers.

Is it a wonder that the mightiest and most noble men and women traversed the globe to hear the wisdom of this man?

***

Against You Only Have I Sinned

David writes Psalm 51 after he sinned with Bathsheba and murdered her husband, Uriah. One of the verses we like to quote is verse 10, where David pleads with God to create in him a clean heart. We can identify with this desire because we all want to rid ourselves of the guilt and soil of sin. We know we do not have the power within us to make our hearts clean, but the blood of Jesus can wash us whiter than snow.

But in verse 4, David makes a bold proclamation concerning his adulterous affair with Bathsheba and the murder of her husband when he speaks this to God:

> "Against you, you only, have I sinned and done what is evil in your sight, so that you may be justified in your words and blameless in your judgment." (Psalm 51:4 ESV).

To many, this declaration seems clinical and perhaps even inaccurate. Was it really only against God whom David sinned when he committed these acts of adultery and murder?

Well, he certainly did sin against God. The sixth commandment says,

> "You shall not murder." (Exodus 20:13 ESV).

And the seventh commandment says,

> "You shall not commit adultery." (Exodus 20:14 ESV).

Even the tenth commandment, with all that we are not to covet, says,

> "You shall not covet your neighbor's house; you shall not covet your neighbor's wife, or his male servant, or his female servant, or his ox, or his donkey, or anything that is your neighbor's." (Exodus 20:17 ESV).

And if you really wanted to get into the law, he probably violated a few other commandments in this act as well. Trying to cover up one sin led him down the spiral path of sinning to cover up other sins. Have we ever found ourselves there before? Perhaps not with murder, but lying, stealing, falsely accusing, etc... just to try to hide the sins we commit?

This is where David found himself. But was it really against God, and God alone whom he sinned? Let's look at what the prophet tells us.

We know the story. During the season of war, David stayed home while his army, including Uriah, was fighting his battles for him. From the roof of his palace one evening, he sees Bathsheba bathing and sends for her.

> "And David sent and inquired about the woman. And one said, "Is not this Bathsheba, the daughter of Eliam, the wife of Uriah the Hittite?"
> So David sent messengers and took her, and she came to him, and he lay with her. (Now she had been purifying herself from her uncleanness.) Then she returned to her house." (2 Samuel 11:3-4 ESV).

From the beginning, David brazenly involves innocent servants in his evil causing these messengers to facilitate his sin. Have we ever been guilty of involving people to help us facilitate our sins?

After he commits adultery, he gets Bathseba pregnant. Of course, it takes two to tango. But he is the King and should have been Bathsheba's shepherd. Instead, this king uses his power and influence to lead her into sin.

> "And the woman conceived, and she sent and told David, "I am pregnant." (2 Samuel 11:5 ESV).

But it's not just Bathsheba. It's also Uriah her husband, who David sins against. But this man of God hatches a plan to cover his sin from the husband he caused the wife to cheat on.

> "So David sent word to Joab, "Send me Uriah the Hittite." And Joab sent Uriah to David." (2 Samuel 11:6 ESV).

The trail of sins keeps getting worse and worse for David. He involves Joab in his scheme to murder Uriah, and he sins against his advisor, Ahithophel, Bathsheba's grandfather (is it any wonder Ahithophel sided with Absolam in the rebellion against David?) He also causes the death of innocent soldiers as he carries out the murder of Uriah and, of course, the baby dies because of his sins. He even sins against the people by bringing this sin into the land.

So, could David really say in Psalm 51, "Against You Only Have I Sinned?"

I think the story Nathan told him which convicted his heart was ample evidence that David knew his sin was against others. "You are the man!" Nathan said with an accusatory finger pointed at him. Uriah was the poor man who had the little ewe lamb he loved.

When David came to terms with his sin, he stopped compartmentalizing his sins. We often do that when we want to sanitize our sins, don't we?

We say things like, "I'm not sinning against God. I'm just fudging on my taxes against the IRS. I mean, the government is not the bastion of morality anyway."

Or, "Hey, I'm just doing what he did to me."

Or we say things like, "Everyone's doing it. It's just the way things are."

We compartmentalize sins so we don't have to feel the moral weight of sinning against God. But in the end, every sin is against God, aren't they? I think this is what David is coming to grips with. As King, he could have had Bathsheba. No one could have stopped him. But it still would have been a sin against God.

Centuries later, Jesus would say this before He took His place on David's throne as his eternally reigning descendent:

> "And he said to him, "You shall love the Lord your God with all your heart and with all your soul and with all your mind.
> This is the great and first commandment.
> And a second is like it: You shall love your neighbor as yourself.
> On these two commandments depend all the Law and the Prophets." (Matthew 22:37-40 ESV).

Jesus would say that everything hangs on the two greatest commandments: Love God and love neighbor. In his sin against Bathsheba, David broke both of these great commandments and in breaking them, they were a direct sin against God Who gave both commands.

If we are to get to the point where our sins cause godly sorrow to move us to repentance, then we must see all of our sins as sins against God. We must fight the urge to compartmentalize our sins.

When David sinned against all the people we looked at, they were, at their core, sins against God. David knew that. He owned that. David realized that taking the poor man's little ewe lamb he loved was ultimately a sin against God. Until he could see that, there would be hiding, scheming, and denying.

When we sin against others, we need the bony finger of accusation pointed at us. When it is, we need to see our sins as sins against God. Sure, we may be sinning against our neighbor, but at the end of the day, when we do not love God or our neighbor, we are sinning against God.

We too, ultimately sin against God, and God alone.

***

In my daily Bible reading, I read about the tender heart of King Asa who sought the Lord and put his trust in Him. Here is what the prophet said to the king:

"and he went out to meet Asa and said to him, "Hear me, Asa, and all Judah and Benjamin: The LORD is with you while you are with him. If you seek him, he will be found by you, but if you forsake him, he will forsake you." (2 Chronicles 15:2 ESV).

Our God is a God who desires to be sought. But He is also a God who desires to be found. He does not make it difficult for us to find Him.

If we seek Him, He will make Himself be found. In fact, God later says to Asa,

"For the eyes of the LORD run to and fro throughout the whole earth, to give strong support to those whose heart is blameless toward him." (2 Chronicles 16:9c ESV).

If our eyes are seeking the Lord, His eyes also seek us. What great joy when, in us seeking God and God's seeking us, we both find each other!

"And without faith it is impossible to please him, for whoever would draw near to God must believe that he exists and that he rewards those who seek him." (Hebrews 11:6 ESV).

***

If we set our hearts to serve the Lord above all things,
There may come a time in our lives when we will have to make a choice
Between following what we learn from the Word about what Jesus, our King desires from us
Or whether we will follow our family, friends, doctrine, or teachers.
Between hanging on to the things we treasure upon the earth
Or letting everything go to grasp the heavenly treasures where true, lasting value resides.
The men and women who followed Jesus in the days when God walked upon the earth had to choose whether to embrace the Lord
Or hang on to the traditions they were taught.
If that day comes for us,
Will we forsake all to follow Him?

"So therefore, any one of you who does not renounce all that he has cannot be my disciple." (Luke 14:33 ESV).

***

Manasseh was an evil King. Very evil. He set up foreign gods and enticed Judah to worship them. He sacrificed his sons to false gods.

Yet this man was the son of the righteous king Hezekiah. But the goodness of his father did not help him at all in the eyes of the Lord.

God finally brought judgment upon Manasseh and caused the Assyrians to lead him away in hooks.

Finally, this evil king repented and humbled himself in the eyes of God.

"He prayed to him, and God was moved by his entreaty and heard his plea and brought him again to Jerusalem into his kingdom. Then Manasseh knew that the LORD was God." (2 Chronicles 33:13 ESV).

What a great God we serve that we are never too evil, have done too much, or have never gone too far in His eyes to receive His gracious salvation.

Just as God was tender toward the heart of an evil man who repented before Him, so is He tender toward our hearts as we turn from sin and humble ourselves in His eyes today.

***

I am listening to a debate with an atheist. He makes a common accusation against believers called "The God of the Gaps."

He said that we attribute it to God when we don't understand something. But then science explains it, and we understand it wasn't the power of God but simply a natural explanation.

The charge against Christians is that everything has natural explanations and we just have to wait until science can explain it.

But it made me think that the truth works the other way as well. God truly is the God of the Gaps for the atheists too.

When they can't understand how God can do something, they fill in their gaps with natural theories (evolution, the age of the universe, etc...).

But as soon as science disproves their theories, instead of acknowledging God, they revise their theories.

In the end, they are guilty of the same thing they accuse Christians of being guilty of.

***

In my daily Bible reading, Ezra is in sorrow over the sins that the people had committed in the presence of God. Listen to the way he puts it in Chapter 9:

> "And after all that has come upon us for our evil deeds and for our great guilt, seeing that you, our God, have punished us less than our iniquities deserved and have given us such a remnant as this," (Ezra 9:13 ESV).

Ezra calls their sins evil and places guilt upon themselves. Then, Ezra praises God for His disposition toward the people calling out the Lord's grace:

"Seeing that you, our God, have punished us less than our iniquities deserved."

Isn't this God's disposition toward us today? Doesn't God punish us less than our iniquities deserve?

The more I read the Old Testament, the more I see that God is the same yesterday, today, and forever. He is a God full of grace and quick to give that grace to His created image bearers.

The ultimate expression of God's grace is seen when He sent His Son who willingly laid down His life upon the cross so we could be punished far less than we deserve.

In fact, His grace is shown toward us to such a degree that the punishment we deserve is fully taken away from us. How can we not embrace and appreciate this matchless grace?

I think Ezra truly understood some measure of God's great grace.

> "but God shows his love for us in that while we were still sinners, Christ died for us." (Romans 5:8 ESV).

***

Jacob I Have Loved and Esau I Have Hated

I have to tell you that the passage in Malachi about God hating Esau has always troubled me. And what troubles me more is that I know it shouldn't trouble me. Nothing that God does or says should trouble me.

Yet, for some reason, this does. And as I closed out the Old Testament in my daily Bible reading, the passage came up again.

> "I have loved you," says the LORD. But you say, "How have you loved us?" "Is not Esau Jacob's brother?" declares the LORD. "Yet I have loved Jacob
> but Esau I have hated. I have laid waste his hill country and left his heritage to jackals of the desert." (Malachi 1:2-3 ESV).

This doesn't sound fair, does it? Perhaps my preconceived notions of God have a lot to do with how I feel when I hear that phrase. God is love, right? God is no respecter of persons. God loves the world. All of these sentiments are bedrocks of our Christian faith that are taught in Scripture.

And when God came to earth, wasn't it Jesus Himself who said He would make a place at the table for the Gentiles?

> "I tell you, many will come from east and west and recline at table with Abraham, Isaac, and Jacob in the kingdom of heaven," (Matthew 8:11 ESV).

Doesn't Scripture say that God would make Gentile believers sons of Abraham and thus, heirs of the promise to Abraham?

> "Know then that it is those of faith who are the sons of Abraham.
> And the Scripture, foreseeing that God would justify the Gentiles by faith, preached the gospel beforehand to Abraham, saying, "In you shall all the nations be blessed."
> So then, those who are of faith are blessed along with Abraham, the man of faith." (Galatians 3:7-9 ESV).

And who can forget this:

> "For God shows no partiality." (Romans 2:11 ESV).

But it is just a little further in Romans when Paul, the same apostle who wrote that God is not a respecter of persons and who wrote in Galatians that Gentiles are made the sons of Abraham, quotes Malachi:

> "As it is written, "Jacob I loved, but Esau I hated." (Romans 9:13 ESV).

What is the Lord trying to say? A reading of Romans 9 helps us understand what God means when he says this. God makes a choice on who to choose to be His special people and who He will reject. This is precisely what happened to Esau and Jacob.

Some may ask if God is unfair when He makes this kind of choice between Jacob and Esau. As I said when we started this discussion, for many of us, it just doesn't feel right that God would love one person and hate another. And Paul addresses this very natural thought we might have about this:

"What shall we say then? Is there injustice on God's part? By no means!" (Romans 9:14 ESV).

Paul goes on to say,

"For he says to Moses, "I will have mercy on whom I have mercy, and I will have compassion on whom I have compassion."
So then it depends not on human will or exertion, but on God, who has mercy." (Romans 9:15-16 ESV).

It is God's prerogative to whom He extends grace and to whom He rejects. God did not make Esau His chosen people, nor did He restore them to their land. That grace was reserved for the descendants of his brother, Jacob. Why? Because God chose it to be that way.

But even the Edomites had the right to join as proselytes with the Jews. They could still choose to submit themselves to God as did any Gentile. God did not shut the door for them just as He didn't shut the door for any Gentile. Yet the simple truth is this: God chose to extend grace to one people by selecting them as His chosen people while rejecting to do so to other people.

Jacob was not chosen based on merit. He was not chosen based on works. He was chosen because God chose to extend mercy and compassion to him and not to his brother. That should teach us all a powerful lesson.

When the Lord rejects the goats on the Day of Judgment, it is His prerogative. When He accepts the sheep, it is His prerogative. It is up to God to whom He will extend grace and upon whom He will reject.

None of us are in a position to tell God who He has to accept, yet we try to do this all the time, don't we? Even our society attempts to co-op God's prerogative. We think we can mandate to God who will be accepted by Him and who will not be accepted by Him. Whether we are woke or not, whether we are politically correct or not, we feel that we can dictate who God should and should not accept, who God will and won't extend mercy and compassion on.

But the same truth that Malachi spoke and the same truth that Paul spoke still applies today. God will love who He will love, and He will hate who He will hate. He will extend mercy and compassion to those He chooses because it is His prerogative to do so.

Grace is His gift. He can extend it to whoever He wishes and withhold it from whoever He wishes. That is His prerogative. We will not earn His favor. We will not be able to demand His judgment in our favor. He extends grace to whomever He wishes.

In the days of Malachi, God told the people, "I loved Jacob, but I hated Esau." The people of Edom could not demand God's grace, but neither could the people of Jacob. God always gave the people of the earth a path to Him, but only to the people of Jacob, this path was given by birth.

Today, it is still God's prerogative to give grace to whom He wishes and to reject whom He wishes. No one will be in a position to demand anything from God.

Today, God loves whom He loves and hates whom He hates. But as another extension of His grace, God invites all men to His table. He has told us to whom He will extend grace.

May we humble ourselves before our Creator and choose to be among those whom the Lord loves and not among those whom the Lord hates.

***

God's sovereignty demonstrated. There is none like Him! Praise God for being above all. This is the One in whom I put my trust.

"A Psalm of Asaph. God has taken his place in the divine council; in the midst of the gods he holds judgment:

"How long will you judge unjustly and show partiality to the wicked? Selah

Give justice to the weak and the fatherless; maintain the right of the afflicted and the destitute.

Rescue the weak and the needy; deliver them from the hand of the wicked."

They have neither knowledge nor understanding, they walk about in darkness; all the foundations of the earth are shaken.

I said, "You are gods, sons of the Most High, all of you;

nevertheless, like men you shall die, and fall like any prince."

Arise, O God, judge the earth; for you shall inherit all the nations!" (Psalm 82:1-8 ESV).

If King Jesus returned in 15 minutes, would you be ready? One day, He will be 15 minutes away from His return. That day could be today.

***

Love Believes All Things

I Corinthians 13 is often called the "love" chapter. In it, Paul defines what love is by showing how we will interact with others if we have love for them. The Greek word that he uses is agape. This is a love that we choose to have for someone, not one that we have from an obligation or attraction. It is often described as self-sacrificial love that is given without the expectation of getting anything in return. Many describe agape as the highest form of love we can have for someone.

In 1 Corinthians, Paul is writing to a group of brothers and sisters in Christ who seem to lack agape love for each other. They are full of division, envy, sin, fornication, litigation, separation, and other activities that demonstrate a lack of love.

Paul's point when he gets to chapter 13 is that if they have love for each other, then many of the problems they are experiencing in their congregation will take care of themselves. When he gets to this great chapter of love, Paul paints a portrait of what a loving person will exhibit toward others. And when compared to some of the most wonderful gifts the Spirit has blessed them with, love is greater than all of them. In fact, Paul says,

> "If I speak in the tongues of men and of angels, but have not love, I am a noisy gong or a clanging cymbal.
> And if I have prophetic powers, and understand all mysteries and all knowledge, and if I have all faith, so as to remove mountains, but have not love, I am nothing.
> If I give away all I have, and if I deliver up my body to be burned, but have not love, I gain nothing." (1 Corinthians 13:1-3 ESV).

It would be a worthy study to examine everything Paul says love is. But in this post, I want to focus on one thing he says, not because it is the greatest expression of love, but because it is one I have been working on for almost two years. It seems simple enough, but it is hard to always put into practice.

Love believes all things (vs. 7).

This is such a wonderful expression of love because to truly manifest this aspect of love requires self-sacrifice, putting others before ourselves, forgiveness, grace, and self-control, all rolled up into one simple, powerful action of service.

What does it mean to believe all things? In my experience, it is a spectrum of service that Jesus touches on throughout His ministry, culminating in the second greatest commandment of loving our neighbors as ourselves. At its essence, love "believing all things" incorporates giving others the benefit of the doubt. When given the choice of ascribing the best or worse motives, we choose to ascribe the best in others. This is the aspiration we all should want in our relationship with each other.

What makes "believing all things" love is that others won't always have the best motives, but we still assume they do when they ask us to. Jesus shows us how to put this aspect of love into action when He has this interaction with Peter:

> "Then Peter came to Him and said, "Lord, how often shall my brother sin against me, and I forgive him? Up to seven times?"
> Jesus said to him, "I do not say to you, up to seven times, but up to seventy times seven." (Matthew 18:21-22 NKJV).

How can we forgive someone over and over when they come to us over and over asking for our forgiveness? Doesn't there come a point when we say, "Look, I'm tired of forgiving you when you keep sinning against me. If you are serious, you would stop sinning." This is where "love believes all things" comes in.

You see, believing all things is our choice. It's not dependent on what others do or do not do. Jesus says if someone sins over and over, love dictates that we choose over and over to believe all things. Agape lays down our own hurts and defenses to give grace to others. Love gives our brothers and sisters the benefit of the doubt when they tell us they are sorry without us looking for evidence to the contrary.

Love believes all things.

When someone tells us they will do something, do we give them the grace of believing all things, or do we hold their past over their heads and cast doubt over their likelihood of delivering what they promise? Agape will forgive and give the grace they need to repent.

But there is a risk in this kind of love, isn't there? The risk is that we will be on the receiving end of betrayal and lies. Again. And again. And again.

Hence our King's words to Peter, "I do not say to you, up to seven times, but up to seventy times seven."

That's a lot of betrayals, isn't it? That's a lot of lies we may have to endure. But that is what agape love is. It is believing all things, and it is a hard aspect of love to manifest. Oh sure, the first two or three times, we can manage it. Or if we are as righteous as Peter thought he was, we might be able to forgive seven times. But Jesus' message is that we believe all things as many times as it takes.

But how? How do we believe all things when the person proves to be unbelievable? Isn't that the real questions we ask ourselves in the back of our minds? When is enough enough? When do we stop being someone's patsy, someone's walking mat, someone's stooge?

To understand what Paul teaches in 1 Corinthians 13, we must understand the real purpose behind agape love. It is self-sacrificial, and it is a choice. It is an act of grace on our part, not an act of obligation. As we learn to give others the benefit of the doubt when all they deserve is doubt, or when we believe all things when they are unbelievable, we begin to take on the image of our Lord and King, Jesus.

When we are unbelievable, He believes all things. When we do not deserve grace, He gives us the benefit of the doubt. When we tell Him, "I'm sorry" 490 times, He believes all things and forgives us 490 times. He made the greatest agape sacrifice when we were least worthy of it.

> "but God shows his love for us in that while we were still sinners, Christ died for us." (Romans 5:8 ESV).

Is Jesus a stooge, a patsy, a walking mat when He receives us back over, and over, and over, and over? None of us would think that. We know He does that because He is full of grace. He agapes us. When it comes to us, He believes all things and gives us His grace to prove it.

How do we believe all things when people are unbelievable? We agape them. We give them grace. We give them the benefit of the doubt. We sacrifice for them and make ourselves vulnerable. And we will do it over, and over, and over.

We do it for each other because Jesus does it for us.

Every day.

As many times as He needs to.

We love each other that way because He loves us that way.

> "Love is patient and kind; love does not envy or boast; it is not arrogant or rude. It does not insist on its own way; it is not irritable or resentful; it does not rejoice at wrongdoing, but rejoices with the truth. Love bears all things, believes all things, hopes all things, endures all things. Love never ends." (1 Corinthians 13:4-8a ESV).

Tuesdays With Tony

ABOUT THE AUTHOR

Tony Eldridge has written 5 books, including his most recent before this volume, The Sovereignty of God. He has been a full-time minister and has taught many Bible classes at various churches. He currently attends the Campbell Road Church of Christ in Garland, TX. He is married to his wife of 23 years, Emily, and he has 17-year-old twin boys, Connor and Landon, and a 7-year-old son, Ryder. Tony and his family live in Wylie, TX.

Made in the USA
Columbia, SC
14 June 2023